Jörg Dünne / Gesine Hindemith / Judith Kasper (eds)

Catastrophe & Spectacle

Variations of a Conceptual Relation from the 17th to the 21st Century

Jörg Dünne / Gesine Hindemith / Judith Kasper (eds)

Catastrophe & Spectacle

Variations of a Conceptual Relation from the 17th to the 21st Century

Neofelis Verlag

Contents

NECESSARY
EVIL
91

Introduction

Jörg Dünne / Gesine Hindemith / Judith Kasper

At the beginning of each essay in this volume, there is an image. Some of these images, which have been brought together and combined within the montage of this introductory chapter, depict so-called 'natural catastrophes', some refer to technical or historical events, while others display a theatrical scene or simply a seemingly peaceful meadow. In most cases, if not all, the 'catastrophic' aspect of these images calls for some explanation, meaning that the images are dependent upon an annotative text that situates the initial image within a historical, philological or pragmatic context.

With this combination of iconic depiction and textual commentary, the contributions in this volume provide a form of critical commentary on recent theoretical discussions concerning the modern understanding of catastrophe in the 18th century as a phenomenon emerging from these images. From the perspective of the contributions in this volume, this assumption requires a number of modifications:

1) Spectacularity: Catastrophes are inseparably bound to their modes of visual display, and yet these modes of display are not simply the product of one specific medium as opposed to another. The essays in this volume seek the genealogy of a modern understanding of the catastrophe in medial practices of staging, rather than solely within the medium of the image (Trempler[1]). They thus closely relate the history of the term 'catastrophe' (Briese / Günther) to that of the spectacle and the spectacular (Hamon-Siréjols / Gardies, Moindrot), and assume that, in variating the title of Hans Blumenberg's essay on the shipwreck metaphor, catastrophes are always already "catastrophes with spectators". This new emphasis also accompanies a return to the theatrical origins of the term catastrophe.

2) Historicity: Recent studies assert that the catastrophe was an "invention" (Mercier-Faivre/Thomas) of the 18th century. Indeed, the term undergoes a significant semantic change during the 18th century when the theatrical origins of the term are expanded to include both geological and political-historical events. The hypothesis regarding the creation of the catastrophe during the 18th century, however, must include the observation that narratives of catastrophe in the fields of both fiction and non-fiction had already been evolving during the 16th and 17th centuries (Lavocat). Whether an epidemic, a fire or a shipwreck: The catastrophe is always written from the perspective of the witness and thus exhibits an inherent observer constellation. And, especially in the age of so-called 'technical' media, such techniques of the observer (Crary) serve to intensify the tension between the catastrophe and the spectacular, thus facilitating the "society of the spectacle" according to Guy Debord.

3) Reflexivity: The combination of image and textual commentary in this volume ultimately refers to a critical approach toward the nexus of catastrophe and spectacularity, perhaps most prominently figured in Guy Debord's well-known criticism of what he refers to as the "society of the spectacle", which is fueled by an endless series of catastrophic moments. In the course of this criticism, the desire for catastrophic staging is increasingly confronted by skepticism toward catastrophic images, which finds expression in philological work on the term "cata/strophe" (Kasper), that is, within the search for alternative concepts (such as those of the unspectacular 'disaster'), as well as in images themselves, which refuse to be embedded within a spectacular staging.

The essays in this volume are arranged in chronological order according to the relationship between spectacularity and catastrophe, taking the relationship between image and text as a starting point for considering the changes that have taken place in literature, in the media and cultural history. Starting with the representation of catastrophes in the early modern period, that is, in baroque theatrical stagings (Françoise Lavocat, Bettine Menke), two subsequent essays (Jörg Dünne, Walburga Hülk) then deal with the interdependence between natural and cultural history during the Enlightenment, before attention shifts to a major focal point of the contributions in the volume at hand (Kati Röttger, Marie-Hélène Huet, Gesine Hindemith, Johannes Ungelenk, Giulia Palladini), which is examining the culture of the spectacular catastrophe in the 19th and early 20th centuries. A striking rupture in our fascination with the spectacularity of the catastrophic is documented in the contributions that describe the catastrophic spectacle and its criticism from the middle of the 20th century on (Jean-Pierre Dupuy, Martina Bengert, Vittoria Borsò, Davide Caliaro, Judith Kasper) – an ambivalence that is clearly recognizable in the search for new forms of engagement with the spectacular in the sense of global or planetary catastrophes since September 11, 2001 (Markus Ophälders, Gianluca Solla, Jörn Etzold).

***

Although these collected essays take different approaches toward the relationship between spectacularity and catastrophe, they all process a relationship of tension in the same way (variously accentuated depending upon the chosen subject and its historical localization). On the one hand, the contributions show to which extent the process of visualization provides a basis for understanding catastrophic events. In addition, they analyze visual procedures with regard to their inadequacy as well as their collapse in light of the catastrophe being observed. At times, the imagery itself becomes affected by something catastrophic, making the iconic depiction of catastrophes impossible at a representational level, even causing depictions to implode in themselves. (Martina Bengert explains in her essay that even the rhombus within the pictorial montage of this introductory chapter can bring forth an implicit challenge to the imagery.) The spectacularization of catastrophes on the one hand and the challenge to the spectacular as a catastrophe of a second order on the other both follow, as will become apparent in this volume, a clear historical arrangement.

The spectacular staging of the catastrophe and the critique of catastrophe within the impossible image reorganize the human relationship to the past as early as during the early modern period and the Enlightenment, but increasingly from the 19th century onward (Huet). They contemplate history from its contingent end, from its sudden interruption and its hopeless downfall. It is a disruptive presentation of history, which is epistemologically formed from the images of the spectacular catastrophe (Dünne). History becomes a sequence of time periods that overlap and that are separated from each other by catastrophes, for example, by catastrophes of a geological nature. This assumption also corresponds with the idea of a geological *deep time* which is catastrophically separated from *human time* and can no longer be made historically perceivable. History is no longer a continuous narrative, but rather appears as a sequence of discontinuous tableaus whose appearance and disappearance seem at times to possess spectacular traits in themselves (Rudwick).

An affinity for catastrophe and spectacle can be found in the theater as well. Although the concept of the spectacular is explicitly established for the first time within the context of the 19th-century theater (Roger), its roots go back to the baroque machine theater. Having inherited the intensive use of theater machinery from the baroque theater, popular theater since the French Revolution has been particularly affected by the affinity between catastrophe and spectacle, a factor which is evident in the popular French genre of the *féerie* (Dünne / Hindemith). Originating on the theatrical Parisian stage, the culture of spectacular theater begins to take over urban spaces in the 19th century, and new forms of entertainment are born (Schwartz). Spectacle and catastrophe thus find their place in the consumer culture of flourishing capitalism.

Moving past theatrical catastrophe, which was merely a (downward) turning point and could also be found in comedy (Briese), the essays in this volume also ask to which extent the spectacular is inherent to the catastrophe: Does the spectacularization of the modern catastrophe occur as a part of consumer culture? And does it inevitably lead to Debord's society of the spectacle? Or does the spectacular itself have the potential to defy the simple consumption of the catastrophes presented? Is what we would call modernity in an aesthetic and epistemic sense perhaps based on the articulation of spectacle and catastrophe?

While spectacular catastrophes function as a historical foundation for the modern episteme and for aesthetics, they are also challenged by a movement of unfounding (what Deleuze calls *effondement*). In the 20th century, the two World Wars and the annihilation of the Jews in Nazi concentration camps marked critical watersheds in European history and its representation of catastrophes, forcing us to ask what it means to speak of events without end and to probe the limits of representation (Benjamin, Adorno). New ways of working at and on these limits have included the use of non-linear, multidirectional narratives, visual and verbal fragmentation, and belated, traumatic temporality.

The fact that it was possible to kill six million Jews in Nazi camps spread throughout Europe without that annihilation being *effectively* documented – that is, without it leading to attempts by the Allies and others to stop it – is a scandal that has shattered the relationship between catastrophe and visibility, seeing and knowing, representation and responsibility.

The Shoah – the Hebrew word for catastrophe – has been described as a "historical attack on perception" (Felman). Such an attack has made it necessary to reconceptualize the relationship between catastrophic events and their perception. The devastating experience of the Shoah cannot be represented by conventional means or can only be 'represented' to the extent that it shatters these means. Its traumatic impact registers belatedly and often elsewhere than one might expect it. Here it is important to stress that the traditional mimetic ordering of an event and its representation may itself be shattered, making it necessary to view the former paradoxically as an after-effect of the latter. One could argue in this regard that the catastrophe emerges as an after-effect of its depiction and visualization. In short, with the Shoah, the catastrophe itself breaks into its depiction, smashing not only the means of representation but the very relationship between before and after, event and image.

The historical catastrophe as an absolute, even ontological disaster (Blanchot) cannot be portrayed as a discrete event. Indeed, it is the historical catastrophe that destroys everything – including the perception of the radical loss itself. The catastrophe as a disaster no longer brings about the collapse of the heavens as a firmament, but instead the demise of each subjective observer position. The catastrophe as disaster is the alarming experience that images and reality, as well as words and things, constantly disintegrate. The catastrophe as a disaster is above all an infinite void that leaves one disoriented, traumatized and anesthetized throughout space, time and history.

Given this completely faceless catastrophe, the task of art, science and philosophy is no longer to present the catastrophe, which will never be anything else than an act of trivialization that bestows a face and a history upon a destruction that can no longer be captured by any image, face or story. Their task is rather to interrupt the anesthetic reporting with their rhetorical constructions of language and image, which are all placed on the image like a shroud hung over a catastrophe that has long since become normal. Viewed as such, the spectacle is not a means of increasing awareness, but rather a perfect defensive shield against it – unless we can ascribe to the spectacular (or at least some of its manifestations) a character of staging beyond Debord's critique of the spectacle, a staging that is in itself already disrupted. In this context, the importance of writing and oral testimony returns: In writing and the spoken word, something of this catastrophe can be articulated, which tends to be negated by images. As such, the critique of the spectacle in light of the Shoah sharpens our awareness of those structurally resistant moments in potentially every form of the spectacularization of catastrophes, in which the images, recalled once more, fail: in that the language of tropes begins to stutter, or the images called upon suddenly begin to blur or in any other form prove to be disrupted precisely because the Real of the catastrophe penetrates the medium of illustration.

But has the last word in the complex history of the nexus of catastrophe and spectacle already been spoken with the 20th-century crisis of catastrophic spectacularity? Faced with current figurations of global or even planetary catastrophe (cf. Dupuy, Horn), it seems that, in light of the 'Anthropocene', the catastrophic spectacularity of human history inextricably refers back to natural history, thus picking up aspects of the catastrophe theories of the 18th century. Will this shift in understandings of the catastrophic also, for its part, shift the boundaries of their ability to stage the spectacular? The melodramatic apocalypse in Lars von Trier's film *Melancholia*, which the last essay in this volume addresses, calls forth the assumption that new modern forms of the relationship between spectacle and catastrophe are being established, as does the title image of this volume, a reactor merry-go-round which is built inside the cooling tower of a planned atomic reactor, the main attraction of the "Wunderland Kalkar" amusement park in Niederrhein. While this may certainly be understood as a late-capitalist product of the society of the spectacle according to Guy Debord, it may also be understood as an entirely ironic repurposing that contrasts the reflexive force of the spectacular with the life-threatening catastrophic agency of mankind in the atomic age.

Be that as it may: In their confrontations with the spectacularity of catastrophes, art, science, philosophy and perhaps even popular culture, the contributions in this volume become seismographs that document shocks affecting not only the geologic dimensions of Earth and larger historical changes, but also ways of dealing with theatricality and imagery, language and thought themselves.

***

Most of the essays in this volume were first presented at the international conference "Spectacular Catastrophes, Catastrophic Spectacles", which was held from March 4 to March 7, 2015, in Erfurt and funded by the Deutsche Forschungsgemeinschaft (DFG). The conference was the joint concluding event to two DFG-funded research projects with related questions: the project "Die katastrophische Feerie" (Jörg Dünne and Gesine Hindemith) at the University of Erfurt and the project "Der traumatisierte Raum" (Judith Kasper) at the University of Potsdam. The English-language publication of this volume was also made possible by DFG funding.

For the support they provided during the preparation of the publication, the editor would like to thank Michael C. Noto, who translated several essays (Martina Bengert, Jörg Dünne, Gesine Hindemith) into English and carried out the linguistic revision of others; and Andrew Kirwin and Marlene Klein, who translated the essays by Bettine Menke and Judith Kasper. Additional bibliographic research and final linguistic corrections were carried out by Jonathan Schmidt-Dominé and Andrew Patten. Very special thanks go out to Lydia White, Matthias Naumann and all employees of the Neofelis Verlag who have patiently and competently accompanied the publication of this volume, from initial inquiries all the way up to its actual publication.

*

1 For detailed bibliographic references see the bibliography of this introduction which is supposed to give an overview of basic readings on the subject of this book.

Bibliography

Adorno, Theodor W.: *Minima Moralia. Reflexionen aus dem beschädigten Leben* [1951]. *Gesammelte Schriften*, vol. 4, ed. by Rolf Tiedemann. Frankfurt am Main: Suhrkamp 1970.

Benjamin, Walter: Über den Begriff der Geschichte. In: W. B.: *Gesammelte Schriften*, vol. I.2, ed. by Rolf Tiedemann / Hermann Schweppenhäuser. Frankfurt am Main: Suhrkamp 1974, pp. 690–708.

Blanchot, Maurice: *L'Écriture du désastre*. Paris: Gallimard 1980.

Blumenberg, Hans: *Schiffbruch mit Zuschauer*. Frankfurt am Main: Suhrkamp 1979.

Briese, Olaf: "Genommen auß den Comoedien". Katastrophenbegriffe der neuzeitlichen Geologie. In: Michael Eggers / Matthias Rothe (eds): *Wissenschaftsgeschichte als Begriffsgeschichte. Terminologische Umbrüche im Entstehungsprozess der modernen Wissenschaften*. Bielefeld: Transcript 2009, pp. 23–50.

Briese, Olaf / Timo Günther: Katastrophe. Terminologische Vergangenheit, Gegenwart und Zukunft. In: *Archiv für Begriffsgeschichte* 51 (2009), pp. 155–195.

Crary, Jonathan: *Techniques of the Observer. On Vision and Modernity in the Nineteenth century*. Cambridge: MIT Press 1990.

// *Suspensions of Perception. Attention, Spectacle, and Modern Culture.* Cambridge: MIT Press 1999.

Debord, Guy: *La Société du spectacle* [1971]. Paris: Gallimard 1996.

Deleuze, Gilles: *Différence et répétition*. Paris: PUF 1968.

Dünne, Jörg / Gesine Hindemith (eds): *La Féerie autour de 1900 – une figure de la modernité*. Dossier in: *Lendemains* 38:152 (2013).

Dupuy, Jean-Pierre: *Pour un catastrophisme éclairé. Quand l'impossible est certain*. Paris: Seuil 2002.

Felman, Shoshana: In an Era of Testimony: Claude Lanzmann's *Shoah*. In: *Yale French Studies* 97 (2000): 50 Years of Yale French Studies: A Commemorative Anthology, part 2: 1980–1998, pp. 103–150.

Hamon-Siréjols, Christine / André Gardies (eds): *Le Spectaculaire*. Lyon: Cahiers du Gritec / Aléas 1997.

Horn, Eva: *Zukunft als Katastrophe*. Frankfurt am Main: Fischer 2014.

Huet, Marie-Hélène: *The Culture of Disaster*. Chicago / London: University of Chicago Press 2012.

Kasper, Judith: Für eine Philologie der Kata/strophe. In: Ottmar Ette / J. K. (eds): *Unfälle der Sprache. Literarische und philologische Erkundungen der Katastrophe*. Wien / Berlin: Turia + Kant 2014, pp. 7–20.

Lavocat, Françoise (ed.): *Pestes, incendies, naufrages. Écritures du désastre au dix-septième siècle*. Turnhout: Brepols 2011.

Mercier-Faivre, Anne-Marie / Chantal Thomas (eds): *L'Invention de la catastrophe au XVIIIe siècle: du châtiment divin au désastre naturel*. Genève: Droz 2008.

Moindrot, Isabelle (ed.): *Le Spectaculaire dans les arts de la scène du romantisme à la Belle Époque*. Paris: CNRS Éditions 2006.

Roger, Philippe: Spectaculaire, histoire d'un mot. In: Christine Hamon-Siréjols / André Gardies (eds): *Le Spectaculaire*. Lyon: Cahiers du Gritec / Aléas 1997, pp. 9–14.

Rudwick, Martin: *Scenes from Deep Time. Early Pictorial Representations of the Prehistoric World*. Chicago / London: University of Chicago Press 1992.

Schwartz, Vanessa: *Spectacular Realities. Early Mass Culture in Fin-de-Siècle Paris*. Berkeley: University of California Press 1999.

Trempler, Jörg: *Katastrophen. Ihre Entstehung aus dem Bild*. Berlin: Wagenbach 2013.

Fig. 1: Domenico Gargiulo (called Micco Spadaro): *Largo Mercatello durante la peste del 1656* (c. 1657).

The Spectacularity of Mass Death

Françoise Lavocat

Domenico Gargiulo, also known as Micco Spadaro, dedicated several paintings to the historical and natural catastrophes that shook the city of Naples in the middle of the 17th century: the revolt of Masaniello, the eruption of Vesuvius in 1631 and the plague of 1656.[1] He devoted two paintings to the latter, each of which significantly different in its fundamental conception. The first painting (not pictured in this article), *Rendimento di grazie per lo scampato pericolo della peste* (*Thanksgiving After the Plague*), shows the priests of Certosa de San Martino and Cardinal Ascanio Filomarino arranged in a semi-circle comprised of three rows, grouped around a commemorative stone that has just been created, while, on the left, standing to the side of the group, a figure in a red coat, armed with a sword (St. Martin), chases away an emaciated feminine figure – an incarnation of the plague. The scene is reproduced a little farther off, beneath the imaginary arcades the painter had added to St. Martin's Charterhouse. The celestial sphere is rather crowded; half-way up, the Virgin and St. Bruno, in the company of angels, fly toward an angry God, who is surrounded by a number of saints. All of the human figures (including the painter himself, standing at the back of the painting and watching the scene) are real and identifiable. This large format painting (81" x 120"),[2] commissioned by the priests of St. Martin's Charterhouse, reinterprets ancient models for representing catastrophe; it enlists allegory, privileges the intercession scene, and almost the entire space is occupied – in a highly-organized manner – by the painting's commissioners, along with representatives of the ecclesiastical hierarchy and supernatural powers.[3]

Gargiulo's second painting, *Largo Mercatello durante la peste del 1656,* however, breaks with almost all previous codes for representing the plague. The contrast between these two works is striking. In the latter, allegory has disappeared, and divine presence is but a distant echo – out of communication with the human world, which has fallen prey to chaos. The painting's spectacularity no longer resides in the careful ordering of what is represented – however magnificent – nor in the prestige of those being represented. On the contrary, it basks in a certain disorientation of perspective, condemned to roam a partly indecipherable terrain. Largo Mercatello itself was a space located at the gates of the city that was usually given over to grain trade, but was officially transformed into a hospital during the plague epidemic.[4] In this painting, it has become a mortuary and cemetery.

To a certain degree, it is impossible to make sense of the chaos that reigns here, both because the tangle of bodies, particularly at the center of the painting, cannot be unraveled, and also because it is often impossible to interpret the gestures and attitudes of the depicted figures. One of the most distinct groups (found on the right side of the painting, in front of a cart from which bodies are being unloaded) is comprised of two or three men holding up another figure, who is struggling with his mouth open – crying out. Is he a sick man being dragged by force to the quarantine zone? Or a relative of one of the victims, whom they are preventing from entering the diseased quarters and perhaps killing himself in doing so?[5] The corpses in their winding sheets cover the surface of the canvas in innumerable and increasingly small horizontal groups. Piles of them can be made out. In the background, to the left, a dark patch seems to reveal a grave. All the way in the back, against a wall, a fire is burning; the viewer cannot tell whether it is a funeral pyre. We do not know what is being done with the dead nor do we always understand what the living are doing; many of them are carrying bodies on their backs, grasping them tightly in their arms, dragging them by their feet, pulling them by the arms, probably by means of a rope. Others are raising their arms towards the heavens. In the distance, a sedan chair can be seen arriving, but we cannot tell whether it is carrying an authority figure or an ill person of noble stature.

In the sky above the fray are the roofs and bell-towers of the city. In a little yellow bubble, placed close to the upper edge of the painting, miniature celestial figures play out a familiar scene. The Virgin, in a supplicatory posture, is turned toward God, whose raised arm wields a staff held back by an angel. This shows that the Virgin's intercession has been successful; God's plague will no longer scourge the city – the punishment is coming to an end.

But on earth, no one is taking any notice of this distant supernatural presence. There is a striking difference in the treatment of the two spheres – terrestrial and supernatural – in these paintings that deal with the plague of 1656. Another of Micco Spadaro's paintings, depicting the eruption of Vesuvius in 1631, exhibits a similar distance to that exemplified in *Largo Mercatello*, with the same non-communication between the terrestrial and the heavenly planes. Up in the sky, San Gennaro is flying toward Vesuvius, whose dark form can barely be discerned in the distance, while the crowd down below is turned toward the meandering procession that is the center of everybody's attention, including ours. The depiction of the eruption of Vesuvius, completed 20 years after the event, has no votive function. But the presence of representatives of temporal and ecclesiastical Neapolitan authority at the heart of the procession gives the painting historical, documentary, commemorative and no doubt political value.

While the authority figures in *Largo Mercatello* do not occupy the same position of dominance as those of the Vesuvius painting, they are nonetheless present. Two figures in black at the core of the central tangle of bodies – one on horseback, the other on foot – may be representatives of Neapolitan civil authority: Carlo Pagano and Felice Basile.[6] Each one has an arm lifted, as if to point something out. The presence of these two men at the heart of the confused mass of dead, dying and living figures bears witness to their courage and likely involvement in dealing with the catastrophe. What the eye sees, however, is the engulfing chaos that surrounds them. The presence of authority figures does not generate any order in this scenario. Two other historical figures can also be identified in this disorder. One of them is the painter himself on horseback in the shadows, entering through one of the two doors (Porta Reale)[7] at the far left of the painting.[8] On the opposite side, to the right, one of the figures on the ground can be identified as the painter Massimo Stanzione, who had worked with Spadaro on the frescos of St. Martin's Charterhouse. These few referential facts lend a testimonial and autobiographical weight to the work – even if the presence of the painter, priest and authority figures in such a highly contaminated place points to probable fiction.[9]

In order to appreciate the innovation of *Largo Mercatello*, it must be placed in relation to established codes for painting the plague. These can be divided into two unequally represented categories.[10] The first, of which there are far more examples, is made up of paintings depicting scenes of intercession or pastoral care, carried out by at least one ancient or modern saint (Saints Sebastien, Roch, Charles Borromeo, Jean de Dieu, Louis Gonzago, Macaire, Bernardo Tolomei, François-Xavier, Francis de Sales, Thecla and Genevieve). These works belong to the votive genre and comprise part of the 17th-century Catholic Church's extensive program for coping with catastrophes – in a physical, symbolic and memorial manner.[11] The second category of 16th and 17th century plague paintings belongs to a different agenda, one that can be described as aesthetic: It involves paintings that skip over contemporary incarnations of the plague and are not concerned with intercession. This is the case in *The Plague of Phrygia* (named after a passage in the *Aeneid*) – a famous engraving by Marcantonio Raimondi (1507), modeled after a drawing by Raphael – as well as in *The Plague at Ashdod* (based on a Biblical episode) by Nicolas Poussin. The epidemics depicted here have neither historical ties nor remote references to anything resembling a contemporary plague (Poussin painted *The Plague at Ashdod* right in the middle of the European pandemic of 1630–1631). This distance from reference favors painting plague subjects for their own sake – that is to say, for the beauty of the forms and bodies. Beginning with Raphael's drawing, we witness an iconic group of figures – formed by a dead young woman and a living child, often held apart from the corpse by a man plugging his nose – that is reproduced in a great number of subsequent works on the plague.

Now if, as we have seen, *Largo Mercatello* does not fit into the first category (the intercession of the Virgin not being its principal subject), it is just as difficult to place it in the second. However, at the center of the painting, along its lower edge, lies the body of a dead woman with a child at her breast. This is almost certainly an allusion to the *Plague of Phrygia*, made all the more likely by the fact that there is a nearly naked man standing a little way off from the corpse, toward which he appears to be moving. But he is not holding his nose. This detail is not the only variation from the Raphaelesque topos: neither the green color of the corpse nor the posture of the body in any way exalt feminine beauty. Moreover, the referential and historical anchoring made clear by the very title of the work inscribes it within a completely different genre to that of fiction, devotional paintings and aestheticized depiction of the plague. In this kind of paintings, the presence of corpses is always limited. The corpse of the young woman with the child functions as a synecdoche for mass death. In the frontispieces of certain works, such as *La Peste di Milano del 1630* (*The Plague of Milan of 1630*) by Benedetto Cinquanta, an open grave occupies one third of the page, but only holds three intertwined bodies. Another painting, almost contemporaneous with that of Micco Spadaro, can also be cited here: *La vergine appare agli appestati* (*The Virgin Appears to the Plague Victims*) by Venetian artist Antonio Zanchi.[12] This painting is similarly cluttered with corpses – seven of them, to be precise. But in Micco Spadaro's painting, there are dozens of dead bodies, the exact number of which is impossible to determine, piled up and spread out over the vast grey-green space – the same color as the corpses – that is Largo Mercatello. They are fated to lose all differentiation. Class and sex mix together, becoming almost indiscernible, which makes this mass death very different from the triumphs of medieval death, such as that of the Camposanto of Pisa, painted by Buonamico in the middle of the 14th century. While in Buonamico's painting angels and devils fight over the souls fleeing from each mouth, a monk can be made out among the pile of the dead by virtue of his tonsure, a bishop by his miter and a patrician woman by her headdress. In Breughel's painting (1562), carts of skulls and armies of dead bodies portray death in a disembodied manner, which supports the reassuring fantasy of the dead really being alive in the form of animated skeletons. Micco Spadaro's depiction of death, however, paints it as a process, a continuum between the state of dying, the state of being a corpse – whose former characteristics can still be surmised by its clothes – the state of being a simple human form wrapped in a sheet (we can clearly make out the legs of the corpse under the white cloth, held between two men in black) – and the state of being a larva, a mere shadow and residue, as the sheet, now seen off in the distance, diminishes into a thin white line. The intense activity around the bodies spotlights a process by which individuality is erased and forms are rapidly destroyed. It is perhaps for this reason that Spadaro's painting of the plague seems anachronistically modern to us (insofar as it shares certain characteristics with what we imagine to be genocidal industries).

Micco Spadaro's painting thus inaugurates a new mode for representing catastrophe: mass death. Are we, then, entitled to speak of a certain "catastrophe of meaning"?[13] The continued presence of the supernatural (however reduced and remote) as well as the scene's foundations in historical and geographical fact, supported by its autobiographical references (minimal though they are), do not allow us to say that we can. But by virtue of the strategic disorientation of the viewer's gaze, the spectacle of collective death, such as it is presented here, still manages to approximate the multiplicity of all these cases, which are impossible to grasp, and forces the suspension of interpretation when confronted with the ambiguity of their gestures and situations, which might otherwise favor empathy (we do not always know whether someone is sick or in mourning). So, is Micco Spadaro's aesthetic choice – the form of realism that he privileges in painting disasters, with a strong emphasis on the collective rather than the individual – totally isolated? Or is it a promise of things to come in the literary and iconographic realm?

A literary work of the same period, which is also a singular case, echoes this aesthetic: *La Peste di Milano del 1630* by Benedetto Cinquanta, a play whose frontispiece depicts the open grave we referred to earlier. Written at the end of the plague epidemic (which was probably also the time period of Micco Spadaro's paintings), we do not know whether the work was ever performed. In the prologue, the author expresses his awareness of the fact that he is dealing with a subject that defies representation, an unintelligible chaos, by virtue both of the number and variety of the victims and of the eradication of all distinctions of age, rank and sex. To display "the thousandth part of this chaos",[14] the author creates a variety of characters (no less than 19), a multiplicity of scenes and weaves together different stories.[15] The central throng of people in Micco Spadaro's painting, living and dead mixed together, reminds us of the "monstrous monster" and "confused confusion"[16] that, according to Cinquanta, characterize the representative challenge posed by the plague.

This challenge is interpreted and thematized in moral terms by Daniel Defoe some years later. In *The Journal of the Plague Year* (1722), the narrator, who voluntarily remains in plague-ridden London, is gripped by the irrepressible desire to visit the mass grave, whose horror is explicitly related to the unbearable, obscene confusion of bodies, where sex and class are mixed together. Despite the warnings he receives, his scopic drive wins out.[17] Once he arrives at the grave, however, this drive is mitigated, as his attention is drawn to a father watching a mass of bodies containing his wife and children as they are rolled into a grave. Once again, the height of horror, amplified by the experience of an empathetic figure, is incarnated in a mass of intermingled bodies that annuls individual histories and human bonds.

These two literary works, as well as all of Micco Spadaro's catastrophe paintings – whether of the plague or the eruption of Vesuvius – have one thing in common: The crowd is the object of someone's gaze, itself thematized by the systematic presence of a witness, narrator or spectator within the work. When the catastrophe is an epidemic, which characteristically manifests itself in bodies, the decision to depict the multitude permits the painter to display, perhaps even interrogate, the essence of humanity in the spectacle of its destruction. This display of collectivity in catastrophe also usually makes its political implications evident. Such is the case in all of the literary works dealing with the plague and in many graphic and pictorial works,[18] but not in *Largo Mercatello*.[19] The presence of the spectator within the spectacle allows us to appreciate the value of witness accounts (this is probably the case with Spadaro, as well as Cinquanta) and, in Defoe's case, to problematize the legitimacy of the spectator's gaze.

The integration of the spectator into the image also serves to further underline the spectacularity of the event before us. This is notably the case for the engraved edicts with vignettes that were produced at the same time for the same plague epidemic (1656) in Rome.[20] These printed images, which were widely distributed and resemble *vedute*, form a record of the places and practices transformed at the time of the plague (e. g. small boats transporting corpses – themselves pulled by other, uninfected boats – sick zones, decontamination sites, punishments, lists of the dead posted on walls for crowds to read etc.). A small figure (found in Callot's engravings) at the edge of the vignette's frame is almost always integrated into a scene that it is observing and sometimes showing us. These engraved prints were sold to Romans who could afford them as souvenirs.[21] Immediately after the plague, the engravings were incorporated into collections of Roman vistas and sold to travelers as touristic items.

The final European plagues therefore resulted in all sorts of visual, aesthetic and technical innovations. Within their category, almost all the works we have cited are very particular cases and there are only a few works that resemble them. Benedetto Cinquanta's play, entirely devoted to the plague of 1630 in Milan, which he personally witnessed, is the only one of its kind ever written (and can in no way be compared with the 19th century historical reconstitutions of the Black Death). The only remaining engraved edicts with vignettes were produced for the Roman plague of 1656, even if there are also a few prints of the London plague of 1665 in existence.[22] Micco Spadaro's work and his particular type of plague representation are equally unique. The inventiveness displayed in each of his works does not, however, prevent us from noting some of their common traits, which share a spectacularity that relies on the problematized representation of multitudes. I am convinced that the painting's foundation in a real event and anchoring in a particular historical context (marked by urbanization and the institutional management of catastrophe) explains its formal inventiveness, as well as its particularities and resemblances. It is nevertheless somewhat paradoxical that Daniel Defoe, in a fictive testimony (albeit inspired by the memory of the London plague of 1665 and writings on it), was the one to take the moral, political and aesthetic interrogation of the plague in its collective dimension to its highest level. In the 18th and 19th centuries, once the plague of Marseilles was over, painting radically distanced itself from this Baroque realism that focused on collectivity.

The historical reconstitutions of past plagues instead privileged the individual's fanciful and emotional experience of catastrophe.[23]

My intention here has been to contribute to ongoing reflections on the spectacularity of catastrophes, particularly the epidemic that affected human and social bodies on such a vast scale and its depiction prior to the 18th century, alongside the classic hyperbolic mechanisms of tribute – columns, votive churches, ceremonies and commemorations – which have inscribed the memory of the plague into the heart of most European cities.

Translation from the French by Mark Cohen and Auni Chovet

1 Micco Spadaro (1612–1675 or 1677) also painted a number of landscapes and paintings about ancient and religious themes. Cf. Giancarlo Sestieri / Brigitte Daprà: *Domenico Gargiulo detto Micco Spadaro: paesaggista e "cronista" napoletano*. Milan / Rome: Jandi Sapi 1994.

2 *Largo Mercatello durante la peste del 1657* (*Market Square, Plague of 1657*) is smaller, but still a rather large canvas (49" x 69").

3 Giancarlo Sestieri and Brigitte Daprà's hypothesis, according to which this depiction must be ironic, is, however, highly improbable (Sestieri / Daprà: *Domenico Gargiulo detto Micco Spadaro*, pp. 42–43). Why would the painter have wanted to mock the patrons who had offered him refuge during the epidemic?

4 This location in Naples is now the Piazza Dante in the center of the city. It was completely reconstructed during the 18th century. The walls around it, built by the Spanish in the 16th century, were torn down in 1787.

5 A similar scene is described in Daniel Defoe's *Journal of a Plague Year*, in which the gravediggers overpower a father gripped by the fear that he will throw himself into the pit alive.

6 Sestieri / Daprà: *Domenico Gargiulo detto Micco Spadaro*, p. 145.

7 The other gate, the Alba Gate, can be seen at the right of the picture in the distance.

8 This identification, which Sestieri and Daprà adopted tentatively in their catalogue record for this painting (Sestieri / Daprà: *Domenico Gargiulo detto Micco Spadaro*, p. 145), is borrowed from Wilhelm Rolfs: *Geschichte der Malerei Neapels*. Leipzig: Seemann 1910, p. 327. It was made on the basis of this figure's resemblance to the artist's self-portrait.

9 Contrary to what is shown in many paintings, priests did not administer communion before coming into contact with sick

people during a plague. They administered the host from a distance at the end of a staff or by placing it on a dividing wall.

10 Dominique Aicardi-Cheve (*Les corps de la contagion. Etude anthropologique des représentations iconographiques de la peste, XVI–XXe siècle en Europe*. Doctoral thesis, Université d'Aix Marseille II, Faculté de Médecine, October 30, 2003) has catalogued 177 for the 17th century, mainly made in Italy and France.

11 Cf. Louise Marshall: Manipulating the Sacred: Image and Plague in Renaissance Italy. In: *Renaissance Quarterly* 47:3 (1994), pp. 485–532; Christine M. Boeckl: *Images of Plague and Pestilence: Iconography and Iconology*. Kirksville: Truman State UP 2000.

12 Today, this painting hangs in the Scuola Grande di San Rocco. Although it dates from 1666, it is also catalogued under the title *La peste del 1630 a Venezia* (*The Plague of 1630 in Venice*). We can therefore surmise that the painter created this work 30 years after the epidemic. Despite its subject matter, it no longer had any obvious votive function (even if Venice was still living in fear of an epidemic, one having ravaged Italy in 1656, then London in 1666 and finally Vienna in 1679).

13 In this expression, we designate the projection of the idea of destruction onto the medium itself and its means of expression (associated with a metaphysical postulate about the unintelligibility of the world). This understanding of the concept of catastrophe marks its evolution, especially in the 20th century.

14 "Protesto però che non dissi la millesima parte delle miserie occorse" (Benedetto Cinquanta: A benigni lettori. In: B. C.: *La peste del 1630*. Milan: Malatesta 1632, p. 16).

15 Cf. Françoise Lavocat: Donner forme au Chaos. Le théâtre de la peste de Benedetto Cinquanta. In F. L. (ed.): *Pestes, incendies, naufrages. Ecritures du désastre au XVIIe siècle.* Turnhout: Brépols 2011, pp. 451–588.

16 "confuse confusione"; "mostruoso monstro" (Cinquanta: A benigni lettori, pp. 10, 12).

17 "[A] terrible Pit it was, and I could not resist my Curiosity to go and see it." Daniel Defoe: *A Journal of the Plague Year*, ed. by Louis Landa. Oxford / New York: Oxford UP, p. 59.

18 It is, indeed, present in the etched strips of vignettes of Rome and London, which will be discussed later on. For more on this point, I will take the liberty of referring to my forthcoming article: Françoise Lavocat: Avant la bande dessinée: les bandes gravées des pestes de Rome (1656) et de Londres (1665). In: F. L. / Charlotte Krauss (eds): *Art séquentiel et catastrophes*. Paris: Presses universitaires de La Sorbonne Nouvelle [forthcoming].

19 On the other hand, with regard to the same plague, another Neapolitan painter, Carlo Coppola, portrayed a vast scene of repression: *Scena della peste del 1656* (*Scene from the plague of 1656*). Micco Spadaro's painting concerning Vesuvius instead focuses on the political response of the city of Naples to the catastrophe.

20 Cf. Ellen B. Wells: Prints Commemorating the Rome Plague Epidemic. In: *Annali dell Instituto e Museo di Storia della Scienza di Firenze* 10:1 (1985), pp. 15–21.

21 We know of three series of etched edicts with vignettes featuring the Roman plague. The most remarkable (14 edicts and 26 vignettes) was made by Louis Rouhier and published by Giovanni Giacomo de' Rossi in Rome (the leading center for prints and engravings in the 17th century) in February 1656. Cf. Ibid.

22 Cf. Lavocat: Avant la bande dessinée [forthcoming].

23 I am alluding here to works such as Edouard Picot's painting (*Episode Plague in Florence*, 1839) and John Franklin's engraving (*The Plague Pit*, 1855), which use the Black Death of the Middle Ages and the London plague of 1665 as their theme.

Fig. 1: Pierre Corneille: *Andromède*, scenery for the second act,
as first performed on February 1, 1650 by the Troupe Royale at the Petit-Bourbon in Paris.

The Catastrophic Spectacle of the Theater Machines – and Its Destruction

Bettine Menke

A copper engraving by François Chauveau published in 1651 depicts Giacomo Torelli's scenery for the second act of Pierre Corneille's *Andromède, "representée avec les Machines sur le Theatre Royal de Bourbon"*.[1] It presents a spectacular cloud formation high above the stage whose noisy thunder cuts short Phinée's 'blasphempous' talk as he complains about being cheated of his promised bride:

> *Ici le tonnere commence à rouler avec un si grand bruit, et accompagné d'éclairs redoublés avec tant de promptitude, que cette feinte donne de l'épouvante, aussi bien que de l'admiration, tant elle approche du naturel* (A, II.4, p. 64).

Joining the thunderstorm of special effects[2] are eight wind gods, commanded by Aeolus, who float around in theatrical flying machines while performing "*un spectacle étrange et merveilleux*": a series of complex aerial movements enacting the *raptus* of the title character (A, II.5, p. 66). According to Christian Quaeitzsch, Chauveau's depiction follows Corneille's detailed paratextual notes that outline the flight maneuvers, representing the "rape of the princess by the wind gods as a choreographed tableau."[3] Such *pièces à machines*, machine plays, to which Corneille's *Andromeda* belongs, originated in the interludes or *intermèdes*, and themselves constitute a series of spectacular *tableaux*.

Before Corneille's *Andromeda* was printed in 1650–1651, a booklet was published announcing:

> *Dessein de la tragédie d'Andromède de P. Corneille représentée sur le Theatre Royal de Bourbon, contenant l'ordre des scénes, la description des Theatres & des Machines et les paroles qui se chantent en Musique.*[4]

The machines and their machinations, which make possible the effect of awe, invoke wonder and admiration in their own right. At Cardinal Mazarin's suggestion, Corneille wrote *Andromeda* to make use of the machines and scenery from Luigi Rossis' Opera *l'Orfeo*, designed by the famous Giacomo Torelli, who had transferred the stage architecture and machinery of the Italian opera to Paris. Corneille praises Torelli, who recycled and tailored the machinery of *l'Orfeo* to fit *Andromeda*,[5] for being an ingenious inventor who outdid himself with this work (cf. A, Argument, p. 12). The *pièces à machines* translate to the Parisian theater the kind of apparatuses used in the spectacles held at King Louis XIV's court festivals, with their "suggestive synergy between language, music, dance and artistic stage design".[6] They also constitute a *contrapposto* to the understanding of 17th century French theater in terms of the classicist canon, because another aesthetic takes shape in them, a "different, Baroque aesthetic of the spectacular, the irregular, the diverse and heterogenous".[7] *Pièces à machines* with mythological themes allow a multitude of pagan gods to take the stage; the list of dramatis personae for *Andromeda* refers to them as "dieux dans les machines" – gods in the machines (A, Argument, p. 14). As divine and demonic figures were transported magically through the air by flying machines, and while flying chariots, theophanies and terrifying monsters appeared, new visual spaces emerged. These spaces of wonder and of the *merveilleux* were not merely populated with images. Rather, the magic of the machine made the invisible visible, and through the transformations it performed, made the "transition into the imagination".[8] These spaces were thus brought into being as *other*, *artificial* theatrical spaces, supplied and animated by the machines. They corresponded to hybrid theatrical forms: inserted musical pieces, choruses and ballets, the entire legacy of the *intermèdes*,[9] which broke the boundaries of genre. From a dramatic perspective, the secondary literature has conceived of this using the notion of the natural catastrophe: a flooding of the stage by something foreign to the plot, a presumed accessory to the main drama that ultimately destroyed it.[10] Notably, this catastrophic flooding of the stage (conceived as the catastrophe of the forms of spectacle) had also become the object of spectacular representation: the spectacle of catastrophe threatened to become a 'catastrophe', undoing representation itself.[11]

When Corneille praises Torelli, he is also praising his own inventiveness, "[qui] donne lieu à une machine tout extraordinaire et merveilleuse" (A, Examen d'*Andromède*, p. 144):

> J'ay été assez heureux à les [les machines] inventer et à leur donner place dans la tissure de ce Poème, mais aussi faut-il que j'avoüe que le sieur Torrelli s'est surmonté lui-même à en exécuter les desseins, et qu'il a eu des inventions admirables pour les faire agir à propos, de sorte que s'il m'est dû quelque gloire pour avoir introduit cette Venus dans le premier Acte, qui fait le nœud de cette Tragédie par l'Oracle ingénieux qu'elle prononce, il lui en est dû bien davantage pour l'avoir fait venir de si loin et descendre au milieu de l'air dans cette magnifique étoile, avec tant d'art et de pompe, qu'elle remplit tout l'monde d'étonnement et d'admiration. (A, Argument, p. 12)

He thus creates a 'line of defense' for the machine: He justifies what appears to be *ex machina* as not merely a pleasant accessory, but rather necessary for the coherence of the drama. He employs the traditional metaphors of tying and untying a knot to describe the dramatic process in which, according to the *doctrine classique,* the *catastrophe* functions as a turning point.[12] At the same time, he reveals the other purpose of the machine play: "mon principal but ici a été de satisfaire la vue par l'éclat et la diversité du spectacle" (A, Argument, p. 13).

If the 'knot'is tied, it may be at the point where Venus materializes out of the machine, causing alarm and wonder (which Chauveau depicts as the reverence of the play's personnel

Fig. 2: Pierre Corneille: *Andromède*, scenery for the first act.

for her appearance, see Fig. 2), and delivers an oracle that remains misunderstood, at least throughout the second act and up until the abduction. But if the knot is tied there, it rather resembles a *coup (de théâtre)* that breaks in as if 'from outside'. And instead of initiating the continuous untying of the knot, this decisive turning point launches a whole series

Fig. 3: Pierre Corneille: *Andromède*, scenery for the fifth act.

of peripeteias, which include Andromeda's abduction. These *coups de théâtre machinés* then punctuate the action.[13]

The spectacles produced by the theater machines allow for the characters' awe-inspiring and triumphant entrance. The machine is the exteriorization of the techniques from the *entrée d'éclat*, which is supposed to blind us to the frailness of the natural body with the *éclat* – the dazzle of a triumphant *mise en scène*,[14] like the triumphant appearance of gods: "Iupiter descend du Ciel dans un Trône tout éclatant d'or et de lumières". (A, V.7, p. 127, see Fig. 3) The appearance 'in the machine' produces a *different* artificial body. The artifice of the machine elevates the image of the one entering into the jubilatory and into a stellar or cosmic image in order to make the risks of the entrance, the fragile construction, which it indeed is, forgotten in the *éclat* that the entrance creates, the "triumphant overpowering of all who are present".[15]

However, the machines were not just a technique for elevating appearances to the realm of the gods; in fact, it was mainly due to the "magic of the machines" that the gods appeared.[16] The *éclat* of rhetorical and mechanical arts, a "festive theophany", brought about an overwhelming effect "that [could] be summarized by the term *miracle*".[17] This *éclat* nevertheless came from the machine that made it – and which was hidden by it. The effect of wonder produced by these hidden means was nevertheless directed at precisely those concealed devices whose operations allowed for the "radiant visibility of their result", a bursting forth in "multiple images". But the physical risks and contingencies of the devices were latent in all of the images. *Éclat* refers to a shining and glittering that is, at the same time, a dazzling that 'obscures'; an outburst of images, and also a 'shattering' (*éclater*) of images no longer graspable as a shape.

When theater machines make something appear, as media, they model that which appears within them and they create a different space and a different time. *Ex machina* effects create artificial 'intermediate worlds' that are bound to other places located elsewhere, offstage, where the devices are installed. The stage of *this* theater was not the closed 'container' of classicism. It was rather "perforated, full of slits," through which the machines intervened.[18] Corneille called attention to the fact that scenes such as Andromeda's abduction, in which miraculous wind and weather phenomena intervened, do not (and cannot, in the sense of the verisimilitude of the representation) present a closed inner space (cf. A, Examen d'*Andromède*, pp. 150–151). The visible is linked to what is hidden from view and thereby divided in itself and to that whose hidden spaces are widely expanded for the sake of the machine's operations. The *mise-en-abyme* of this division within itself of all that is presented onstage, preventing it from closing itself and achieving self-identical presence, are the ghosts. This is why d'Aubignac wanted to banish from theaters all 'magical' events that were implemented by machines and thereby controlled externally. According to d'Aubignac, demons that required the 'external' 'magic' of the machines should "never" be the main protagonists; the *pièces à machines*, however, did exactly that: they made "the machine the main actor".[19]

The theater machines were characterized by an undecidable duality: On the one hand they produced the illusion of a flying goddess or sorceress and, thus, as a deceptive *machination* from offstage, they remained as invisible as possible. On the other hand, they were praised as a technically brilliant achievement and revealed themselves to be *ingenious* inventions due to their amazing and astonishing *effects*, which were directed toward their 'madeness' and artificiality itself. The spectacle of thunder and lightning that initiated Andromeda's *raptus* is called a *feint*, fictitious and fabricated (cf. A, II.4, p. 64). The "playful spectacle" of the winds was not meant to resemble nature, but rather to surpass nature, calling attention to representation and its media.[20] The *machinations* were the actual object of pleasure. Paratexts praised the art of the machines that had surpassed everything that had so far been seen on the stage in terms of *nouveauté*, creating artful flight manoeuvres and complex aerial choreographies involving numerous flying characters in crisscrossing orbits (cf. A, III.3, pp. 78–83; IV.4, p. 102), and the complex aerial spectacle of Æolus on the eight winds (cf. A, II.5, pp. 66–67). What the audience was seeing was explicitly attributed to the machines, whose 'art' turned out to be that of *self-concealment*.

The allegorical prologue to *Andromeda* marks an interruptive pause that opens up a *different* time and space, which becomes explicit when Melpomène calls out to le Soleil to get him to watch the great scene of homage: "Arrête un peu ta course impétueuse,/ Mon Théâtre, Soleil, mérite bien tes yeux, / Tu n'en vis jamais en ces lieux/ La pompe plus majestueuse" (A, Prologue, p. 16). Le Soleil explictly provides the reason for his pause: "Pour contempler ce Prince, / Je me suis arrêté" (A, Prologue, p. 22) – that is, taking the time it takes to watch. When le Soleil needs to make a fast exit at the end of the prologue, to make up for the delay with "ma rapidité" and continue his run, he takes Melpomène with him in his carriage, "pour aller publier ensemble la même chose [they just have seen] au reste de l'Univers" (A, Prologue, p. 22). Subsequently the action in *Andromeda* is interrupted again and again by inserted 'spaces of time', which are dedicated to pausing and observing the extensive flight choreographies.

Torelli's machine theater did not just set up 'space-consuming' machines that encompassed the visual space and allowed for increasingly complex aeriel movements from above as well as the appearance and disappearance of demons and spirits from below. Rather, a much broader concept of the theater machine becomes apparent: now the scenery turned out to be a *machine*. As *machinations,* the sceneries were not so much merely a 'means of illusion', as in Torelli's scenes of unfathomable perspective with their "enormous, strictly axial depth", "vanishing alleyways which can artificially create any type of illusionary effect and depth."[21] Rather, they were given to *transformation* at any time. *Machines,* according to Torelli and in Torelli's work, determine what can be seen, determine the scene by its potential for transformations and dynamics. By technically optimizing the way the theatrical machines operated, Torelli made it possible to "change [the] scenery on the open stage", which Walter Benjamin compared to the "special scenes put under glaring light" that were devoted to the plotter of intrigues: the theatrical exposition of what is presumed to determine the action from 'behind the scenes'.[22]

The transformation of scenery before the audience's eyes makes every scene a potential other: Everything has the potential to turn into something different. The ropes can be pulled at any time and the theatrical events will be subject to an 'immediate' scene change. Corneille's descriptions of the "Décorations" of *Andromeda* address the changes the scenery will undergo, all of a sudden, "en un moment par un merveilleux artifice" (A, Décoration du premier acte, p. 23), "s'évanouit en un instant" (A, Décoration du second acte, p. 45), and "Voici une étrange Métamorphose" (A, Décoration du troisième acte, p. 69) into a wild natural landscape (that will be the scenery of the third act), occuring like a 'caprice of nature', an event that, if represented, would be a catastrophe, as in: "Les vagues fondent sous le Theâtre, et ces hideuses masses de pierre dont elles battaient le pied, font place à la magnificence d'un Palais Royal" (A, Décoration du quatrième acte, p. 87). The transformations of the represented 'world', which "suddenly relocate us from Earth to heaven, from ocean to hell, from heaven to Earth",[23] presented this world as wonderfully changeable by means of the apparently self-moving equipment, "[c]omme, par un Enchantement".[24] Corneille (occasionally) folds these transformation into the 'inside' of the 'plot' as if by magic. He does this in the allegorical plot of the prologue from *La Conquête de la Toison d'or* (1660), when Hymenée, when asked by La Paix to change the 'face of this place' ("Chassez de ces débris les funestes images, / Et formez des jardins"), transforms the scenery into a magnificent garden: "tels qu'avec quatre mots / Le grand Art de Medée en fit naître à Colchos".[25] In Medée's magic, the 'secret' and the 'power' of the mechanical arts, the operations of the invisible apparatuses, are thematized *inside* the plot. In similar fashion, the Prince's *Fête* represented its host Louis XIV (who controlled its preparations, the apparatuses and their secret) as the *arcana* of power, as a magician.[26] In the third act of Corneille's *Toison d'or*, the way the machinery changes the scenery becomes an impressive theatrical *mise-en-abyme*, when Medée's magical act totally transforms the exhaustively expounded magnificence of the "Palais du Roy Aœte" into a horrific scene: "*Ce Palais doré se change en un Palais d'horreur, sitôt que Medée a dit*" (T, p. 161).[27] It becomes a theatrical *mise en abyme* as the artifice is exposed as a trick by Medée, which gives her brother the opportunity to spectacularly 'rescue' the distraught Hypsipyles. "[T]out d'un coup", all of a sudden, the changes in scenery (cf. T, Décoration du second acte, p. 138) are *theatrical* in their effects; they model the turning points in the course of the drama as something breaking in from the outside, as *coups de théatre*, in which the theater presents 'itself'.

By means of the "mechanical [...] permeation of the theatrical space", Torelli "unleashed unrestrained dynamism".[28] "The performance with machines becomes the presentation of the machines",[29] manifesting themselves through their seemingly 'autonomous movements'. In this ballet of things and characters, the stage is presented as a 'system of kinetic objects'. On the one hand, the action of the *machines* is manifest in the effect of sudden change, "tout d'un coup," which *temporalizes* the space and pushes any space into the "virtual space" of the "kinetics of the machines".[30] On the other hand, the action of the machines in extended aerial ballets of considerable complexity, which should evoke astonishment and admiration for the invisible inventions, creates a different kind of temporality, in conflict with the plot. Corneille had music played for the duration of the detailed choreographed aerial ballets that interrupt and divide the plot. This music, Corneille argues, is there to 'please the audience's ears',

> tandis que leurs yeux sont arrêtés à voir descendre ou remonter une machine, ou s'attachent à quelque chose qui leur empêche de prêter attention à ce que pourraient dire les Acteurs, comme fait le combat de Persée contre le Monstre. (A, Argument, p. 11)

The aerial performance arrests the eyes and makes 'room' for the music, which would otherwise be out of place in a theater, where it is necessary to understand words. This is the argument (directed, incidentally, against the Italian opera and carried out in the *mélodrame*) for the separation and disjunctive coupling of media.[31] There is 'room' for music for the duration of the aerial performance, but the music does not merely accompany the scene: With its extension in time, it also interrupts the plot for an extended period of time and prolongs the time dedicated to seeing and listening, which is extraneous to the plot. This is what the *tableaux* of melodramas do (they often included music and ballet parts); and these *pièces à grand spectacle*, the machine plays, can be seen as a succession of such spectacular *tableaux*.

The musical accompaniment to the flight manoeuvres had another important function, namely to 'cover up' disturbances in the illusion, which were inseparable from the grand effects of the apparatuses.[32] While they were operating, the apparatuses caused visual and acoustic disturbances despite efforts to conceal the noise, the ropes and the metal rods. The music, songs and choruses that accompanied the flight manoeuvres "drowned out the noise of the stage machines"[33] in order to hide the fact that the aerial movements were attached to invisible machinations that revealed themselves in the noise. The disturbances of the creation of perspectival space are even inherent to the modes of this 'creation' itself, because it does not take place as an illusion on the surface of a picture, but rather by combining spaces (the front stage, rear stages, the backdrop) that rarely create *one* illusionary space for the spectator (as Chauveau imagined it in his engravings). All movements through these spaces highlight the composite nature of the spaces. Flying movements, particularly those highly praised ones originating in the depths of the stage, cross through "the illusion of space [...] as a disruptive moment", writes Viktoria Tkaczyk, and this "play between the illusion of perspective and its dissolution through disturbing effects" made "the flight machines a theater effect par excellence during the 17th century".[34]

Theatrical machines that make the spectacle possible in spectacular fashion articulate theater's relationship to the non-visible, to the 'off'. These machines encompass and penetrate the scene, rendering it dynamic. They usurp space; for their sake, the 'off' is expanded immensely on all sides of the stage. The spectacle is bound to what it is not, to its media, which manifest themselves in disturbances. Its effects are self-referential theater effects. If it is to become an *event*, it has to destroy the spectacularity that would be contained in an image: in the *éclat*, in which the construction itself dissolves, shattering into multiple 'images' like the fireworks that concluded the *Toison d'or* or in the festivities of *Les Plaisirs de l'île enchantée* (1664, see Fig. 4), a *mise en abyme* of festive transformations.[35]

But only in the crossing-out of the simulacra, in the destruction that strikes the 'real' of the machines that make it possible, can the spectacle free itself from the machines, as in Félibiens description of the festival in *Les Plaisirs de l'île enchantée*:

> As one also let the whole Machine on the Canal burn along with the seven large boats that carried it, this burning was a new spectacle that surprised those who did not expect it and that made the grandeur and magnificence of the *divertissement* appear to even greater advantage.[36]

Fig. 4: Israël Silvestre: *Les Plaisirs de l'île enchantée* (1664).

Louis Marin points out here that "the simulacrum, in an instant, is turned around and poured back into the real itself, whose consummation is represented in an ultimate spectacle"[37]. This would be *the spectacular catastrophe* that breaks with the "catastrophic imaginary" that Eva Horn addresses,[38] the imaginary that figures and thereby covers over and erases the catastrophic disruption (the disruptive event) through its spectacular representation. Apparently, the catastrophe of the *spectacle* (subjective genitive) that is not restricted by the conception of the internally autonomous and self-contained drama[39] (as in the concept of catastrophe in classical doctrine), but rather threatens to 'flood' and exceed the boundaries of representation, aims at the *catastrophe* of the spectacle (objective genitive). That would be the catastrophe that is *between* and *beyond* imaginary representations and representative images as their medium, which manifests as a hole: the empty, gaping stage. But, the tension between the event and the representation still does not dissolve in the actual destruction of the apparatuses, on the one hand, because in this overturning of the spectacle, as Marin remarks, there is an "act of gratitious giving, that will attempt to make of the staged representation an *infinite* presence [...]", that might 'give' the "epiphany of the glorious body of the king" to the 'portrait of the king' – *beyond* all images.[40] On the other hand, the 'gesture' that reveals the apparatus that produces the illusions also shows that it is just an illusion: a 'play', thus repeating and repeatable – and not a catastrophe. It is not at all clear whether this spectacular destruction of the machines, the supposedly grand gesture of excess, is nothing more than pure coincidence, an accident, or simply a debacle that refers the spectacle back to the physical nature of its apparatuses. The suspension of the frame of dramatic representation does not necessarily accomplish anything overpowering, but does instead reveal the contingencies of the theater, even its banal embarassment.

Translation from the German by Andrew Kirwin

1 Pierre Corneille: *Andromède. Tragedie*. Rouen / Paris: Charles de Sercy 1650; 2nd edition 1651, with the series of six copperplates (source: http://catalogue.bnf.fr/ark:/12148/cb30271434t; accessed April 21, 2017; copperplate for décoration du second acte: p. 30); the series of copperplates by Chauveau was also separately edited in Rouen in 1651 (available at: https://en.wikipedia.org/wiki/Androm%C3%A8de; accessed April 21, 2017). All texts referring to *Andromeda* are here quoted from the following edition: *Andromède*, ed. by Christian Delmas. Paris: Marcel Didier 1974 (hereafter: A). A long version of the following will be published under the title: Was das Theater möglich macht: Theater-Maschinen. In: Nicola Gess et al. (eds): *Archäologie der Spezialeffekte*. Munich: Fink 2018, p. 113–144. The work on the actual version of this text has been made possible by a fellowship of the Excellenzcluster "Kulturelle Grundlagen von Integration" of the University of Konstanz in 2015/16.

2 Staged thunder is a paradigm of accoustic special effects, cf. Florian Nelle: Theaterdonner – Geräusch und Illusion um 1800. In: Hans-Peter Bayerdörfer (ed.): *Stimmen, Klänge. Synergien im szenischen Spiel*. Tübingen: Narr 2002, pp. 493–506, here pp. 493–495.

3 Christian Quaeitzsch: *"Une société de plaisirs": Festkultur und Bühnenbilder am Hof Ludwigs XIV und ihr Publikum*. Munich: Deutscher Kunstverlag 2010, p. 265; all traslations of German quotes by Andrew Kirwin.

4 Rouen / Paris: Augustin Courbé 1650 (source: http://catalogue.bnf.fr/ark:/12148/bpt6k717446; accessed April 21, 2017). Cf. A, pp. 170–189.

5 Cf. Margret Dietrich: Der barocke Corneille. Ein Beitrag zum Maschinen-Theater des 17. Jahrhunderts. In: *Maske und Kothurn* 4 (1958), pp. 199–219 and 316–445, here pp. 207–209; John S. Powell: *Music and Theatre in France 1600–1680*. Oxford: Oxford UP 2000, pp. 23–27, 226–229, 241–244; William D. Howarth (ed.): *French Theatre in the Neo-Classical Era, 1550–1789*. Cambridge: Cambridge UP 1997, pp. 205–210.

6 Quaeitzsch: *Une société de plaisirs*, pp. 16–20.

7 Nikola Roßbach: *Die Poiesis der Maschine. Barocke Konfigurationen von Technik, Literatur und Theater*. Berlin: Akademie 2013, p. 22.

8 Ulrike Haß: *Drama des Sehens. Auge, Blick und Bühnenform*. Munich: Fink 2005, p. 338, pp. 345–346.

9 Cf. Powell: *Music and Theatre in France*, pp. III–IX; Delmas: Introduction. In: A, pp. XV–XXVI. The connection between machines and intermedia is documented by Nicola Sabbatini's *Practica di fabricar scene, e machine ne'teatri* (1637), 2nd part. Cf. Haß: *Drama des Sehens*, p. 338.

10 Albrecht Schöne: *Emblematik und Drama*. Munich: Beck ³1993, pp. 162–185, here pp. 167–168.

11 The theatrical spectacle can be traced back to Bernini's 'simulation of a catastrophe' during the carnival season of 1638: the spectacle of an astonishing flooding of the city of Rome. Cf. Florian Nelle: *Künstliche Paradiese. Vom Barocktheater zum Filmpalast*. Würzburg: Königshausen & Neumann 2005, pp. 19–23.

12 In poetics, the *kata-strophé* became the decisive turning point that produced a meaningful conclusion, the 'solution' or 'untying' in the metaphors *lysis*, *dénouement*; cf. Olaf Briese / Timo Günther: Katastrophe. Terminologische Vergangenheit, Gegenwart und Zukunft. In: *Archiv für Begriffsgeschichte* 51 (2009), pp. 155–195, here pp. 161–164. For the classical link between 'catastrophe' and (nœud and) dénouement, cf. François Hédelin d'Aubignac: *La Pratique du Théâtre* [1657/1715], book II, chap. 9, ed. by Hélène Baby. Paris: Honoré Champion 2001, pp. 203–208.

13 Delmas: Introduction. In: A, p. LXXXVIII; Christian Delmas: Corneille et la tragédie à machines ou le problem de structure d'un genre. In: *Pierre Corneille, Actes du colloque tenu a Rouen* (October 2–6, 1984), ed. by Alain Niederst. Paris: PUF 1985, pp. 393–405.
14 Juliane Vogel characterizes the "Glanzauftritt" in this way. Juliane Vogel: "Who's there?" Zur Krisenstruktur des Auftritts in Drama und Theater. In: J. V. / Christopher Wild (eds): *Auftreten. Wege auf die Bühne*. Berlin: Theater der Zeit 2014, pp. 22–37, here p. 33.
15 Cf. ibid., p. 33.
16 Viktoria Tkaczyk: *Himmels-Falten. Zur Theatralität des Fliegens in der Frühen Neuzeit*. Munich: Fink 2011, p. 164.
17 Louis Marin: The Magician King, or the Prince's Fête. In L. M.: *Portrait of the King*, transl. from the French by Martha M. House. Minneapolis: University of Minnesota Press 1988, pp. 193–205, here and the following pp. 196 and 197.
18 Cf. Ulrike Haß: Vom Wahnsinn des Sehens in geschlossenen Räumen. Raumdebatten und Szenografie im 17. Jahrhundert. In: Nicola Gess / Tina Hartmann / Dominika Hens (eds): *Barocktheater als Spektakel*. Munich: Fink 2015, pp. 139–161, here pp. 144–146, cf. p. 158; cf. also Haß: *Drama des Sehens*, p. 321.
19 Roßbach: *Poiesis der Maschine*, p. 30.
20 Viktoria Tkaczyk: Cumulus ex machina. Wolkeninszenierungen in Theater und Wissenschaft. In: Helmar Schramm / Ludger Schwarte / Jan Lazardzig (eds): *Spektakuläre Experimente. Praktiken der Evidenzproduktion im 17. Jahrhundert*. Berlin / New York: De Gruyter 2006, pp. 43–77, here pp. 61–62, 73.
21 Haß: *Drama des Sehens*, p. 351.
22 Cf. Walter Benjamin: Ursprung des deutschen Trauerspiels. In: W. B.: *Gesammelte Schriften*, vol. 1, ed. by Rolf Tiedemann / Hermann Schweppenhäuser. Frankfurt am Main: Suhrkamp 1974, p. 254. If "the machine is the intrigue" (Delmas: Corneille et la tragédie à machines, p. 397), then this is not just seen as "ruse et tromperie" (ibid., pp. 397–401), but it creates a *coup de théâtre*, incompatible with the act borne from within, which is rather dissembled and established by exhibitions.
23 According to Ménestrier (*Des représentations en musique*, 1681), qtd. in Nelle: *Künstliche Paradiese*, p. 21.
24 According to a report of the performance: *Gazette de France* 123 (1645), p. 1180, qtd. in Quaeitzsch: *Une société de plaisirs*, pp. 167–168.
25 Cf. Pierre Corneille: *La Conquête de la Toison d'or*, ed. by Marie-France Wagner. Paris: Honoré Champion 1998 (hereafter: T), p. 124.
26 Marin: The Magician King, pp. 196–197.
27 "Medea interprets the long-established part of the stage magician whose power is displayed, as [...] the self-reflexive power of staging the play-within-a-play"; "[the] stage-specific power of the magician" "is redoubled and conflated with the power of the machinist" (Amy Wygant: Pierre Corneille's Medea-Machine. In: *The Romanic Review* 85:4 (2004), pp. 537–552, here pp. 541–542).
28 Cf. Jan Lazardzig: *Theatermaschine und Festungsbau. Paradoxien der Wissensproduktion im 17. Jahrhundert*. Berlin: Akademie 2007, p. 36; Ulrike Haß: Von der Schaubühne zur Architektur und über das Theater hinaus. Raumbildende Prozesse bei Sabbattini, Torelli, Pozzo und Appia. In: Norbert Eke / U. H. / Irina Kaldrack (eds): *Bühne: Raumbildende Prozesse im Theater*. Munich: Fink 2014, pp. 345–368, here p. 350.
29 Roßbach: *Poiesis der Maschine*, p. 33.
30 Haß: *Drama des Sehens*, pp. 345–349, here p. 356.

31 Cf. Armin Schäfer / Bettine Menke / Daniel Eschkötter: Das Melodram. Ein Medienbastard (Einleitung). In: A. S. / B. M. / D. E. (eds): *Das Melodram: ein Medienbastard*. Berlin: Theater der Zeit 2013, pp. 7–17.

32 Robert M. Isherwood: *Music in the Service of the King. France in the Seventeenth century*. Ithaca / London: Cornell UP 1973, p. 126; cf. Powell: *Music and Theatre in France*, pp. 262, 230, 244, 258; Quaeitzsch: *Une société de plaisirs*, pp. 166–167.

33 Cf. Dietrich: Der barocke Corneille, p. 321, on Orphée's singing in *La Toison d'or* (cf. T, I.4, p. 136, and V.4, p. 185).

34 Tkaczyk: *Himmels-Falten*, p. 164.

35 "Alcine the magician [...] indeed ends the festival with her own immolation, her palace 'réduit en cendres par un feu d'artifice, qui met fin à cette aventure, et aux divertissements de l'Ile enchantée'" (Wygant: Pierre Corneille's Medea-Machine, p. 551).

36 Quoted from Marin: The Magician King, pp. 203–204.

37 Ibid., p. 203.

38 Eva Horn: *Zukunft als Katastrophe. Fiktion und Prävention*. Frankfurt am Main: Fischer 2014, pp. 20–22, 26–29.

39 Cf. Bettine Menke / Christoph Menke: Tragödie – Trauerspiel – Spektakel. Drei Weisen des Theatralen. In: B. M. / C. M. (eds): *Tragödie. Trauerspiel. Spektakel*. Berlin: Theater der Zeit 2007, pp. 6–15.

40 Marin: The Magician King, p. 203, cf. pp. 204–205.

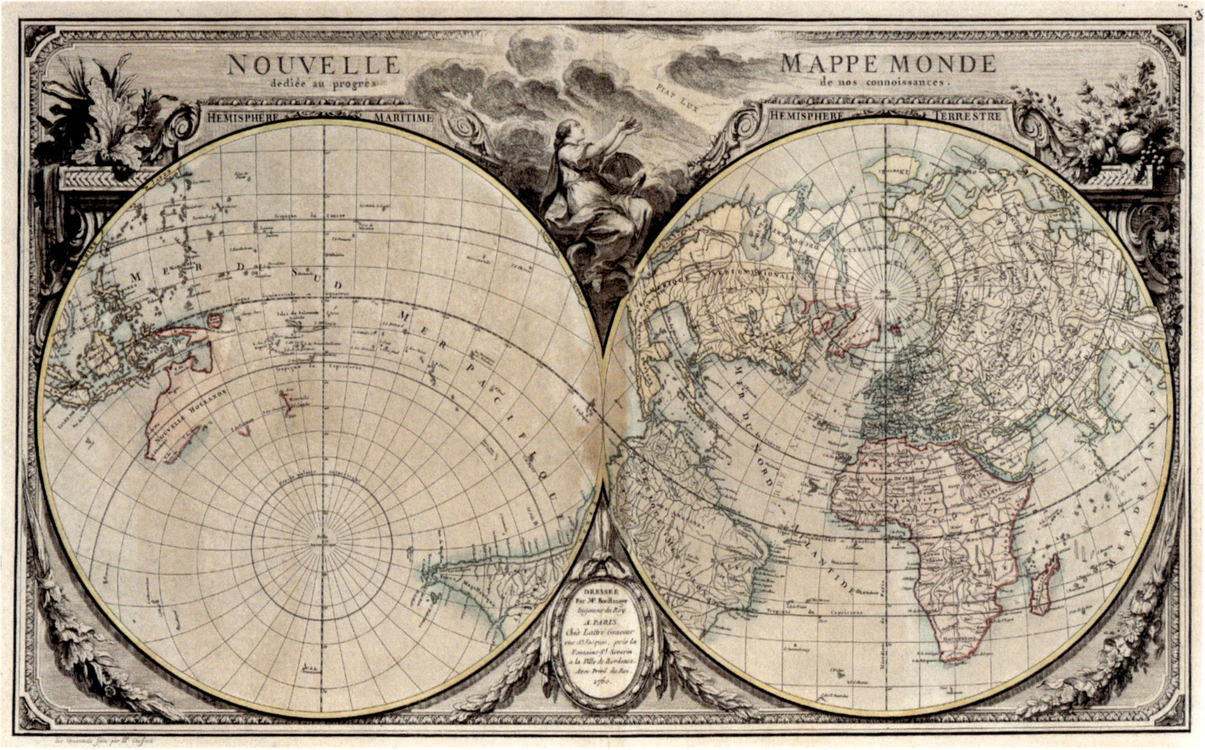

Fig. 1: Nicolas-Antoine Boulanger: *Nouvelle Mappemonde* (1753, here: reprint 1763).

The Elasticity of Earth

On the Precarious Spectacularity of the Catastrophic in Nicolas-Antoine Boulanger's *Nouvelle Mappemonde dédiée au progrès de nos connoissances*

Jörg Dünne

1. What we see: the spectacle of Earth

What we see is a world map divided into two in an azimuthal projection,[1] that is, a projection in which each half of the earth's surface can be displayed on a surface in a circular shape so that, upon observation, it seems as if it is being viewed from outer space. What we can also see is the 'middle line' that divides the two halves into semicircles. By viewing the right half of the map, which shows Europe, the greater part of both Americas and Asia, we can assume that the line is a longitudinal line, the zero meridian to be exact, which runs through the middle of Paris. We can also see that the azimuthal projection is 'tilted', that is, that neither the poles nor any point on the equator are at the center of the illustrated hemispheres. One effect of this projection is that Paris is not only in the middle between the left and right semicircles on the right-hand side of the map, but it also comes rather close to being at the vertical center of the right circle. As the map legend explains, one would have to tilt the earth's axis by 48 degrees, 50 minutes and ten seconds, instead of 45 degrees, for the observatory in Paris to be at the center of the earth's hemisphere, which is illustrated on the right-hand side. Furthermore, we also find the following on the world map: The right half of the map, with the title "hémisphère terrestre", shows one half of the earth's surface, which consists mainly of land masses, whereas the left "hémisphère maritime" depicts the half that is almost completely covered with water (aided by the fact that the contours of Australia have not yet been completely recorded).

What we cannot just see but also read is that this new world map ("Nouvelle Mappemonde") is dedicated to the advances in our knowledge ("dédiée au progrès de nos connoissances") – this title is visualized by way of a typical

Enlightenment allegory that is described in the text that accompanies the map as the "génie des sciences", the genius of science. He stretches his hands toward the cloud-covered sky and with the exclamation "Fiat lux", borrowed from the biblical story of creation, he expresses his wish for the blanket of clouds around the sun to disperse and to allow the desired advances in knowledge, synonymous with looking into the sun, to be made. The viewer of this new world map thus does not merely gain a new perspective on the earth, but, as long as he identifies with the "génie des sciences", he also gains a view of the unobstructed sun, which bestows upon him the blinding light of knowledge. And, we are not wrong to assume that Paris' central position on this world map is a statement that the lifting of this veil, or the elimination of ignorance, predominantly emanates from this city.

The world map thus offers the viewer a showroom, a *theatrum*, as book titles of the early modern period were commonly called, or rather a spectacle – as in the abbé Pluche's metaphor for the encyclopedic summary of human knowledge about nature propagated in the 18th century, primarily throughout France, under the title *Spectacle de la nature*. What immediately catches our eye on this map is that it does not just focus on Europe, or rather France; instead, there is a division between the terrestrial and maritime halves of the earth. This division is arguably the basis for the immediately recognizable idea of progress that is meant to lift the veil of previous blindness for humanity – more on this later.

However, the author of this map and of the accompanying *Mémoire*[2] remains anonymous, unlike the copper engraver Pierre-Philippe Choffard and the publisher, who is mentioned in the cartouche centered at the bottom. This also has something to do with the author profaning the idea of God as the creator while serving to improve human knowledge, which was not appreciated by all of those who read the map or its accompanying text. It was the young Parisian engineer Nicolas-Antoine Boulanger (1722–1759) who, among the *encyclopédistes*, took up the cause to free humanity from its millennia of religious and political illusions. The map and the memorandum serve as an accompaniment to his *Anecdotes physiques de l'histoire de la nature*, a manuscript first published in its entirety in 2006, which was part of a larger project initially called "Anecdotes de la nature".[3]

In this context, the term 'anecdote' has a rather specific meaning, which the contemporary *Dictionnaire de Trévoux* describes as "Choses qui n'ont pas paruës, qui ont été tenuës secretes" ("things not released to the public, which are kept secret").[4] With this secret dimension and the revealing of secrets, the scenes the map suggests of visual insights into the shape of the world are simultaneously challenged by the fact that the surface of the earth, as will be shown, clearly does not reveal the entirety of that which, in spatial terms, can be seen 'below' it, and that which, in the temporal sense, occurs 'before' the current state of things as it is depicted here. This is the point at which the (geological) catastrophe enters this spectacle, which thus far has been as distanced as it has been apparently peaceful: It is that which we do not see on the map – or at least not at first glance.

2. What we do not see (directly): the secret catastrophic history of Earth

It is not geography that is the focus of Boulanger's actual interest, but rather geology – not the depiction of the earth's surface on the map, but rather its 'depth', which, however, is first revealed by the memorandum accompanying the map with the title *Memoire sur une nouvelle mappemonde*. Modern 19th-century geology developed different conventions through which the earth's depth came to be scientifically visualized, ranging from maps depicting the rock types at the surface of the earth to vertical cuts through the earth's crust.[5] For Boulanger, however, such conventions are not yet available; everything below the earth's surface is only tangible to him as phantasmatic and not directly perceivable 'depth'. Long before theoreticians of history perceived the 'depth dimension' as a new historical turn in the 19th century, this depth dimension emerged for Boulanger from geological "deep time",[6] which refers to the spatial depth below the earth's surface. Boulanger thus created a mode of historical thinking that harks back to an ancient geological catastrophe, which he believed could be seen through traces found on the earth's surface.

The secret history of Earth, which Boulanger wanted to present to his readers in his revealing *Anecdotes* report, is quite dynamic. Even though the *Anecdotes* were never published during his lifetime, Boulanger influenced the mode of thinking about Earth's history adopted by renowned natural scientists of the time with his assumption that the earth's surface had been the stage for numerous larger catastrophes, as made clear in the *Époques de la nature* by the Comte de Buffon. But he also influenced the catastrophe theory of the 19th century.

Boulanger's main theory was that the history of humanity had to have seen larger upheavals and catastrophes, and he specifically referenced contemporary and still heavily theologically influenced discussions about the form and the effects of the biblical flood.[7] However, instead of basing his own geological assumptions upon biblical assumptions, which he viewed as pure "imagination" (A, p. 280), Boulanger viewed himself as a scientific observer in the mechanist tradition of "faits sensibles" ("facts based on sensory impressions")[8] and as an analyst of such ideas as a symptom of completely different founding events.

Boulanger suggests nothing less than the ability to connect the world's myths, customs and religious traditions with the real existence of gigantic geological catastrophes that would have so permanently shocked humanity's survivors that the resulting testimonies thereto could only be derived indirectly, requiring an expert 'archaeologist' of imagined human worlds to carry out a revealing process of reading.[9] Thus, he saw himself, anachronistically speaking, not only as an archaeologist of knowledge, but directly as a depth psychologist *avant la lettre*, who had to use his works to 'relieve' humanity as a whole of its collective but unconscious trauma:

> Pour moi, j'ai vu écrit dans la nature que l'homme a été vivement affecté & profondément pénétré de ses malheurs; j'ai vu qu'il a tremblé; j'ai vu qu'il est devenu triste, mélancolique & religieux à l'excès; j'ai vu qu'il a conçu un dégoût total pour cette terre malheureuse [...]. (A, p. 13)
>
> (As far as I am concerned, I have seen, as it is written in nature, that man was actively affected and deeply permeated by his misfortune; I have seen how he trembled, how he became sad, melancholic and overly religious; I have seen him develop a total disgust toward this ill-fated Earth.)

The surviving part of the *Anecdotes* primarily explains the changes to Earth's surface, but it already hints at Boulanger's criticism of the "fables" of humanity, which he would ultimately like to trace back to founding "facts".[10] In the *Anecdotes*, the evidence that Boulanger believes to have found of such catastrophes ranges from the festival of the Hydrophoria in ancient Athens to the Caribbean myths of origin, as well as a daring re-reading of the story of creation in the Old Testament (cf. A, pp. 228–256) – Boulanger is completely convinced that the *tohu wa-bohu* of the story of creation does not describe the original chaotic state of the earth's surface, but rather a much later moment of total destruction after a catastrophe.

Boulanger traces all of humanity's religions, and even the forms of political rule that have developed out of such a traumatized world, back to a 'founding catastrophe'[11] that is not, however, the starting point in the history of Earth as a whole, but rather marks a break that contingently befalls humanity. Thus, Boulanger does not explicitly go beyond the narrow 6,000-year time frame of theologically influenced *geotheory*,[12] which his thoughts are based on. However, he shifts the actual creation of Earth to an inconceivable time in the past, meaning that his assumption that there was a founding catastrophe of historical significance goes hand in hand with his rejection of an initial act of creation carried out by God.

But, what does this catastrophic prehistory of humanity in the *Anecdotes de la nature* have to do with the presentation of Boulanger's world map and the accompanying text to this *Nouvelle Mappemonde*? The catastrophe is what we do not see on the *Nouvelle Mappemonde* or that which we can only see when we read 'beneath the surface' of the map: This is where Boulanger hides his highly speculative explanation as to why the earth's surface was not just subject to all-encompassing catastrophes in the past, but also why such catastrophes can be expected in the future (cf. A, p. 351). However, in order to understand this explanation, we have to accept a different perspective when viewing the world with Boulanger, which does not originate from a limited perspective of a humanity traumatized by various catastrophes. According to Boulanger, we have to discover the history of Earth as 'physicians', or as engineers who wish to peek behind the fundamental principles of the earth's construction and "considérer la terre comme spectateur et non comme habitant" ("view Earth as a spectator and not an inhabitant") (M, p. 392).

Contrary to the popular theory of the time that the earth was originally more fluid and, over time, increasingly became a solid celestial body, Boulanger assumes that the earth has always been a "masse souple et flexible dans son tout" ("moveable and through and through flexible mass") (M, p. 385) and that it possesses a constitutive "élasticité", which Boulanger – entirely the engineer he was by profession – compares with the statics of specific buildings that he by no means considers immovable. Using this comparison, it is his intention to show that an 'elastic' entity such as an arch has more of a curve at one position if another position tends to give way (cf. M, pp. 390–391). According to Boulanger, something similar must have happened to Earth's surface: Such major changes to the statics of the planet are either the result of a sudden change in Earth's interior or rather, according to a popular 18th-century belief, to a sudden change in the tilt of the earth's axis. For Boulanger, such changes must have caused the flattening of Earth at the poles and, moreover, resulted in a lowering of one hemisphere, which has been compensated for by the rising of the surface of the other hemisphere, which, in turn, changed the even distribution of land masses and water between the two hemispheres. We have to get used to the idea, Boulanger writes,

> qu'elle n'est aplatie sur ses pôle et élevée sous son équateur que par une suite de la souplesse générale de toute sa masse, que la division de ses deux hemisphères est l'effet d'une force qui a agi sur elle, comme une force agirait sur une courbe ordinaire. (M, p. 392)
> (that the flattening at the poles and the bulging at the equator are only a consequence of the general flexibility of the earth's overall mass and that the division into two different hemispheres can be traced back to forces that had such an effect on the earth as one would expect on a curved surface.)

This, according to Boulanger, is the physical foundation of the gigantic floods that Earth's history must have experienced since, he later writes, water always makes its way along the deepest paths and thus flows where the surface of the earth is at its deepest (cf. M, p. 393).

The apparently so orderly and stable image of the surface of Earth depicted by the *Nouvelle Mappemonde* can thus, if we assume the distant perspective of a 'spectator' who understands how to read the traces of catastrophes in the history of Earth, be viewed as a catastrophic scenario in which an elastic body has been 'pushed in' on its left side and raised on its right side. The catastrophe is thus hidden within this dynamic compensatory movement that we must imagine having taken place between the right and left hemispheres of the earth. And, above all, the continuous elasticity of Earth allows for such a shifting to occur in the future at any time – for Boulanger, the change between high and low tide is an obvious sign for the ever-present, though somewhat mute vibration of the elastic Earth mass, which could easily tip the scales toward a full-blown catastrophe… However, at first glance, this once again questions the optimism about progress carefully centered around Paris in the *Nouvelle Mappemonde*. Such a geological event of global or cosmic proportions could completely shift the centrality of the French metropolis from its location at the core of Earth's "hémisphère terrestre" at any time and send flood waters rushing through the salons of the Enlightenment thinkers and encyclopedists. The Boulangerian "spectator" must learn to take this deep dimension into consideration while viewing the *Nouvelle Mappemonde*. The catastrophic spectacularity of the spectacle of Earth is made up of a specific combination of the visible and the invisible, of a visible surface and various forms of a barely traceable depth.

3. Conclusion: the catastrophe 'beneath' the images

In conclusion, when viewing the *Nouvelle Mappemonde* and the accompanying comments by Nicolas Antoine Boulanger, we realize that the medial and epistemological conditions for the "invention of the catastrophe", which arguably dates to the 18th century,[13] are not only rooted in visibility and, accordingly, the immediate pictorial character of the catastrophe. The geological theory of catastrophe, which shaped the geological theories of the 18th and 19th centuries starting with Boulanger and which would become the prototype of literary and cultural catastrophe figurations[14], does not emerge – at least not exclusively – "from the image" as the art historian Jörg Trempler describes.[15] If we follow the Boulangerian genealogy of catastrophism, modernity's fascination with spectacular catastrophes is not a result of the linking of image and event to a purely presentist "image-acte", meaning images of the moment of catastrophe,[16] as Trempler suggests, but rather from a collision between different temporalities erupting out of both images of and texts about catastrophes. Here, the catastrophic occurs at a point where a normally inaccessible geological deep time for humanity is immediately linked to a form of historical eventfulness, where latency meets presence. Specifically, one must understand the *Nouvelle Mappemonde* – as considered in this context – together with the opposition it posits between the left and right hemispheres of the world as a type of picture puzzle, in order to discover in it not a permanent order, but rather the earth's ability to change on account of its special 'elasticity'. This is, however, only possible if we read the commentary in the *Mémoire*, which accompanies the *Nouvelle Mappemonde* and refers to a 'revealing' of the deepest secrets of Earth in Boulanger's *Anecdotes de la terre*.

Nowadays, we might smile at Nicolas-Antoine Boulanger's obsession with geological catastrophes, but the vividness with which he describes the deep-time processes as thoroughly historical and the consistency with which he relates various temporalities to each other by means of the way he thinks about catastrophe are more topical than ever before, especially within the context currently being described as the 'Anthropocene'.[17]

Translation from the German by Michael C. Noto

1 Nicolas-Antoine Boulanger: *Nouvelle Mappemonde dédiée au progrès de nos connoissances* [1753]. In: N.-A. B.: *Œuvres complètes*, vol. 2, ed. by Pierre Boutin. Paris: Honoré Champion 2006, s. p.

2 Mr B… [Nicolas-Antoine Boulanger]: *Mémoire sur une nouvelle Mappemonde* [1753]. In: Boulanger: *Œuvres complètes*, vol. 2, pp. 381–399 (hereafter: M; all English translations by Michael C. Noto).

3 Nicolas-Antoine Boulanger: *Anecdotes physiques de l'histoire de la nature*. In: Boulanger: *Œuvres complètes*, vol. 2, pp. 105–372 (hereafter: A).

4 Cf. http://www.cnrtl.fr/dictionnaires/anciens/trevoux/ (accessed March 7, 2016).

5 Cf. Martin Rudwick: The Emergence of a Visual Language for Geological Science 1760–1840. In: *History of Science* 14 (1976), pp. 149–195.

6 Cf. Stephen Jay Gould: *Time's Arrow, Time's Cycle: Myth and Metaphor in the Discovery of Geological Time*. Cambridge: Harvard UP 1987.

7 Concerning the flood in Boulanger, see Paul Sadrin: *Nicolas-Antoine Boulanger ou avant nous le déluge*. Oxford: Voltaire Foundation 1986. On the flood in the 18th century in general, cf. Maria Susana Seguin: *Science et religion dans la pensée française du XVIIIe siècle: le mythe du Déluge universel*. Paris: Honoré Champion 2001.

8 See Pierre Boutin's introduction in: Boulanger: *Œuvres complètes*, vol. 2, pp. 9–102, here pp. 26–34.

9 On Boulanger's catastrophe theory, see Sonja Asal: "Eine neue Art, die Menschengeschichte zu schreiben." Nicolas-Antoine Boulangers Theorie der Sintflut zwischen Mythos und Naturgeschichte. In: Walter Schmitz / Carsten Zelle (eds): *Innovation und Transfer. Naturwissenschaften, Anthropologie und Literatur im 18. Jahrhundert*. Dresden: Thelem 2004, pp. 97–119. Cf. also Martin Mulsow: Sintflut und Gedächtnis: Hermann von der Hardt und Nicolas-Antoine Boulanger. In: M. M. / Jan Assmann (eds): *Sintflut und Gedächtnis. Erinnern und Vergessen des Ursprungs*. Munich: Fink 2006, pp. 131–161.

10 Boulanger elaborates on his criticism of myth in his posthumously published works *Recherches sur l'origine du despotisme oriental* [1761], ed. by Paul Sadrin. Paris: Les Belles Lettres 1988; and *L'Antiquité devoilée par ses usages* [1766], ed. by Paul Sadrin. Paris: Les Belles Lettres 1978.

11 Concerning the 'founding catastrophe' that gave birth to the art of memory, see Louis Marin: Le trou de mémoire de Simonide. In: L. M.: *Lectures traversières*. Paris: Albin Michel 1992, pp. 197–209. On the parallel dynamics of foundation and unfounding, see also the neologism "effondement" coined by Gilles Deleuze in *Différence et repetition*. Paris: PUF 1996, pp. 92–93; see also the introduction to this volume, p. 10.

12 On the history of geology in the 18th century in general, see Martin Rudwick: *Bursting the Limits of Time. The Reconstruction of Geohistory in the Age of Revolution*. Chicago / London: University of Chicago Press 2005.

13 Cf. Anne-Marie Mercier-Faivre / Chantal Thomas (eds): *L'Invention de la catastrophe au XVIIIe siècle. Du châtiment divin au désastre naturel*. Genève: Droz 2008.

14 Cf. Jörg Dünne: *Die katastrophische Feerie. Geschichte, Geologie und Spektakel in der modernen französischen Literatur*. Konstanz: Konstanz UP 2016.

15 Jörg Trempler: *Katastrophen. Ihre Entstehung aus dem Bild*. Berlin: Wagenbach 2013.

16 Cf. ibid., pp. 59–63.

17 For a more detailed account of how Boulanger's theory might be crucial to reflections on the 'Anthropocene', see the modified German version of this contribution: Jörg Dünne: Paris 1753: L'Anthropo-scène – eine katastrophische Mediologie der Menschheitsgeschichte. In: Christian Kiening / Martina Stercken (eds): *Medialität. Historische Konstellationen*. Zurich: Chronos [forthcoming].

Fig. 1: The Ruins of Palmyra (2016).

Spectacular Catastrophes

Representations of Suddenness and Distance

Walburga Hülk

Contemporary catastrophes appear as the unmediated depictions of catastrophes, frozen moments or even livestreams of periods of time. Most of us are lucky to read about or share in catastrophes from a distance, and yet, in a globalized world, they do hit home. These images do more than just brush against our indifference: They excite our imagination, our empathy and fear. They are, according to Stephen Greenblatt's term, loaded with social and cultural energy,[1] and their *punctum* can touch or affect us, as Roland Barthes would have said.[2] Today's catastrophes and disasters are visible in shots of destroyed cities, of a single victim, several victims, uncountable victims, whether Germans are among them or not. Perhaps the contemporary catastrophe is most vividly symbolized by the ruins of Palmyra, and, since even those ruins have now been destroyed, by nothingness. Palmyra's ruins and nothingness are icons of our time; they belong to a war of images, unheard of until the 21st century, and make us fear the apocalypse.[3] Most of all, according to Susan Sontag, they make the pain of others present and make us look at it and the suddenness of terror.[4]

'Depictions of catastrophe' are not an invention of technical media, though technical media have had a decisive influence on the way disasters are perceived. Today, natural and political catastrophes might seem ubiquitous or at least in direct proximity to us, even if they happen thousands of miles away. Yet, depicted disasters belong to the history of iconography, and we wonder which media, which formal or compositional techniques inform our impression of proximity or distance. Visual representations of disasters were a central issue in the 18th century. Painters like Claude-Joseph Vernet, Pierre-Jacques Volaire and, later on, Caspar David Friedrich and Théodore Géricault frequently depicted natural and human disasters, sea storms and shipwrecks, volcanic eruptions, firestorms and ruined cities. They transformed allegorical traditions or chose specific historic moments to memorialize, and they created an atmosphere of astonishment and awe. These paintings were closely related to the emergence of the aesthetics of 'greatness' or the 'sublime' proposed in an article by Joseph Addison in *Spectator* 412 in 1712 and elaborated upon by Edmund Burke in 1757.[5] Burke's treatise *A Philosophical Enquiry into the Origins of Our Ideas of the Sublime and Beautiful* was published two years after the Lisbon earthquake,[6] and although the book and the disaster were not directly related, we believe that both correspond with a specific interest in the spectacular that was popular in the 18th century.

The Lisbon earthquake, which was immediately followed by a large fire and a tsunami, occurred on Catholic All Saints' Day on November 1, 1755, in one of the oldest, largest and most flourishing European cities at that time, which was also the capital of a huge colonial empire. The catastrophe, which killed an unknown but certainly enormous number of victims and caused material damage on an astonishing scale, was generally considered an overwhelming disaster, a 'great' event.[7] And whereas the term 'catastrophe' had designated the final act of a tragedy up until then, it was used as a term for a natural calamity from that moment on. The immediate responses of witnesses to the Lisbon earthquake, from admonishers and accusers alike, were multiple, a huge number of leaflets went into circulation, and reactions all over Europe were enduring.[8] When news of the disaster finally arrived in Cologne, Amsterdam, Genova, Paris and Königsberg only a few weeks later, the intellectual world was thrilled. The prevailing philosophy of optimism and the concept of theodicy, as represented by Alexander Pope and Gottfried Wilhelm Leibniz, as well as geological questions were debated energetically by the most eminent European thinkers, such as Voltaire and Jean-Jacques Rousseau, who found new reason to argue with each other, while the young Immanuel Kant discussed the ecological origins and consequences of the earthquake and considered the greatness of the event to be inspiration for fantasy and narration. The Lisbon earthquake, the sudden rage and uncontrolled outbreaks of the earth that are always, as Michel de Montaigne pointed out, in motion and never stop trembling even slightly, had a unique influence on theological and philosophical ideas.[9] It spurred on geological studies and kindled narratives of oceanic secrets and the tumultuous interior of the earth. It also became a source of reference for important literary texts, such as Voltaire's *Poème sur le désastre de Lisbonne* (*Poem on the Lisbon Disaster*, 1756) and his philosophical narrative *Candide* (1759); Heinrich von

Kleist's novella *Das Erdbeben von Chili* (*The Earthquake in Chile*, 1807); Johann Peter Hebel's calendar story *Unverhofftes Wiedersehen* (*Unexpected Reunion,* 1811); and Theodor Fontane's late novel *Der Stechlin* (*The Stechlin*, 1897/98). Never before had a natural catastrophe that had actually taken place evoked such an abundance of texts – competing with those about the flood myth – nor has any since.

The Lisbon earthquake was not just a privileged issue for writers, but also for artists. In 1757, the French engraver Jacques-Philippe Le Bas, a member of the Cabinet du Roi and scholar of Vernet, referred to as the "painter of shipwrecks", published a series of six plates, *Recueil des plus belles ruines de Lisbonne causées par le tremblement et par le feu du premier novembre 1755* (*Collection of the Most Beautiful Ruins of Lisbon Caused by the Earthquake and the Firestorm of the 1st of November, 1755*). At that time, the aesthetics of ruins was in vogue, being one of the strongest impressions of those who returned from their *grand tours*, and also a privileged impulse for imagination. Giovanni Battista Piranesi had recently published two widely observed graphic series, *Antiquità Romane de Tempi della Repubblica* (*Roman Antiquities of the Time of the Republic*, 1748) and *Antichità Romane* (*Roman Antiquities,* 1756); David Le Ruys' *Les Ruines des plus beaux monuments de la Grèce* (*The Ruins of the Most Beautiful Monuments of Greece*) appeared in print in 1758; and Robert Wood and James Dawkins published their engravings *The Ruins of Palmyre, Otherwise Tedmor in the Desert* in 1753. In 1751, the article on "Antiquités" in Denis Diderot's and d'Alembert's *Encyclopédie* stated that, in architecture, the term "antiquities" was also used for fragments of monuments ruined by time or by barbarians, as in Rome.[10] And when, on his first trip to Italy in 1787–88, Johann Wolfgang von Goethe met the draughtsman and engraver Louis-François Cassas,[11] who had returned from his journeys to Rome and to Pompeii, where the Herculaneum had recently been discovered, and further afield to the Orient, it was a real highlight for him. In 1784, Cassas had published his travel report *Voyage pittoresque de la Syrie, de la Phénicie, de la Palestine et de la Basse-Égypte* (*A Picturesque Tour through Syria, Phoenicia, Palestine and Lower Egypt*), with images of the ruins of Balbec and Palmyra, which were already sites of amazing beauty and decay at the time. Goethe was thrilled.[12] In his letters to Charlotte von Stein from September 1887, he expressed his "delight" about Cassas' drawings and his almost contemporaneous *Roman Elegies*, due to the imaginative portrayals of the power of ruins in Italy and abroad. He began as follows: "Speak to me, stones, o say, you lofty palaces, tell me – Streets, are you lost for a word? Spirit of Rome, are you dumb?"[13] Cassas'

Fig. 2: Jacques-Philippe Le Bas: *Recueil des plus belles ruines de Lisbonne causées par le tremblement et par le feu du premier Novembre 1755*, plate 4: Ópera do Tejo (Paris, 1757).

drawings inspired Goethe's own aesthetic experiences and, several years later, in his *Italienische Reise* (*Italian Journey*), he confessed to having stolen some of Cassas' ideas.

Ruins were, so to speak, 'in the air' when Le Bas decided to engrave his *Most Beautiful Ruins of Lisbon*. The two years since the earthquake had not been enough to reconstruct the Portuguese capital, and politicians, urbanists and architects now had to take into account the tectonic risks of the coast and the lower Tajus river, which run across a fault line. As Jörg Trempler has pointed out, Le Bas' series of engravings, in their graphic rigor and pure and sophisticated composition, differ decisively from representations of previous earthquakes that had taken place in the middle ages and in early modern times – such as Sebastian Münzer's copperplate of the earthquake of Basel, published in 1356.[14] Le Bas' views of the ruins of the opera house, St. Nicolas Church, the Tower of St. Roch and the Royal Palace also stand out in an anonymous engraving, dated 1755, that portrays the immediate chaos following the disaster and the immediacy of total confusion, bewilderment and horror in the particularly detailed and dynamic composition of a 'Wimmelbild' – a 'teeming picture' – a technique that, incidentally, can be observed, transferred into another medium, in some passages of Kleist's novella *The Earthquake in Chile*.

No doubt: Le Bas' *Most Beautiful Ruins* differs significantly from all representations of previous earthquakes and even of the Lisbon disaster. But while Trempler argues that Le Bas' series reveals the first examples of modern "catastrophe pictures", I would object that precisely this technique of compositional reduction and formal rigor suggests another interpretation: Instead of staging directness and proximity, as modern catastrophe pictures easily do, Le Bas' series cites and reinvents previous pictures of reflection and distance. As some of them show the spectator in the painting, they also emphasize the iconography of memory. They look at what remains, vestiges of the past that suggest what has happened, *what was*. And although they are sometimes considered to be the documentation or the autopsies of architectural damage, we need to consider the fact that they do not represent the exact location of the buildings in the urban space and not even precise architectural proportions. This suggests that they do not merely figure as autopsies of damage and destruction, but become *memento mori* and a source of aesthetic experience – of melancholy, imagination and self-reflection. They also remind us of the freedom of art, the freedom Shakespeare evokes in the *Winter's Tale* where Bohemia is described as a desert country near the sea.[15]

Fig. 3: Anon.: *La destruction de Lisbone* (The Lisbon Earthquake of 1755).

Just one century after the Lisbon earthquake and the iconographic vogue of portraying ruins, the Parisian prefect Georges-Eugène Haussmann engaged the photographer Charles Marville[16] to record 'Haussmannisation', the destruction of old Paris and the construction of the new capital. Marville's multiple series documents the unique urban conversion that damaged the old quarters of Paris and created a modern and elegant urban space. Haussmannisation incited a range of different reactions. Even though it reduced the incidence of the regular cholera outbreaks and made it possible for the ubiquitously praised elegance of the globalized capital to emerge, it was also considered a disaster by many inhabitants and artists who complained about a process that we today refer to as 'gentrification'. Whatever this titanic operation was, like Haussmann, Marville left us an

Fig. 4: Charles Marville: *Between Rue de l'Échelle and Rue Saint Augustin: demolition*. From the photo series *Percement de l'Avenue de l'Opéra* (1876).

amazing legacy, and the most impressive photographs are to be found in the series *Percement de l'Avenue de l'Opéra* (*Construction for the Avenue de l'Opéra*, about 1870).

When Marville photographed the city's destruction and rebuilding, he created much more than a meticulous autopsy of historical moments observed in close proximity. Like his predecessor Le Bas, he sometimes put the spectator in the picture and thus showed, in the early years of a new technical media, a deep understanding of pictorial composition and self-reflexivity as well as a sense of aesthetic distance. Roland Barthes declared this distance the essence of photography: to represent that what *was* and what still touches us because it is lost.[17]

And Palmyra? It is part of the memory of the world, as it was when Friedrich Hölderlin wrote his poem *Lebensalter* (*Ages of Life*, about 1803/04) and asked in the first verses: "Euphrates' cities and / Palmyra's streets and you / Forests of columns in the level desert / What are you now?"[18] In a distant future, the ruins and nothingness of Palmyra might again be praised as an inspiration, a sublime site in the desert and a source of delight. Today, their real presence *hurts*.

1 Stephen Greenblatt: *Shakespearean Negotiations. The Circulation of Social Energy in Renaissance England*. Oxford: Clarendon 1988, pp. 1–20.

2 Roland Barthes: *Camera lucida*, transl. from the French by Richard Howard. London: Fontana 1984, pp. 43–46; *La chambre claire. Note sur la photographie*. Paris: Seuil 1980.

3 Paul Veyne: *Palmyre. L'irremplaçable trésor*. Paris: Albin Michel 2015.

4 Susan Sontag: *Regarding the Pain of Others*. New York: Picador / Farrar, Strauss & Giroux 2003.

5 Joseph Addison: *Pleasures of the Imagination. Papers from the Spectator (1712)*. http://web.mnstate.edu/gracyk/courses/phil%20306/addison_index.htm (accessed April 23, 2017).

6 Edmund Burke: *A Philosophical Enquiry into the Origin of Our Ideas of the Sublime and the Beautiful*, ed. by J. T. Boulton. London: Routledge / Kegan Paul 1958.

7 Harald Weinrich: Literaturgeschichte eines Weltereignisses: Das Erdbeben von Lissabon. In: H. W.: *Literatur für Leser. Essays und Aufsätze zur Literaturwissenschaft*. Stuttgart: Kohlhammer 1971, pp. 64–76.

8 Theodore E. D. Braun / John B. Radner (eds): *The Lisbon Earthquake of 1755. Representations and Reactions*. Oxford / Richmond: Voltaire Foundation 2005.

9 Michel de Montaigne: *The Complete Essays*, ed. and transl. from the French by Michael A. Screech. London: Penguin Classics 2003, book III, chapter 2, pp. 907–922; *Essais*, vol. 2, ed. by Maurice Rat. Paris: Garnier 1962, pp. 222–237.

10 Jacques-François Blondel: Antiquités. In: Denis Diderot / Jean-Baptiste le Rond d'Alembert: *Encyclopédie ou Dictionnaire raisonné des sciences, des arts et des métiers*. http://www.encyclopédie.eu/A.html. (accessed April 23, 2017).

11 Thomas Ketelsen (ed.): *Palmyra, was bleibt? Louis-François Cassas und seine Reise in den Orient*. Cologne: Museum Wallraf 2016.

12 Mathias Énard: *Boussole*. Arles / Paris: Actes Sud 2015.

13 Johann Wolfgang von Goethe: *Roman Elegies*, ed. and transl. from the German by David Luke. New York: Barnes 1977, p. 25; Römische Elegien. In: *Werke*, vol. 1: *Gedichte und Epen 1*, ed. by Erich Trunz. München: Beck 1981, pp. 157.

14 Jörg Trempler: *Katastrophe. Ihre Entstehung aus dem Bild*. Berlin: Wagenbach 2013, pp. 64–78.

15 William Shakespeare: *The Winter's Tale*. In: *The Norton Shakespeare*, ed. by Stephen Greenblatt. New York / London: Norton 1997, Act III, Scene 3, p. 2913.

16 Sarah Kennel (ed.): *Charles Marville: Photographer of Paris*. Chicago: University of Chicago Press 2013.

17 Cf. Barthes: *Camera lucida*.

18 Friedrich Hölderlin: Ages of Life. In: *Selected Poems*, transl. from the German by David Constantine. Newcastle: Bloodaxe 1996, p. 71; Lebensalter. In: *Werke*, vol. 1: Gedichte, ed. by Friedrich Beißner / Jochen Schmidt. Frankfurt am Main: Insel 1983, pp. 133–134.

Fig. 1: Théodore Gericault: *The Raft of the Medusa* (1819, oil on canvas, 16' x 23', Musée du Louvre).

The Eventization of Tragic Experience at the Threshold of the 19th Century: *The Raft of the Medusa*

Kati Röttger

"A shipwreck ends in a human tragedy. *The Raft of the Medusa* by Jean Louis Théodore Géricault both moves and shocks the viewer today like it did 200 years ago."[1] So begins the introduction to this painting on the website of the Schirn Museum in Frankfurt. According to Ekkehard Tanner, it is the painting's timeless expression of tragic experience that is so deeply moving. Back then, in 1819, it reported on the utmost desperate moment of the last 15 survivors of the naval disaster that had taken place on the French flagship Medusa in 1816, which had resulted in the death of at least 135 people. Now, it is evocative of the shipwrecks and the loss of so many of those who have crossed the Mediterranean Sea to seek asylum in Europe.

Right from the beginning, *The Raft of the Medusa* became a modern myth. Only a few paintings have provoked so many and such enduring responses. In her rich collection of material on the shipwreck motif, Sabine Mertens writes that "this, for its time, most spectacular picture was a milestone in the history of the motif. Never before had the suffering and death of people been depicted in such an impressive way."[2] It qualifies it as a key artwork of modernity, be it as a symbol of the condition of modern life (Peter Weiss), of modern society (Jules Michelet) or as a milestone for modern painting (Hans Belting). The biblical flood motif, which dominated depictions of catastrophe until the late 18th century, was – combined with classical techniques – replaced by the depiction of a real event for the first time. Consequently, the actors of this event were neither Napoleonic heroes according to the traditional manner of historical painting, nor were they biblical figures. They were common, everyday people, but portrayed in poses like those painted by Rubens or Michelangelo. This indicates a turning point: the transition to Romantic painting.

The painting is based on a report about the catastrophe of the *Shipwreck of the Medusa on her voyage to Senegal in the year 1816*, which was published by two survivors, Jean-Baptiste Henri Savigny and Alexandre Corréard in 1817, to "uncover the cruel truth" of the disaster that was caused by the irresponsible and incompetent command of the Royalist captain Hugues Duroy Vicomte de Chaumaneys.[3] The report immediately became a political scandal. On the one hand, the whole enterprise that the Medusa – the most precious ship in the French Navy – and three other ships had been part of had failed. Its aim had been to recapture Senegal, the colonial African territory that had been taken by England and then taken back again by France. On the other hand, the disaster was also seen as proof of the malfunction of the restored monarchy, "a symbol of the shattered French ship of state under Louis XVIII."[4]

Géricault had not personally witnessed the events. Without taking this fact into consideration, his painting went down in history as the most intriguing document of the fatal shipwreck. In fact, it was not the report but the painting that entered collective memory. But without the report that Géricault himself had read, the painting would never have come into being. It became an event in its own right, praised as a key work of the catastrophic imaginary of Western modernity. The fact that this was possible was due, as I would like to argue in the following, to its specific contribution to the spectacularization of catastrophe in its time – a spectacularization that went hand in hand with the eventization of tragic experience. This link to tragedy was not new. Jörg Trempler, for instance, elucidates the impact of this painting by comparing its essence with the "primary matter of tragedy".[5] A single catastrophe, a current event, becomes a metaphor for human destiny. The survivors on the raft went into the fatal accident innocently when they embarked the ship together with 220 other passengers on June 17, 1816, and they came out of it weighed down by guilt due to the tragic decisions they had to make about life and death. They were only able to survive the 12-day passage on the raft by killing other passengers and even eating their dead flesh. They were forced to fight and kill a large number of their shipmates. Others had been swept out to sea, died of hunger or had lost their sanity. Those who had been saved had been feeding on human flesh for several days. They had become cannibals and murderers – held captive in between barbarism and sacrifice.

Géricault's monumental painting, at 16x23 feet, portrays the horrific events that took place on the raft on the day of rescue. It leaves aside the monstrous details of human behavior, concentrating instead on the climax of the situation between hope and despair, between the prospect of survival and that of going under. The painter decided to choose the 'fruitful' or 'pregnant moment' when those left on the raft finally spotted one of the ships from their convoy. The brig Argus was searching for the remains of the Medusa in the hopes of recovering its survivors. At first, it appeared and then disappeared on the horizon. The final rescue only took place when the Argus appeared a second time. The moment being depicted is still at the stage of cruel existential uncertainty. At this point, nobody on the raft knows if they will be discovered and thus recovered, if they will live or die. By selecting this scene, Géricault chose the moment that is identical with the literal translation of the Greek word catastrophe, derived from *kata* (reversing or downwards) and *strophe* (turn around): the turning point. However, in Aristotle's *Poetics* this moment is described as *peripeteia* and not as catastrophe. Whereas *peripeteia* means the turning point of the dramatic curve of suspense, the climax in which the action is reversed reaching either a happy or a fatal end, catastrophe denotes the *result* of the climatic situation, *the end* of the suspense curve. As Eva Horn so aptly writes, it is only from the perspective of its ending that the whole dramatic scenario can be surveyed.[6] Géricault combines both: Observing from such an end, he places his actors right at the turning point where they themselves do not know the outcome, the result of their drama. This extreme dramatic tension at the turning point in the narrative is enhanced by the painting's spatial composition. The forefront of the monumental canvas is dominated by a pyramidal composition of human bodies that seem to be piled up like a pyre. The more than life-sized bodies that fill the entire bottom half of the painting are turned toward the gaze of the beholder, with one figure idly glancing straight at the viewer. These bodies express pure misery, total exhaustion, starvation and near death. Those in the upper half direct their gaze toward the horizon, in the opposite direction, outside of the picture, where the rescue boat seems to have just appeared, a minuscule point far away in the ocean. All of their bodies are stretched toward it; some lift their arms in the same direction, like blazing flames. They are crowned by a flittering cloth held up to the sky by the black man who forms, supported by his comrades, the top of the pyramid of bodies. This composition divides the scene on the raft into two opposite parts, one shaped by an attitude of strained, animate hope and the other by slack, inanimate despair. Yet both sides are part of the same pyramid. "A single horizontal diagonal rhythm [leads] us from the dead at the bottom left, to the living at the apex."[7] It is a visualization of the turning point, which will reach its end in either sacrifice or rescue.

The apocalyptic, but still undecided situation is stressed by the dark-colored overtones that define the painting, which seem even more threatening in contrast with the glowing horizontal line that seems to shed light on some of the body parts. The entire raft is fully exposed to the forces of nature. It is helplessly abandoned to the heavily moving waves. It is especially striking that the whole group, together with the sail, is painted as if it forms a gigantic wave in itself that is moving toward the horizon.
In this sense, *The Raft of the Medusa* made history, because the single tragic moment of human suffering that Géricault's painting depicted was a simultaneous incarnation of the catastrophic implications of the historical turn of its time. This historical turn is marked by a certain tension, as it stands for the invention of history as the overall episteme of the 19th century as well as the experience of the loss of a stable historical foundation. Both were caused by the political and industrial revolutions at the end of the 18th century. By dismissing salvation history, a modernity begins that is defined by the paradox of the belief in a manmade future and in the irreversibility of history. The more man deems himself able to create the future and the further that future progresses, the more he perceives himself to be at the mercy of the events to come. In this constellation, the predictability and inexperience of human destiny are closely linked to each other. Consequently, the period around 1800 was the first time that historical catastrophes were contemplated as specific events. According to Dieter Groh et al.,[8] the semantic field covering the notion of catastrophe changed in the early 19th century. Its former poetological meaning was now transformed to describe everyday life experiences. On the one hand, it referred to human forms of drama and sorrow. On the other hand, it indicated a disaster that pointed to the loss of future prospects. The eighth edition of the *Brockhaus Enzyklopädie* from 1835 is similar in its definition but stresses the notion of the turn even more:

> The word catastrophe roughly translates to turn. Hence, it refers to the moment in an individual's life or in the life of a group of individuals that marks a definite and crucial turning point. This can be a turn for the better or for the worse, toward fortune or misfortune.[9]

Nearly parallel to this, we can see that "in the first half of the 19th century," in the aftermath of the French revolution, "the terms catastrophe and revolution could be explained with each other".[10] A similar reading can be found in Hannah Arendt's extensive study *On Revolution*. Here, Arendt establishes a relationship between the contexts of natural history and human history to which the French revolution and the ensuing permanent revolutions in the 19th century (1789, 1792, 1830, 1848, 1851, 1871). From the experience of the historical necessity of those "who first made and then enacted the Revolution in France,"[11] she derives a new metaphorical meaning for the word. This new meaning relates to celestial bodies that rotate and, according to the laws of physics, must move by necessity. Furthermore, it is for this very reason that the (permanent) revolution behaves like a great spectacle.

> It has obviously carried an even greater plausibility for those who watched its course, as if it were a spectacle, from outside. What appeared to be most manifest in this spectacle was that none of its actors could control the course of events.[12]

Along with the spectacle, the category of the spectator emerges, as well as the category of the observer of historical events who is carried away with them. This experience of historical necessity and the irreversibility of events paves the way for a philosophy of history. Or, to put it as Jacob Burckhardt did, these shocks give birth to the historico-philosophical spectator who increasingly loses his position as mere spectator in the face of expected catastrophes, be they social catastrophes, natural catastrophes or technological catastrophes resulting from the progress of modernity. This catastrophic experience of modernity manifests itself in the image of the *Raft of the Medusa*, as I have described. However, what must be stressed here is that, in precisely that crack in time that is the caesura at the threshold of the 19th century, from which that what we call modernity arises, the painting contributes in a specific way to the formation of a self-referential catastrophic iconographic program. By depicting an event *as catastrophic*, it *produces* catastrophic experiences, which in the sequel – as Groh et al. put it – created awareness for certain perils. The demands of history and poetics become intertwined challenges to the claims of reality.

Géricault did this by transferring the catastrophic moment from the realm of the poetological, the literary, into the realm of the visual, the pictorial. Here we witness a turn away from the textual dramaturgy of the tragic toward a pictorial dramaturgy of the tragic. At its core, we find the technique of *eventizing* catastrophic experience. This means that the fictive plot of tragic poetics is substituted for a real event. But at the same time, Géricault's attempt to depict reality in his painting also drew on the theatricalization of the event. Not having experienced the scene of the catastrophe himself, he re-created it as though on stage. To combine the effect of the

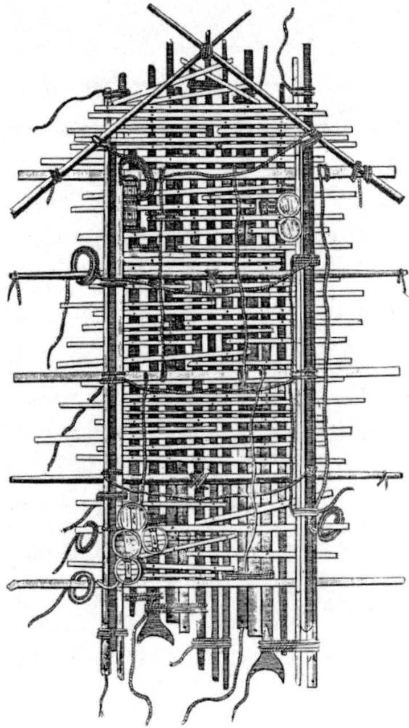

Fig. 2: Layout of the Raft of the Medusa (attributed to Alexandre Corréard). In: Alexandre Corréard / Jean-Baptiste-Henri Savigny: *Naufrage de la frégate La Méduse*. Paris: Corréard 1821, s. p.

real (i. e. of presence as well) in the image, both the event and the input of the event had to temporally coincide. He put in a great deal of effort to achieve this realistic effect, taking more than a year to get there. He was especially interested in painting a topic of social relevance, which he had, however, never done before. He had largely trained in detailed naturalistic studies of horses and military topics. Only after *The Raft* did he dedicate himself to painting those excluded from society, like in his well-known studies of *Portraits of the Insane* (*Les Monomanes*) between 1822 and 1823. He decided on the topic of *The Raft* shortly after he returned from an extended tour of Italy at the end of 1817. The report on the shipwreck had been published in November of the same year. He must have made his decision immediately after having read it. He bought the canvas on February 24, 1818, and four months later he transferred it to a bigger studio. He was so obsessed with getting all details of the event as true to life as possible that he convinced a carpenter, one of the survivors of the Medusa, to build him a model of the raft in his studio. "On this, he positioned wax models of the figures, while sketches of dead bodies were hung on the studio walls."[13] It is even said that his studio was filled with the disgusting stench of decaying corpses because, in search of detail, he had been extensively studying the remains of several dead bodies.

Additionally, he did a great deal of archival work to get the most accurate information about the events on the raft, also collecting contemporary prints that documented it. Although he knew from the beginning that it was the shipwreck that he wanted to paint, he was not at all certain about which moment to choose. It is interesting to review the series of scenes that he drafted, which emerge chronologically along the timeline of the report. As if he was following the dramaturgy of a three-act play, he concentrated on three crucial moments. The first drawing was dedicated to the first days on the raft when the mutiny broke out and many people drowned. The second drawing depicted the stage of cannibalism.

For every scene, he carried out an abundance of preparatory work and immersed himself in pre-painting the flesh tones of the decaying body parts he obtained from Hôpital Beaujon. In the last phase, he concentrated on the scene of the rescue, drawing several versions of the appearance of the brig Argus. During that time, he finally decided to leave all direct allusions to cannibalism aside. When the painting was exhibited at the Salon of 1819, it sparked very contradictory reactions. Although Géricault deliberately chose the more general title *Shipwreck Scene*, the reference to the factual event was clear for many of his contemporaries and was perceived either as a revolutionary composition that called for defiance or as a

Fig. 3: Theodore Gericault: *Cannibalism* (1818, black chalk, ink wash, watercolor and white gouache on light brown paper, 11" x 15", Paris, Gobin Collection).

defamation of the French Navy. In any case, the historical reference was obvious and, with this, Géricault had introduced an "analogic technology"[14] that helped to inaugurate a new collective and an individual experience that departed from historicity by giving it the status of a catastrophic event. In this sense, the painting preconfigured what would later be identified as a specific (reality-)effect of reproduction media and their power of spectacularization. If we are to believe Bernard Stiegler, this coincides with the "industrial retention of memory":

> [These] media are not satisfied with 'co-producing' events, but, more and more frequently, actually integrally produce them, in a veritable inversion by which media recount everyday events so forcefully that their 'life-story' seems not only to anticipate but ineluctably to precede – to determine – life itself.[15]

The single, spatiotemporal reality that Géricault cuts out of the documentary story of the shipwreck is composed in accordance with the poetological law of tragedy by visualizing the pregnant moment of catastrophe. But interestingly enough, this picture, in turn, did not inspire any tragedies. There is no record of a classical tragedy based on the *Raft of the Medusa*. However, what we do know is that several melodramas and other kinds of spectacular technologies, such as the panorama, were inspired by it throughout Europe.[16] This is a clear argument in favor of Stiegler's observations. It started with one of the first examples of the nautical melodrama in full rig, W. T. Moncrieff's *Shipwreck of the Medusa; or, The Fatal Raft*, performed in London at the same time that Géricaut's painting was being exhibited there, on June 12, 1820. Although Moncrieff mainly based his play on the report, both the play and the painting were quickly set in relation to each other.

> The painting itself was now a sensational event, to be capitalized upon if not competed with; and at this point it may have influenced the staging of the play. A decade later, however, a painting so well-known was bound to influence the staging. Accordingly, when the play was revived in 1831, the frontispiece in Richardson's contemporary edition, "from a Drawing taken in the Theatre by Mr. Seymour', shows the influence of the painting on gesture, attitude, and design, and on the choice of the moment depicted.[17]

The same thing happened in Paris and other European metropolises in the first half of the 19th century.[18] In conclusion, while the painting breathed "new life into art",[19] it did not enter the art of tragedy. Instead, through the technique of eventization and the pictorial dramaturgy that Géricault had developed, the picture became part of the iconographic program and the catastrophic imaginary performed by the melodramatic popular media of the 19th century.

1 Ekkehard Tanner: Das Floß der Medusa. http://www.schirn.de/magazin/kontext/das_floss_der_medusa_1/ (accessed August 8, 2016); all translations of German texts by K.R. unless otherwise indicated.

2 Sabine Merten: *Seesturm und Schiffbruch. Eine motivgeschichtliche Studie*. Rostock: VEB Hinstorff 1987, p. 95.

3 Alexander Corréard / J.B. Henry Savigny: *Narrative of a Voyage to Senegal in 1816*. London: Dawsons 1968. I have consulted the most recent German edition: *Der Schiffbruch der Fregatte Medusa*. Berlin: Matthes & Seitz 2005.

4 Jörg Trempler: *Katastrophen. Ihre Entstehung aus dem Bild*. Berlin: Wagenbach 2013, p. 21.

5 Ibid.

6 Eva Horn: *Zukunft als Katastrophe*. Frankfurt am Main: Fischer 2014, p. 15.

7 Justin Wintle: *Makers of Nineteenth Century Culture*. London: Routledge 2001, p. 246.

8 Dieter Groh / Michael Kempe / Franz Mauelshagen (eds): Einleitung. In: D.G. / M.K. / F.M. (eds): *Naturkatastrophen. Beiträge zu ihrer Deutung, Wahrnehmung und Darstellung in Text und Bild von der Antike bis ins 20. Jahrhundert*. Tübingen: Narr 2003, pp. 11–36.

9 *Allgemeine Deutsche Real-Encyklopädie für die gebildeten Stände*, vol. 6. Leipzig: Brockhaus 1835, p. 135.

10 Otto Brunner / Werner Conze / Reinhart Koselleck (eds): *Geschichtliche Grundbegriffe. Historisches Lexikon zur politisch-sozialen Sprache in Deutschland*, vol. 5. Stuttgart: Klett-Cotta 1984, pp. 653–788, here p. 755 [s.v. Revolution].

11 Hannah Arendt: *On Revolution*. London: Penguin 1977, p. 41.

12 Ibid.

13 Hans Belting: *The Invisible Masterpiece*. London: Reaktion 2001, p. 89.

14 See Bernard Stiegler: *Technics and Time 2. Disorientation*. Stanford: Stanford UP 2009, p. 9.

15 Ibid., p. 114.

16 See the detailed account of this by Christine Riding: Staging *The Raft of the Medusa*. In: *Visual Culture in Britain* 5:2 (Winter 2004), pp. 1–26.

17 Martin Meisel: *Realizations. Narrative, Pictorial, and Theatrical Arts in Nineteenth-Century England*. Princeton: Princeton UP 1983, p. 190.

18 See Kati Röttger: Kritik des Spektakels. In: *Forum Modernes Theater* 23:2 (2009), pp. 83–96.

19 Belting: *The Invisible Masterpiece*, p. 88.

Fig. 1: François-Nicolas Chifflart: *Cholera in Paris* (1865, etching with drypoint on laid paper, 22.7 x 31.3 cm).

Twilight

Disaster after Enlightenment

Marie-Hélène Huet

Paris lies low on the horizon. We recognize the outlines of Notre-Dame cathedral, the Saint-Jacques tower and the dome of the Pantheon. The observer is standing on a stony outlook high above a city that seems strangely immobilized. By contrast, a vast storm is whirling above. Clouds are spiraling in a large ellipse, which occupies most of the space and saturates the skies. The clouds' rotating movement and the clear opening in their midst additionally suggest that we are looking into the eye of the storm, the brief and dangerous period of calm that precedes the deadliest part of a hurricane.

The atmospheric disturbances are made more threatening still by the disproportion between the tormented sky and the low-lying city. The spatial emphasis on the storm alone warns us of the darkness looming over the city. The specific nature of the threat slowly emerges in the shape of dead bodies in various poses of despair and supplication being carried away by the winds. Their arms are raised toward the heavens; their hands are extended as if to reach out toward an absent savior; limbs disappear in the cloud formations, while other bodies, abandoned to their fate, float without resistance in an apocalyptic twilight. This engraving by François Nicolas Chifflart was completed in 1865 and is said to have been inspired by the cholera epidemic that started in Paris on March 18, 1849. This outbreak was more severe than the pandemic of 1831–1832; it caused more than 20,000 deaths in Paris alone, and in London, as Philip Alcabes notes, "[m]ore than three hundred people died each day in the first week of September 1849".[1] Far less frequently discussed than the first epidemic – Catherine J. Kudlick speaks of the "silence of 1849"[2] – the second cholera epidemic brought back all the fears and terrors caused by largely unknown and mysteriously spreading diseases.

Chifflart's engraving first expresses the fury of natural forces far beyond human control: it illustrates the original meaning of the word *disaster*, from the Italian *dis-astrato*, disowned, abandoned by the protective stars that secure a safe passage through life. The natural world, which the Enlightenment philosophers believed could be mastered, strikes a passive city with impunity – a city with its vain monuments to the glory of God and its greatest men. But the etching also relates directly to the theory that epidemic diseases spread through the air and enter the body through the lungs. The stormy weather depicted above Paris carries the deadly miasma responsible for the devastating illness called *cholera morbus*. It echoes the study commissioned in 1831 by the French Royal Academy of Medicine that had explained the rapid and capricious spread of the disease in these terms:

> Annals of astronomy record the stories of a number of various meteors that, in a manner similar to the epidemic we have just discussed, traversed vast areas. Their constant effect was felt successively throughout a number of countries, within various limits, leaving intact some districts and striking others more or less severely.[3]

As the *Gazette médicale* had reported in the same year: "[T]he disease is due to cosmic considerations."[4]

By 1849, questions about the origins of the cholera outbreak remained unanswered. As Charles Rousset asks in the introduction to his *Traité du choléra-morbus de 1849*: "Is cholera morbus, like the celestial bodies, subject to periodic revolutions that would come to decimate our terrified populations at regular times?"[5] He later adds: "The disease's power surpasses medical art's power."[6] Another medical observer writes:

> Ignorant as we are about the primary nature of the epidemic cholera-morbus, it makes sense to locate its germ and transmission agent in atmospheric air, in the vast atmosphere that surrounds us and presses us from all sides; that ceaselessly penetrates our deepest viscera, not only through respiration, but also due to the way it reacts with what we drink and eat; an atmosphere whose agitation, changing directions press upon men's skin and radically modify their health.[7]

A group of doctors, commissioned to write a report for the city of Lyon on the best ways to prepare for the epidemic of 1849 that had just begun in Paris, echo the view that the disease arrives and spreads through the air, much like the storm threatening Paris. "There is no doubt that cholera results from miasmatic poisoning", wrote the commission.

> What we know is that it is a formidable pestilence, all the more dangerous because its immediate cause is unknown. It breaks out; it strikes and disappears without leaving behind any indication of the ways to avert its outbreak or to prevent its return. [...] Men have not been given the power to penetrate the origins or to know about the principles of pestilential diseases. All is invisible, mysterious; all results from powers whose effects alone are revealed to us.[8]

Formidable and threatening as it was, the theory that cholera was an epidemic disease, that is was a disease transmitted through the air, provided powerful reassurance to those who had been stricken and sought treatment. In 1849, as in 1831, the far more frightening theory that cholera was a contagious disease was vigorously rejected by officials who feared both panic in their cities and an obstacle to commercial exchange. Similar debates had taken place during the plague no doubt, but the political and philosophical nature of these controversies had been considerably modified by the time Europe suffered its first cholera epidemics. The doctrine of contagion was rejected as inhuman, leading to barbarian practices such as isolating patients without care and leaving them to die, as had often been the case during the plagues that had previously struck the country. The opposition between the doctrine of contagion and that of the epidemic spreading of the disease was also political. During the first pandemic, the leading author of medical texts that described cholera as a contagious disease was Alexandre Moreau de Jonnès, who also happened to be a royalist and, moreover, a legitimist. He was in fact a supporter of King Charles X, who had been forced to relinquish his throne during the 1830 revolution. In his repeated calls for the government to enact measures that would effectively protect the population, Moreau de Jonnès, a highly respected member of *Académie des sciences*, attacked both officials and revolutionaries:

> There are no reasons to believe that cholera morbus can be transmitted through the air beyond a distance of a few feet, and it is at least quite certain that there is no justification for the belief that it can be carried from one place to another through atmospheric fluctuations.[9]
>
> If it were not for the July Revolution, cholera morbus would still be confined to Asia [...]. Statesmen, from whom we expect the firm and intelligent defense of the territory against cholera morbus, are the very ones who voted against the admirable hygiene legislation proposed by the Restoration government [...]. But then, they preferred the revolt accompanied by the plague.[10]

By 1849, and this is perhaps why this second pandemic has been much less discussed than the previous one, epidemists had won the debates. They figured as the 'moderns' and, as Moreau de Jonnès has rightly asserted, as liberals and revolutionaries. The second time Paris was struck by the disease, France had a Republican regime, and Victor Hugo, elected after June 1848, was addressing the Assembly on a regular basis. But Louis-Napoléon Bonaparte, the leading conservative, had become President. During the spring of 1849, just as cholera was striking Paris, his government began implementing strict restrictions on political activities. Following a series of public political protests, a state of siege was declared in several cities. It must be added that, by imposing decrees meant to control republican activities, the regime was also adopting the very measures requested in vain by those who believed in the contagious nature of cholera, chief among them the prohibition of large gatherings. In cities now under siege and among populations rigorously under control, the risks of spreading both the disease of cholera and that of revolution were met with order and isolation.

It may be helpful to note here that Chifflart had been an enthusiastic supporter of the 1848 Revolution and remained all his life an ardent, if disappointed, Republican. From this perspective, Chifflart's etching, though entitled "Cholera in Paris", also carries a political message. By suggesting that the disease spreads through the air, he sides with those who did not believe in contagion, with the moderns as well as the liberals. But as Chifflart's image dramatically and precisely illustrates, the "cosmic forces" at work during a cholera outbreak also convey a form of oppression to which we will return shortly.

"Chifflart travels among ghosts", wrote Émile Perrin in his review of the *Salon* of 1859, where Chifflart had shown two engravings representing *Faust au Sabbat* (*Faust at the Witches' Sabbath*) and *Faust au combat* (*Faust Fighting*).[11] It was an apt description for an artist haunted by injustice, fate and the search for truth. An obituary published in 1901 by the *Revue Universelle* praised Chifflart's undeniable talent and wondered how anyone would ever understand the artist's complex personality, describing Chifflart as a bitter and restless man, living in a state of permanent frustration. His engravings express "calls for justice and truth, irony, anger, revolt, nightmares and hallucinations".[12] Chifflart was indeed a complex personality. Raised in a working-class family, attracted by both music and painting, he began his career in the most prestigious academic tradition, receiving the *Prix de Rome* in 1851. But his five-year stay in the Villa Medici, to which all laureates were entitled, quickly turned into a nightmare that he would later describe "as a Gehenna, a hell".[13] The Villa Medici was too confined and too traditional a school for him to remain there very long. During his stay, one of the residents died of what was called at the time "the fevers", and Chifflart himself became seriously ill. "By 1855", writes a contemporary

> it had become obvious that the Villa Medici harbored an enemy of its healthy doctrines, which are academic doctrines, an artist who refused limitations: a neo-romantic, and, even worse, a republican.[14]

Unable to endure the Villa's constricting atmosphere or to submit to its academic teachings, Chifflart travelled all over Italy and discovered in Michelangelo his true master. Upon his return to Paris in 1859, where he submitted the two etchings of *Faust* to the *Salon*, Baudelaire praised the artist's "chaotic dream" and his vigorous "rejection of the platitudes of learned melancholia".[15] Théophile Gautier wrote an admirable description of the two etchings, with an emphasis on the skies darkening over the Sabboth: "Above, black clouds, shaped by the swirling winds take on all forms of monstrous shapes."[16] Chifflart had left France just as Louis-Napoléon seized power. Back under a regime his political views could not tolerate, he found a friend in Victor Hugo, whom he visited in Guernsey. He would later illustrate *Notre-Dame de Paris* (*The Hunchback of Notre-Dame*) and *Les Travailleurs de la mer* (*Toilers of the Sea*).

In 1865, at the time Chifflart completed his engraving, Paris was suffering from yet another cholera epidemic. *Le Monde illustré*, to which Chifflart regularly contributed, published several articles on cholera, all of them meant to reassure its readers. On October 21, 1865, the journal stated:

> Yes, cholera is in Paris, but aside from the fact that sudden and acute cases are rare and that the disease can be fought efficiently, the majority of cases are not truly serious. [...] What is the meaning of the panic felt by some? It is imprudent and unnecessary. [...] If you are outside Paris and comfortably installed, stay there and wait for the epidemic to end. If, on the contrary, you are in Paris, stay there and do not move.[17]

While John Snow had long identified the source of the Soho cholera outbreak in contaminated water, his inquiry had not gone unchallenged, and it was only in 1866, years after his death, that British medical authorities accepted the theory that cholera was transmitted by water rather than air. France appears to have been unaware of the discussions taking place in the United Kingdom. In 1865, Chifflart's etching provided a vivid illustration of miasmatic or epidemic theory, a threat likely to descend from the skies to devastate a powerless population.

Untitled

In 1877, the art critic Charles Tardieu described Chifflart as "a talent marked by his chimerical eccentricity", but one who would never make any concession to anything that could potentially degrade his ideal.[18] The perfect example of an *artiste maudit*, "Chifflart has the misfortune of belonging to the family of artists who think," he wrote. For Tardieu, Chifflart was "a genius pursued, if not ostracized, by a relentless and implacable fatality".[19] Léonce Viltard, visiting the artist not long before his death, added: "No one can pretend to know Chifflart," "[h]e has always lived in resolute seclusion. We know he has been in a tête-à-tête with a tempestuous genius that, though it created admirable pages, made his life sad, bitter and tormented."[20] Chifflart rarely showed his works, but Viltard visited his atelier, providing us with the only contemporary evaluation we have of the artist's representation of cholera in Paris: "Most of the etchings do not have a title," Viltard wrote,

> and it is not an easy task to give one to all of them. Besides, one could be content to admire this view of Paris from Montmartre, so clear, so sharp, so precise; a view dominated by a stormy sky carrying a trail of cadavers that rise and fall, whirl and disappear on the horizon.[21]

Viltard is clearly looking at the etching we have discussed as representing "Cholera in Paris", and the lack of title is particularly striking in this case, adding to, rather than detracting from, the scene's dramatic effect. If we consider the *untitled* image as Viltard saw it in Chifflart's atelier, we no longer see the evocation of a dramatic event – cholera – but rather the deeper expression of catastrophe itself, taken in its original sense of a sudden and tragic overturning. We do not know when or how the title was added to the engraving; but in this case, the pure impact of the general upheaval that dominates Chifflart's image can now be given its full meaning: The dead are whirling over a sleeping city, not as resurrection, but as the most unimaginable human downturn.

We know from anthropologists that, from earliest times, humans buried their dead:

> Inhumation was probably the most widespread disposal pattern. Originally earth burials might have been designated to protect the living from contamination, or to prevent wild animals from molesting the body, or, as a sympathetic rift, to promote rebirth,[22]

writes Milton Cohen, summing up observations of early practices. In all cases, the ceremonies that accompany burials or, in other instances, cremation are meant to separate the living from the dead, to ensure that the dead will rest peacefully, away from the circle of the living. Claude Lévi-Strauss interpreted death rituals as a way to convince the souls of the dead to move on. Moreover, up until the middle of the 19th century, traditional rituals prevailed in the French countryside as a symbolic means of ensuring the definitive departure of the deceased, chief among them the veiling of mirrors and, in some cases, the covering of pitchers of milk and water.[23] Such rituals all expressed, in their naïve way, the absolute necessity of letting go of the dead and protecting the living from the restlessness or regrets the deceased might have felt.[24]

At the time Chifflart executed his etching, Paris had had a long and troubled relationship with its dead. By the end of the 18th century, notes Jacqueline Thibaut-Payen, "[c]emeteries were accused of breeding epidemics, and the dead suspected of contaminating the living".[25] Philippe Muray has argued that the 19th-century obsession with death really began on April 7, 1786, when the first nightly tumbrils began to transfer bodies from the Saint-Innocents cemetery – the most crowded in the city – to the catacombs.[26] In 1804, a decree ordered that all burials would now take place in grounds outside Paris' city limits, setting the stage for the purchase of the Père-Lachaise, the Montmartre and the Montparnasse cemeteries. Most cholera victims were buried there in common graves. North of Paris, the Montmartre cemetery, built in an ancient quarry and opened in 1825, dominated the city and seems to provide the viewing point of Chifflart's engraving.

We can now better understand not only the meaning of the stony place where the beholder stands, but the way it frames the radical reversal of the relationship between nature and humans. In Chifflart's engraving, the dead have neither been buried nor appeased. They do not lie underground, out of sight or far beyond the city; not that the dead have risen in some fantastic Hoffmanian epic. They are not ghosts but tortured bodies that whirl over Paris in various poses of despair. Beyond the catastrophic epidemic of 1849 that claimed, among many others, the beautiful Juliette Récamier, we see the representation of pure catastrophe in the contrast between the vain achievements of men and the untamed power of a violent nature. The city's great monuments are dwarfed; they are no more than useless testimonies to human faith confronted by the deadly storm that, from the beginning, threatened human powers and hopes. This engraving also sums up the anxieties that presided over the 19th-century imagination and that Chifflart would illustrate during his career: with Faust, as we mentioned earlier, but also Victor Hugo's Cain, pursued by God inside the grave itself or by the mob gathering in front of Notre-Dame cathedral.

Whether the etching is an illustration or an exorcism somehow depends on the presence or the absence of a title. We may remember Jacques Derrida's remark in "Title To Be Specified" that the title remains foreign to the discourse over which it presides, that it introduces "an abnormal referential function and a violence": the title imposes a law.[27] In Chifflart's case, the title "Cholera in Paris" frames an image that becomes frozen within a specific historical context. It allows the beholder to step back as it were from the dangerous edge of the promontory overlooking Paris in 1849. However, we recognize in the etching a far deeper confrontation with death itself, with the disquiet and despair of loss, that of a humanity doomed to dying at the hands of an unforgiving world.

Rather than deciding when the title was given to the etching and whether the artist himself inscribed it, we would like to add a post scriptum, one far more modern and yet at one with Chifflart's anxieties. It is a song written by John C. Fogerty:

> I see trouble on the way.
> I see earthquakes and lightnin'.
> I see trouble on the way.
> I hear hurricanes a blowing.
> I know the end is coming soon.
> I fear rivers overflowing.
> I hear the voice of rage and ruin.
> Well don't go around tonight
> Well it's bound to take your life.
> There's a bad moon on the rise.

The song was first performed by Creedence Clearwater Revival in 1969, and Fogerty said that it represented the Apocalypse that was about to descend upon us. Catastrophes are still on our mind.

1 Philip Alcabes: *Dread*. New York: Public Affairs 2009, p. 65.
2 Catherine J. Kudlick: *Cholera in Post-Revolutionary Paris. A Cultural History*. Berkeley: University of California Press 1996, pp. 1–30.
3 *Rapport sur le choléra-morbus*, lu à l'Académie de Médecine en séance générale, les 26 et 30 juillet 1831. Paris: Imprimerie royale 1841, pp. 134–135. All translations by M.-H. H.
4 *Gazette médicale* 3:31 (May 12, 1832), p. 242.
5 Charles Rousset: *Traité du choléra-morbus de 1849*. Paris: self-published 1851, p. 7.
6 Ibid. p. 41
7 Paul Reis: *Notice historique et pratique sur le choléra-morbus et particulièrement sur l'épidémie de 1849*. Paris: L. Lévy 1849, p. 10.
8 *Rapport sur le cholera-morbus de Paris: épidémie de 1849*, présenté à M. le Maire et au conseil municipal de Lyon, au nom d'une commission médicale, par MM. Fraisse, Brévard, Candy. Lyon: Rodanet 1849, p. 17.
9 Alexandre Moreau de Jonnès: *Rapport au Conseil supérieur de santé sur le choléra-morbus pestilentiel*. Paris: Cosson 1831, p. 34.
10 *La Gazette de France*, August 22, 1831.
11 Émile Perrin: Le Salon de 1859. In: *Revue Européenne* (1859), p. 879.
12 Léonce Vitard: Chifflart (François-Nicolas). In: *Revue universelle* (1901), pp. 430–431.
13 Léonce Vitard: Nicolas Chifflart. In: *L'Artiste* 14 (August–September 1897), pp. 81–96, 186–201, here p. 87.
14 Ibid., p. 88.
15 Charles Baudelaire: *Variétés critiques*, vol. 1. Paris: Crès 1924, p. 158.
16 Théophile Gautier: Exposition de 1859. In: *Le Moniteur universel*, October 10, 1859.
17 *Le Monde illustré*, October 21, 1865, p. 259.
18 Charles Tardieu: Un improvisateur sur cuivre. In: *L'Art* 1 (1877), p. 199.
19 Ibid., pp. 203, 218.
20 Vitard: F.-N. Chifflart, p. 81.
21 Ibid., p. 197.
22 Milton Cohen: Death Rituals: Anthropological perspectives. http://www2.sunysuffolk.edu/pecorip/SCCCWEB/ETEXTS/DeathandDying_TEXT/Death%20Ritual.pdf, p. 4 (accessed April 17, 2017).
23 See Arnold Van Gennep's classic *Manuel de Folklore contemporain*. Paris: Picard 1946, vol. 1, pp. 672–673.
24 See in particular Claude Lévi-Strauss: *La Pensée sauvage*. Paris: Plon 1962, pp. 44–47, 264.
25 Jacqueline Thibaut-Payen: *Les Morts, l'église et l'état: recherches d'histoire administrative sur la sépulture et les cimetières dans le ressort du Parlement de Paris au XVIIe et XVIIIe siècles*. Paris: Lanore 1977, p. 207.
26 Philippe Muray: *Le Dix-neuvième siècle à travers les âges*. Paris: Denoël 1984, p. 48.
27 Jacques Derrida: Title to Be Specified. In: J. D.: *Parages*, ed. by John P. Leavy, transl. from the French by Tom Conley. Stanford: Stanford UP 2011, pp. 192–215, here p. 197.

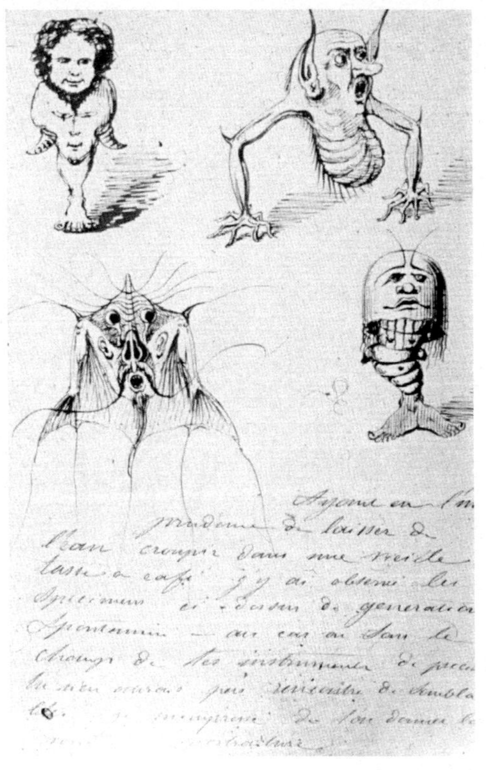

Fig. 1: Caricatures by Félix-Archimède Pouchet for his collaborator Georges Pennetier.

Spontaneous Generation and Cataclysmic Destruction

Louis Pasteur versus Felix-Archimède Pouchet and Jules Michelet

Gesine Hindemith

During his research on the origins of microorganisms in the 1860s, Felix-Archimède Pouchet, professor of natural history in Rouen, performed a momentous experiment. Strange minuscule lifeforms were issuing from a coffee cup full of moldy water: both worm and insect-like, monstrous in their hybrid composition and, above all, anthropomorphous in shape. Pouchet, a scientist with a soft spot for irony, drew sketches of these mini-monsters during his experiments on microorganisms and sent his illustrations to his colleague Georges Pennetier, who must have found them quite amusing indeed. To a certain extent, with his moldy coffee cup, Pouchet anticipated an experiment design that would later write scientific history. In 1928, Alexander Fleming accidentally left a dish vaccinated with staphylococcus on a windowsill and took off on his summer holidays. When he returned, he had accidentally discovered penicillin on that very dish.

The theory of spontaneous generation, which could be observed in the brackish water found in Pouchet's cup, influenced scientific history in a completely different manner than the revolutionary discovery of penicillin. However, Pouchet was already an adherent to this theory, which could be traced all the way back to Aristotle, with the hypothesis that simple lifeforms can take shape in the remains of dead organisms without the involvement of a parental organism. Thus, there is no genetic continuity within this theory. The decay of the one creates the other. Spontaneous generation was a common concept from ancient times throughout the Middle Ages and into the 19th century, and Pouchet tried to prove this concept using his experiments. It was none other than Louis Pasteur who disproved this theory after a 20-year-long debate, which ended in 1864 in front of the Academy of Sciences with one targeted strike.

Still, the theory of spontaneous generation had no less of an afterlife: Pouchet's ideas diffused into the literary world. He was friends with Jules Michelet and with Gustave Flaubert as well, who he taught at the Collège Royal in Rouen. It is plausible that we can find some of Pouchet (theory and person) in *Bouvard and Pecuchet*.[1] His ideas also found their way into the depiction of the parade of monsters in the *Temptation of Saint Anthony*.[2] In 1863, Flaubert conceived of a fantastical micro-scenario: "Microscopic minuscule lifeforms: A scientist studies them. The lifeforms grow little by little, populate the stage, become monsters and finally eat the scientist."[3] It is here that we find ourselves in the middle of an exemplary féerie scenario that experienced its boom on the 19th-century stage, particularly in France, and which fascinated Flaubert above all else.[4]

So typical for the 19th century, natural science and literature once again crossed paths. The (magical) laboratory and the scientist found within were popular subjects of many féeries. Even the transformation and metamorphosis of life forms (it did not matter if they were carrots, fungi or humans) could be traced back to imagination based on natural sciences, just as Flaubert's example shows.

Another strong influence on the 19th-century historical imagination was provided by Georges Cuvier`s theory of catastrophism. In his *Essay on the Theory of the Earth* (1813), Cuvier proposed that new species were created after periodic catastrophic floods. Cuvier studied the strata of the Paris basin and established the basic principles of biostratigraphy. At an aesthetic level, Cuvier's catastrophism seems to have found its way into the féerie's formal structure, especially at points where there were only rudimentary stories of back-to-back adventures interrupted by sudden 'tableaux' changes. This structure can be found in nearly all féerie plays of that time. Each tableau was created like after a natural catastrophe, namely from nothing that had existed on stage before. The works of catastrophe here go hand in hand with theatrical spectacle.

Just how this constellation of the féerie and new scientific theories took shape in the 19th century will be examined using two different but interconnected historiographic cases. In the beginning, there was the scientific debate before the Academy of Science in Paris, where Pouchet competed against his challenger Louis Pasteur and which ended, for Pouchet, in the 'catastrophic' destruction of the theory of spontaneous generation. Jules Michelet's natural history *The Sea* (1861), however, created a literary monument to spontaneous generation. This book declared Pouchet's theory a guarantor of a historic model that vouches for historicity in the sense that history was written by multiple narrators as an ongoing process. This manner of thinking was completely disregarded by Pasteur's claim to write scientific history according to the final discovery he had made himself in front of the Academy, which explained that life could not be created out of dead matter. Interestingly enough, it was Pasteur raising his hand to inflict the final blow at Pouchet that quoted and discredited Michelet. Subsequently, *The Sea* received repeated harsh criticism and sales suffered under Pasteur's verdict.

It is at this point that I would like to examine how the notion of the catastrophe that manifests in the narrative style of *The Sea* and, to a certain extent, in Pasteur's orchestration in front of the academy is closely linked to the aesthetic phenomenon of the féerie and the theatrical spectacle. The performative application of the catastrophe appears to have been decisive for the epistemological form of this dramaturgy, which I would like to analyze as a question of historicity: How can observers come to know what really happened? Observers come to know something by analyzing the storytelling or dramaturgy of scientific performance, which seems to be more important than the supposedly proven fact. This essay draws attention to two protagonists, Pasteur and Michelet, who made history in connection with Pouchet's spontaneous generation, which could not be any more different, yet was fueled by the collective imagination of the 19th century: by the catastrophe and by the theatrical spectacle of the féerie. With his theatrical annihilation of Pouchet, Pasteur set the date for the rebirth of the scientific world. Every form of historicity disappeared in this celebration of victory, which allowed for the contemplation of neither the derivation of his line of argument nor of its influences. Only the final experiment counted! Michelet's presentation of natural history was, however, based on the recently discredited theory of spontaneous generation, which the historian required in order to give his presentation historicity. Here, the change in nature counted, as did the creation and the (individual) experience of a story that had been written by various yet collaborating protagonists.

The first protagonist in the cast to be examined is Félix Archimède Pouchet. At the time of the debate about spontaneous generation, he was at the center of the public's attention, passionately driving the popularity of science. In 1828, he founded the Natural History Museum in Rouen, which played a pioneering role in the development of museums of natural history all the way up until the 20th century. Pouchet was in good company with the Comte de Buffon, Jean-Baptiste Lamarck, Pierre Jean Georges Cabanis and Claude Bernard, who all propagated the theory of spontaneous generation as well. But it was Pouchet, beginning in 1858, who presented experimental proof to the Parisian Academy of Science. He published his results in October 1859 under the title *Heterogenesis or Treatise on Spontaneous Generation* (*Hétérogénie ou traité de la génération spontanée*). The debate took its course in 1862 when the academy decided to award a prize to the first person who could shed new light onto the question of spontaneous generation through experimentation. This was the beginning of a bitter dispute between Pouchet and Pasteur. The latter wanted to prove that germs, which he thought to be carried through the air, undetected by researchers, created microscopic minuscule lifeforms, and that it was by no means possible for life to be generated from nearly dead material, as Pouchet seemed to have proven.

Pouchet cultivated a kind of romantic biology, which was heavily influenced by his friend Geoffroy Saint Hilaire and banked on similar structures, searching for the unifying element behind the facts. He developed an eclectic theory that mediated between the positions of Cuvier and Lamarck: Pouchet added Lamarck's theory of limited transformism under the influence of the environment to Cuvier's theory of catastrophism and his successive re-establishment. Both were complemented by his conceptualization of a force continuously at work, which incessantly manifested itself and allowed for spontaneous generation. In Pouchet's work, the dominance of the vitalistic idea is obvious, his desire to give the organism a unique dignity. Life was not just succession, but could quite possibly spring forth from nothing, be created out of nothing and thus be wholly triumphant over purely physical forces. This was a profoundly anti-Darwinian position. Louis Pasteur, the opponent, attacker and victor over Pouchet, had a completely different view. Life could only come from life and not from dead organic remains.

Bruno Latour has analyzed the debate between Pasteur and Pouchet as an exemplary case of a scientific dispute.[5] Two opponents come together with respect for each other. The debate would find its resolution after two subsequent commissions of the Academy of Science in 1862 and in 1864. Pouchet accepted Pasteur's experimental principles but rejected the commissions, as he found them to be ideologically and politically biased and in favor of Pasteur's position.[6] The debate was open to the public and was followed by the press. Opposing camps were formed. It was a battle between Pasteur's research, legitimized by the capital, and the supposedly provincial and anti-innovative position of Pouchet. Both researchers performed their experiments with the utmost care.

Pasteur developed the goose-neck bottle that did not allow air to enter after the fluids (yeast sugar water, urine, milk) had been brought to the boil, meaning that the contents of the bottle would not change. Pouchet repeated this experiment in the French Alps using a hay infusion as the fluid. The altitude was supposed to reduce the risk of contamination. Still, the contents of the bottle changed. It seemed to be that one only needed pure oxygen to create microorganisms. Pasteur reacted angrily to Pouchet's alleged inaccuracies. One final experiment in front of the Academy of Science would provide the final proof: Pouchet was wrong!

Paris, April 7, 1864, in the great amphitheater of Sorbonne:

> Gentlemen, I am going to show you how the mice got in ....
> *Lights out, please.* Let there be night about us, let everything be dark, and let us illuminate only these tiny bodies, and we shall see them as we see the stars in the evening. *Put on the spotlight.* Ladies and gentlemen, you can see plenty of dust swirling about in the beam of the light. *Shine it onto the bench, please ...*
> If we collect some of this dust on a slide, this is what we see in the microscope. M. Duboscq, will you project the enlargement ...
> Here you see many shapeless objects. But among these shapeless objects, you will see tiny bodies such as these. These, ladies and gentlemen, are the germs of microscopic creatures.[7]

In this passage, Pasteur, with the grace and gestures of a magician, dismantles Pouchet's experiment piece by piece. He works with cauldrons filled with quicksilver and dust and draws in the crowd with his skillfully controlled rhetoric and use of lighting. Ultimately, he inflicts the final blow:

> And consequently, gentlemen, I too can say like Michelet, "From the vastness of creation, I took my drop of water, and I took it full of fecund matter. And I wait, I observe and I question, and I ask it to begin for me the moment of original creation; what a fine sight that would be!" *Exclamations.* But it is silent! It has been silent for many years since these experiments were begun. *Murmuring ...*
> Ah! and this is because I have excluded from it, and still do exclude from it, the one thing it is not to given to man to produce; I have excluded the germs which float in the air, I have excluded life, for live is the germ and the germ is life. The doctrine of spontaneous generation will never recover from the mortal blow inflicted on it by this simple experiment. *Sustaining applause.*[8]

What has happened at the level of science history is, as Bruno Latour tells it, a case of "histoire découverte": A discovery splits history into a before and an after, into the wrongness of the past and truth after the discovery.[9] The situation is irreversible, the past is radically separated from the present and the future. A new age is born. For thousands of years, humans had lived with the idea of spontaneous generation, and now Pasteur had eradicated it in one finely targeted and well-planned attack. He did so by orchestrating his performance to let himself appear as a master magician, drawing in the crowd by artistically controlling light and rhetoric in the amphitheater of the Sorbonne. Pasteur warned his audience at the beginning of his presentation: "You will not leave here tonight without being convinced that the spontaneous generation of microscopic creatures is a chimera".[10] Pasteur was an agent of history as discovery. He, with his method of publicly displaying his experiments, whose results an institution simultaneously recognized, defined a certain style of science. His discovery would defeat his opponents like a natural catastrophe. Everything that had been there before would be annihilated – it would be the rebirth of the scientific world!

This is a model of scientific historiography that is more than ideal for chronologies. It functions as a fairy tale, as Latour has ironically analogized.[11] The truth (microbes could never be spontaneously created without a parent organism) was always there. However, an evil spirit had hidden it. But then it was exposed bit by bit and ultimately set free by Pasteur, the great magician, who revealed the truth to the audience as a scientific show.

The history derived from the discovery, as Latour indicates, is derived without any historicity. It keeps secret the fact that Pasteur himself did not know what his microbes were doing for a long time, that he employed sly tactics, that he was politically positioning himself and egging the academy on in order to perfectly inflict his deathblow. It keeps secret that not everyone was convinced by a long shot. Pasteur was later often challenged and even his team kept looking into the topic of spontaneous generation.

It was not by accident that Pasteur quoted Michelet's *The Sea* while inflicting his final destructive blow; he recognized the adversarial principle of this narration based on the theory of spontaneous generation. Through Pouchet, Michelet propagated a model of history that ran contrary to that of Pasteur. In his third chapter on atoms (Michelet means micro-organisms and microbes), Michelet answers the question pertaining to the continued existence of the living and the creation of new life. His archeology of historical and social life aimed to illuminate the transfer of life from the death of one to the following of the other, not through succession, imitation or the intrinsic identity of form, but rather through transformation.[12] The transition from fleetingness to life marked a point of indifference that was decisive for Michelet as a historian. He set the relationship between all things and universal connectivity against the omnipotence of structures, hierarchies and institutions. For Michelet, this was the only way to think about being and traditions as an ongoing process.

For the structure of Michelet's *The Sea*, Pouchet's bio-philosophy was practically without compare. After all, what would have happened if Michelet had favored Darwin, whose book on the origin of species had already been published two years before *The Sea*? At first glance, Michelet's idea of "work on oneself" ("travail sur soi"), understood as a type of self-creation within natural, historical and social environments, and Darwinian "adaptation" could appear as two views of the same aspect. "But, the blind automatism of selection and adaptation must remain incomprehensible for Michelet. It does not leave room for the unique, non-identical."[13]

For Michelet, even the rotifers had what it took for individualization, when they gained momentum and pursued freedom. Every polyp wanted to be more than it is:

> In yourself, in Polypes, there is an ambition to cease to be one. In your Republic there is a certain creature who in constant anxiety and yearning, repeats that the perfection of this vegetating existence is not real life. It constantly dreams of a freer and more expanded life, navigating hither and thither, penetrating and viewing the unknown world even at the hazard of shipwreck [...].[14]
> Tout polype n'est pas résigné à rester polype. Il y a dans votre république telle créature inquiète, qui dit que la perfection de cette vie végétative ce n'est pas la vie. Elle en rêve une autre à part: - s'en aller et naviguer seule, voir l'inconnu, le vaste monde, se créer, au hasard du naufrage [...].[15]

These minuscule animals search for ways out of the collective indifference towards individuality[16] and remind us, in their implied humanity, of Pouchet's illustration of the microbes in the coffee cup.

Even while Michelet is boasting about the collective indifference and life in harmony using metaphors of love, milk and fertility in his first chapters on the creation of the ocean, noticeably without violence or catastrophe (cf. M, p. 137), another mode of illustration quickly becomes apparent. Just like in Michelet's historiography, polarities play an important role in *The Sea*. The wondrous scene about the underwater world is flooded with horrors of all kinds,

which accompany the growing "individualization" of the higher animal species.[17] The will of creatures already manifests itself in the deep sea around the equator where volcanic soil allows wonderful landscapes to blossom: "[...] [T]hose flowers shrink and shudder with an incipient sensitiveness which promises, perception and will."(S, p. 139) / "[...] ces fleurs frémissent d'une sensibilité naissante, où va poindre la volonté." (M, p. 133)
In this chapter titled "Bloodflower" / "Fleur du Sang", Michelet also introduces the metaphor of the féerie in excess:

> Charming oscillation, fascinating motion, most graceful equivoque! On the confines of the two kingdoms of animal and vegetable life, Mind, under those faëry oscillations gives token of its first awakening, its dawn, its morning twilight, to be followed by a glorious and glowing noon. Those brilliant colors, those pearly and enameled flashings, tell at once of the past night and the thought of the dawning day. Thought! May we venture to call it so? No, it is still a Dream, which by degrees will clear up into thought. (S, pp. 139–140)
> Oscillation pleine de charme, équivoque toute gracieuse! Aux limites des deux règnes, l'esprit, sous ces apparences flottantes d'une fantastique féerie, témoigne de son premier réveil. C'est une aube, c'est une aurore. Par les couleurs éclatantes, les nacres ou les émaux, il dit le songe de la nuit et la pensée du jour qui vient. Pensée! Osons-nous dire ce mot? Non, c'est un songe, un rêve encore, mais qui peu à peu s'éclaircit, comme les rêves du matin. (M, p. 133)

Thought is created in the féerie. Even more: The féerie represents a formal imperative for the presentation of nature: "Nature should only be exhibited as she ever lives, amidst faëry triumphs, enthroning her on a mountain of her own beauties." (S, p. 146) / "On ne devait montrer la Nature que dans la féerie triomphale qui ne la quitte jamais." (M, p. 138)
The magical changes upon the stage of the féerie are enacted in the underwater world using the origins of life. This is carried all the way over to natural scientists, whose theories Michelet refers to. He goes on to describe Ehrenberg – who made it possible to see these minuscule microscopic creatures, and both discovered and classified them – as a magician. The microscopic world that unfolds on a pinhead is a "spectacle" (S, p. 129 / M, p. 125). Spectacular is, above all, the way light is controlled, which is translated into speech during the orchestration of the phosphorescent lifeforms:

> In the great faëry of the illumination of the sea on stormy nights, the Medusa has her separate part. Bathed, like so many other beings, in the phosphoric fluid with which they are all penetrated,

> she returns it in her manner, with a peculiar charm. [...] there their conical lights pirouette upon their own bases, or roll in red balls. A great disc of fire (Pyrosome) commences with an opaline yellow, becomes for a moment greenish, then bursts into red and orange, and at last darkens down into blue. (S, pp. 169 / 171)
> Dans la grande féerie d'illumination que la mer déplie aux nuits orageuses, la méduse a un rôle à part. Plongée, comme dans tant d'autres êtres, dans le phosphore électrique dont ils sont tous pénétrés, elle le rend à sa manière avec un charme personnel. [...] Ici, ces cônes de lumières vont pirouettant sur eux-mêmes, ou roulent en boulets rouges. Un grand disque du feu se fait (pyrosome), qui part du jaune opalin, un moment frappé de vert, puis s'irrite, éclate dans le rouge, l'orange, puis s'assombrit d'azur. (M, pp. 156 / 158)

For Michelet, the Museum of Natural History in Paris is a "faëry palace" (S, p. 150) / "palais de féerie" (M, p. 141), where the spirit of metamorphosis triumphs over the tyranny of immobilism. Lamarck and Geoffroy both confirm this. Michelet repeatedly puts himself in the 'tableaux' that he is creating, as an observer of the ocean from the shores, in his stories of personal experience or as a visitor to the natural history museum. He can join his troops at any time up on stage.[18]

Michelet appears to be a flawless representative of gentle metamorphosis and thus the paradigm of continuity; however, at a very specific point in time, he does introduce some discontinuity to his story. When Michelet, with the help of the parameters of the féerie, repeatedly emphasizes the individualization of life, he is agreeing with Cuvier to a certain extent, as observed by Foucault in *The Order of Things:*

> From Cuvier onward, the living being wraps itself in its own existence, breaks off its taxonomic links of adjacency, tears itself free from the vast, tyrannical plan of continuities, and constitutes itself as a new space [...].[19]

Michelet's stories draw a line of life development from the polyps to the medusas, kraken, crustaceans, fish and sharks that increasingly behave in a warlike manner, looking for intrigue and becoming horrific murderers. Even the microscopic lifeforms show signs of personality, have a sense of humor and a character; some are apathetic, others are quite lively, while others tend to be rebellious.

In the endless web of life metaphorically interwoven into *The Sea*, Michelet describes the upward movements in horrific and violent scenes. It is not just the content and descriptions that take the reader's breath away, rather, the entire story sets a tremendous pace, jumping back and forth in poetic blocks. In his manuscript, Michelet uses white gaps that he marks as *blank* in order to clearly emphasize the break between the preceding and the following 'tableaux' – this results in a structural analogy to the féerie in the theater, whose rudimentary plot is displayed in individual pictures that are loosely motivated as a narrative and pieced together.

In these passages, developments run a zigzag course, for example when the description of development connects and transforms lively infusoria that mature as complete characters into paralysis-stricken polyps.[20] The reader does not just have to deal with gentle, non-violent metamorphoses: Catastrophes do in fact occur, but are projected onto the fate of the individualized animals. Hence, for example, the horrific spectacle in which the crustacean frees itself from its shell:

> When the crustaceans are large they are tyrants and the terror of both land and sea; [...] A strange and pitiful sight it is to see the lobster writhing, twisting, struggling, to get out of its too confining armor. So violent is the struggle that he sometimes actually casts off his claws. Then he remains soft, weak, exhausted. In two or three days a raw shell covers the naked body; but the crab does not so easily repair damages; it takes him much longer to renew his armor, and during that time he is the victim of all that previously were his unspared and unpitied prey. Even handed justice now becomes terrible to him. The victims now have their revenge; the strong is subjected to the law of the weak; falls, as a species, to their level, and pays full share in the great balance between life and death. (S, p. 208)
>
> Dès que le crustacé grossit, il est le tyran, l'effroi des deux éléments. [...] C'est un spectacle de voir l'écrevisse se renverser, s'agiter, se tourmenter, pour s'arracher d'elle-même. L'opération est si violente, qu'elle y brise quelquefois ses pattes. Elle reste épuisée, faible, molle. En deux ou trois jours, le calcaire reparaît, cuirasse la peau. Le crabe n'en est pas quitte ainsi; il lui faut beaucoup de temps pour reprendre sa carapace. Et jusque-là tous les êtres, les plus faible, en font curée. La justice et l'égalité reviennent ici terribles. Les victimes ont leur revanche. Le fort subit la loi des faibles, tombe à leur niveau, comme espèce, au grand balancement de la mort. (M, p. 186)

The creature becomes awash with feelings, fate takes a sharp turn and then reverses again. There is no catastrophic experience within the collective, although there is for the individual. The catastrophe becomes part of the phenomenon of spiritual development; Michelet redefines the term 'historicity' for the 19th century by integrating the catastrophe into

the idea of individual development. It is the subject that experiences history as its own process of life.
Pasteur's model of history as a date and not as an ongoing process with different points of view took its strength from the verdict of the institution that established a hierarchy within the sciences, to which he gave absolute power of control in order to declare his results as valid. Michelet, on the other hand, dealt with the deprivation of power from the institution and the hierarchy. Both narratives took their dramaturgy from the catastrophe, which they staged by means of the theatrical spectacle and the féerie. While the magician of natural science Pasteur conjured truth out of history, which from this time on was another, Michelet portrayed himself instead as a theater practitioner who knew how to stage the spectacular underwater world and how to accompany his troops through their perils. It was this manner of staging the catastrophe from the spectacular that wrote the history models of modern times.

Translation from the German by Michael C. Noto

1 See Maryline Coquidé: Félix-Archimède Pouchet, professeur de sciences naturelle de Flaubert. In: *Flaubert. Revue critique et génétique* 13 (2015). https://flaubert.revues.org/2422 (accessed February 15, 2017).
2 See Judith Wulf: Les sciences naturelles dans *La Tentation de Saint Antoine*: entre esthétique e épistémologie. In: *Flaubert. Revue critique et génétique* 2 (2004). http://flaubert.univ-rouen.fr/revue/revue4/03wulf.pdf (accessed February 17, 2017).
3 Gustave Flaubert: *Les Carnets de travail*, ed. by Pierre-Marc de Biasi. Paris: Balland 1988, Carnet 19, folio 7 (transl. by G. H. / Michael C. Noto).
4 See Gesine Hindemith: Le logos corrompu: La Féerie – Le château des cœurs. In: Pierre-Marc de Biasi / Anne Herschberg Pierrot / Barbara Vinken (eds): *Flaubert. Genèse et poétique du mythe*. Paris: Editions des Archives Contemporaines 2017, pp. 135–148.
5 Bruno Latour: Pasteur et Pouchet: hétérogenèse de l'histoire des sciences. In: Michel Serres (ed.): *Eléments d'histoire des sciences*. Paris: Bordas 1989, pp. 423–445.
6 Ibid., p. 424.
7 Quoted in Bruno Latour: Pasteur and Pouchet: the Heterogenesis of the History of Science. In: Michel Serres (ed.): *History of Scientific Thought. Elements of a History of Science*. London: Blackwell 1995, pp. 526–555, here p. 528.
8 Ibid., p. 530.
9 Latour: Pasteur et Pouchet, pp. 427–430.
10 Ibid., p. 427.
11 Cf. ibid., p. 430.
12 Cf. Rolf Wintermeyer: Nachwort. In: Jules Michelet: *Das Meer*, ed. and transl. from the French by Rolf Wintermeyer. Frankfurt am Main: Campus 2006, pp. 315–351, here p. 327.

13 Ibid., p. 339, transl. from the German by Michael C. Noto.
14 Jules Michelet: *The Sea*. New York: Rudd & Carleton 1861, p.159 (hereafter: S).
15 Jules Michelet: *La Mer*. Paris: Gallimard 1983, p. 149 (hereafter: M).
16 Jean Borie: Préface. In: Ibid., pp. 7–37, here p. 32.
17 Michelet takes the idea of individuality from Giambattista Vico and Johann Gottfried Herder. His personification of the people, the nation and finally the ocean are proof of this.
18 Borie: Préface, p. 25.
19 Michel Foucault: *The Order of Things. An Archaeology of the Human Sciences*. New York: Vintage 1973, p. 274.
20 Wintermeyer: Nachwort, p. 337.

Fig. 1: Sight of Paris in *Cassell's History of the War between France and Germany*, vol. 1. London: Cassell & Company 1873, p. 207.

Catastrophe of Spectacle

Shipwreck of the Spectator or the Debacle of the Sublime in Émile Zola's *Rougon-Macquart*

Johannes Ungelenk

The wood engraving with the caption "The First Sight of Paris", published in *Cassell's History of the War between France and Germany 1870–1871* (1873),[1] does not depict a spectacular catastrophe. Rather, as its title already indicates, it illustrates a visual constellation. What we see is not so much a spectacular vista as the fact *that* someone is seeing – and *how* this works. I would therefore like to use the wood engraving to analyze the basic setting that is formative for every constellation of the 'spectacle'. This will prepare the second step, which will bring in the notion of catastrophe. I will argue that the spectacle of the catastrophe, which gained prominence above all during the 19th century, is not merely a phenomenon of *representing* catastrophe, but involves the constellation of the spectacle as such. Spectacular catastrophes perform and derive their force from the catastrophe of the spectacle – upon which the following will elaborate.

As part of an extensive presentation of the Franco-Prussian war, the wood engraving shows an identifiable historical moment: the Prussian army reaching Paris in September 1870. It is no coincidence that the constellation of 'first sight' is given so much historiographical significance: As a result of the ensuing siege of Paris, the constellation of the city being surrounded by German soldiers, who watch from a certain distance, was maintained for more than four months.

The picture's composition reflects the hierarchies of a siege. The foreground is dominated by a group of Prussian soldiers. They have turned their backs to the viewer's gaze, who is thus looking over their shoulders, making the viewer feel like he or she is part of the group. It is the network of lines formed by the many arms seemingly pointing at an object of interest that guides the viewer to an area in the background of the wood engraving: Apart from half a dozen silhouettes that sketch out a vague skyline, we can only guess that it is the city of Paris in a dark mass that blurs into the surrounding landscape. The picture thus does not use the moment of the Prussians' "First Sight of Paris" to document the historical condition of the city before the siege and its ensuing destructions, instead it chooses to focus on a different theme: on a relationship from a distance. The Prussian soldier around whom the whole scenario is constructed embodies this theme: Positioned the second from right in the golden cut of the picture, he is using field glasses to watch the city that the extended lines of his forearms demarcate. The two elements whose encounter the picture documents are thus placed at the extreme point of the composition: The visual relationship connects the composition from the foreground to the background. However, it is not only distance that the picture's composition emphasizes but also hierarchy. The Prussians – and with them, the viewer – are watching from a superior vantage point. The grouping of the soldiers on different levels emphasizes that they are located on a slope overlooking the landscape. The impression of them looking down on the city is reinforced by the dark crest, presumably a forest, which draws a diagonal line from the two soldiers sitting in the top-left corner down the valley towards the city in the background. The scenario thus also resembles a hunting scenario: An armed group spies prey from a distant (and thus) safe – i. e. superior – position.

The wood engraving's basic composition, with *contre-jour* lighting and the dark backs of the soldiers in the foreground who are looking down on the landscape stretching out in front of them, was likely inspired by a prominent cultural icon: Caspar David Friedrich's *Wanderer above the Sea of Fog* (1818). However, unlike this model, the vista that *The First Sight of Paris* depicts is not clearly identifiable as a paradigm of 'the sublime'. In particular, it is the little houses clearly perceptible in the lighter areas of the wood engraving that instead produce a picturesque impression. Nevertheless, the picture's overall atmosphere is not entirely positive. Partly due to the technique of wood engraving, partly due to its compositional principle, the landscape dissolves into a sea of lighter and darker structures that create a dynamic not dissimilar to Friedrich's vista of fog and rock. Moreover, the picture reflects the historical narrative within which the represented moment is embedded. It is no coincidence that the city of Paris features as a dark, gloomy mass covered by heavy cloud, whereas the sky to the left and above the picturesque middle part is fair or only partly clouded. Moreover, there is one small detail that foreshadows the catastrophe to come: A dark, diagonal 'blot' dominates the upper quarter of the picture dedicated to the representation of the sky. It is a column of black smoke rising from somewhere beyond the diagonal crest, carried by the wind toward the city. Alongside the soldiers in the foreground, this dark cloud of smoke is the only indicator that reminds the viewer of the picture's status as a document of war. Nevertheless, this one hint is very suggestive: The clouds gathering over the dark mass in the background presage the gigantic billows of smoke that will testify to the catastrophe of Paris burning about half a year later, when the fight between the Communards and the Versailles army threw the city into chaos.

Cassell's History of the War between France and Germany does not supplement "The First Sight of Paris" with a 'later sight' of Paris depicting the 'spectacle' of the burning city in May 1871. This might seem surprising, as the peak of the civil war was an important event in French and European history and would have provided a promising – spectacular – motif for the genre of visual war documentation. However, it is not a visual but a literary 'account' that most vividly captures the historical moment of catastrophe at the end of the Commune: the last pages of Émile Zola's *La Débâcle*[2], the penultimate novel of his famous cycle *Les Rougon-Macquart*. It not only 'paints a detailed picture' of the destroyed city, it also narrates why catastrophe cannot be depicted in the same way that "The First Sight of Paris" composes its visual representation: as a spectacle.

In fact, Zola's literary account takes the very constellation of spectacle that structures "The First Sight of Paris" as its point of departure. Henriette is on her way into the city. She fears for her brother's life, who is fighting for the Communards. The Versailles army is successfully retaking the city and it is only a matter of time until the uprising will lose the last quarters still under its control. Henriette's train stops at a station outside Paris; the chaotic circumstances in Paris make it impossible to travel safely into the city. She happens to chance upon a distant relative who is in command of a group of Prussian soldiers controlling the area. Desperate for somebody to help her with her plans to find a way into the city, she addresses Otto, the relative – who, instead of solving Henriette's logistical problems, leads her to a vantage point overlooking the burning city:

> "Paris is burning… Look! Come over here, you can see it perfectly." And he proceeded in front of her, walking out of the station, following the rails for about a hundred paces until he reached an iron footbridge built over the line. When they'd climbed the narrow stairs and found themselves at the top, leaning on the railings, the vast, flat plain stretched before them, over a low hill. (D, p. 489)

What they see, from their superior position "at the top", is the horrible "spectacle of Paris destroyed" (D, p. 490), presumably because the Communards' have set fire to the representative buildings of the old Empire:

> The red glow which had set the heavens on fire was still spreading. To the east, the blood-red flurry of little clouds had disappeared, and high in the sky there remained only an inky stain, in which the distant flames were reflected. The entire expanse of the horizon was now ablaze; in places, though, they could make out the fiercer fires, with bright purple showers of sparks constantly spurting up and streaking the darkness amid the huge billows of smoke. (D, p. 489)

The composition of Zola's literary scene is astonishingly similar to the pictorial composition of "The First Sight of Paris": The reader looks over the shoulders of the two characters, who are watching the city from a safe distance. The catastrophe takes place at the horizon – just a little fiery coloring in the cloudy background would transform the picturesque wood engraving of *Cassell's History* into Zola's sublime literary painting of Paris burning. Zola's account clearly and explicitly characterizes the scene that it narrates as a scene of 'spectacle'. Notions of the visual ("Look!"; "you can see it perfectly") dominate, which emphasize the distance that separates the spectators from the objects of their perception. The "distant flames" are located as far away as at the horizon; some effort is required to spot even the "fiercer fires". The constellation of Henriette and Otto watching the "spectacle of Paris destroyed" is deeply theatrical: "[T]he rails" and the huge distance between the actual spectacle and its viewing audience act as 'fourth wall', separating stage and audience, and thereby clearly demarcating the subject and the object of the gaze. Moreover, Zola creates a typical "Caspar David Friedrich point of view, high above the surging (fog)sea":[3]

> They both fell quiet and a terrified silence reigned. He was right, sudden surges of flames were rising incessantly, overflowing into the sky like fire streaming from a furnace. With every minute the endless sea of flames spread further in an incandescent swell, sending up billows of smoke and piling an enormous, thick cloud of dark copper over the city; and there must have been a slight breeze behind it, for it was slowly crossing the black night, blocking out the heavenly vault with its wicked shower of ash and soot. (D, p. 490)

Although figural, it is nevertheless a typical instance of what Hans Blumenberg has called the "shipwreck with spectator":

Otto, the Prussian soldier, acts as an "undisturbed and reflective observer of other people's shipwrecks."[4] The uncanny emotional dynamic of the constellation that Blumenberg unfolds, i. e. the attraction that the horrific spectacle exercises on its viewers, is closely related to Immanuel Kant's notion of the sublime. In the sublime constellation, the fact that the spectator "stands unimperiled on the solid ground of the shore"[5] plays a decisive role: "[D]istance" is "reward[ed] with enjoyment"[6], writes Hans Blumenberg, reconstructing an argument by Michel de Montaigne. In Kant's words, who more optimistically attributes the horrific pleasure of the sublime to the capacities of the human subject becoming aware of its participation in more than the mere realm of nature, this argument of distance as a condition for the sublime reads very similarly:

> [T]he sight of [the "all-destroying" violence of "volcanoes", "hurricanes" or "the boundless ocean set into rage"] only becomes all the more attractive the more fearful it is, as long as we find ourselves in safety, and we gladly call these objects sublime because they elevate the strength of our soul above its usual level, and allow us to discover within ourselves a capacity for resistance of quite another kind […].[7]

Henriette is shocked by Otto's reaction to the sublime spectacle of Paris burning: "He wasn't shouting or getting excited, and the enormity of his serenity terrified Henriette." (D, p. 489) In contrast to her, Otto is not involved and, indeed, occupies the 'typical' position of the "undisturbed and reflective observer". As the small but weighty comment "as if he'd foreseen this unparalleled disaster and been waiting a long time for it to come" (D, p. 489) indicates, Otto's detached attitude, although it is that of a Prussian foreigner, is loaded with authorial weight: In several of the preceding novels in the cycle, Zola prefigures the catastrophe of Paris burning, so that, in some respects, Otto's distanced but 'reflected' relationship to the events resembles that of the implicit author, to whom we will return.

However, Otto's reaction is not merely an expression of his "cold, harsh, military Protestantism" (D, p. 490), but also displays the common, vulgar traits of the spectacle's lust for voyeurism: He indulges in the horrific sight of Paris burning, "gorging his eyes on the monstrous feast offered by the spectacle of Babylon in flames" (D, p. 491). The catastrophe cannot be *represented* as catastrophe in a spectacular constellation. The "spectacle of Paris destroyed" is not a 'spectacle of catastrophe'; rather, the theatrical, sublime configuration of the spectacle with its strict division between viewers and distant object translates catastrophe into 'triumph'. This holds true for Kant's transcendental subject experiencing its triumph over the realm of nature, as well as for Zola's observer of the decadence of the Second Empire destroying itself:

> In the arrogance of triumph, nothing – neither the conquered provinces nor the five million francs' compensation – nothing rivalled this spectacle of Paris destroyed, struck by rampant madness, setting light to itself and going up in smoke on this clear, spring night. (D, pp. 489–490)

In order to be representable *as catastrophe*, catastrophe must paradoxically seize upon the constellation of representation and its hierarchies: The superior vantage point, "high above the surging (fog)sea" must be 'turned down' (κατα-στρέφειν, *kata-stréphein*); the distance between the spectator and the object of the gaze must be eliminated. Having exposed a prime example of a sublime shipwreck-with-spectator configuration, Zola's novel narrates precisely this *dé-bâcle*, this melting together of the sublime with its position of undisturbed safety.[8] In the midst of Otto's feasting on the spectacle of Paris burning, Henriette brusquely leaves him behind: "And that was it, she climbed down from the footbridge without even bidding him farewell" (D, p. 491). She continues her journey into the chaos-ridden city – i. e. towards the catastrophe, which paradigmatically follows a downward trajectory.

It is not the first time that Zola's *Rougon-Macquart* constructs a constellation of sublime spectacle, whose uncanny attraction cannot be appropriated by the superior and safe position within the topology of the sublime, instead drawing the spectator irresistibly into the center of catastrophic events. In the first novel in the cycle, the protagonists Miette and Silvère watch the sublime spectacle of the Republican insurgents marching by, a "torrent, rolling with living waves that seemed never to end"[9], but they cannot maintain their superior topographical position: "The road below attracted Miette like the depths of a precipice."[10] Every attempt to "avoid slipping down the slope"[11] proves to be of no avail: Miette and Silvère finally join the insurgents – and are killed when the insurgence fails.

In *La Débâcle*, Henriette eventually makes her way into the inner city of Paris. However, it is not from her perspective that the novel narrates the catastrophe. Continuing its movement into the midst of the violent events, it quite seamlessly switches narrative perspectives and focalizes on Henriette's brother Maurice and his old friend Jean. Fighting on opposing sides in the streets of Paris, Jean severely injures a Communard, who turns out to be his old friend Maurice. He immediately tries to rescue Maurice and bring him to his apartment, which is a difficult task due to the chaos and violence reigning in the city:

> He seized Maurice's uninjured arm and held him up, helping him to get to the end of the Rue du Bac, amidst the houses blazing from top to bottom like outsized torches. A shower of burning brands rained down on them, and the heat was so intense that it singed all the hair on their faces. Then, as they came out onto the quayside, they were momentarily blinded by the terrifying brightness of the fires, sending up enormous showers of spark on either side of the Seine. (D, p. 494)

The two are not only "horrified by the dreadful spectacle unfurling before them" (D, p. 495), they are also literally affected, to which their "singed [...] hair" so vividly testifies. The distance between spectator and spectacle has vanished and vision has thus ceased to be the dominant, or even an adequate approach toward this 'spectacle' of catastrophe: "[T]he violence of the fires was blinding, leaving a black abyss behind it. All that could now be seen was an immense darkness, a void" (D, p. 497). And as if to provoke a Blumenbergian reading of the scene, Zola even lets his protagonists experience the catastrophe of Paris burning from a boat on the Seine:

> It was true, the boat floated along as if borne on a river of fire. In the dancing reflections of these enormous blazes, the Seine appeared to be flowing with hot coals. Sudden bursts of red light flickered above it, amid shimmering yellow firebrands. And they went on drifting slowly down, carried on the current of this burning water between the blazing palaces, as if down an outsized road in a city of the damned, as it burned on either side of a path of molten lava. (D, p. 496)

The spectator's impending 'shipwreck', i. e. the absence of distance, is not at all rewarded with any correlation to sublime enjoyment. Countering the fatalist ravings of his lethally injured companion, Jean explicitly voices the impossibility of maintaining or even enjoying their position in the midst of the catastrophic spectacle: "If everything was to be destroyed, wouldn't they die, too? All he wanted now was to get off the river and escape from the dreadful spectacle." (D, p. 497) His wish to regain "the solid ground of the shore", as Blumenberg would put it, is only the first step to re-establishing his "ability to be a spectator"[12] – i. e. to restore the sublime constellation from which the scene, with Henriette and Otto standing "at the top", gazing down on Paris, had started. The topography of Jean's and Maurice's journey confirms this argument: From the lowest point on the river, it continuously leads them upwards, "climbing the steps [up the banks]" (D, p. 498), and up another staircase to Maurice's flat. Finally, as could be expected, the room in which Maurice will die is equipped with a "window onto Paris" (D, p. 500): "From this high position on the Butte des Moulins, at least half of Paris stretched out before" Jean, the spectator, views "a sea of rooftops, treetops, steeples, domes, and towers." (D, p. 501) It is from here that Jean, only moments after his comrade's death, makes a highly ambivalent – but tendentially triumphant – observation: "[A]s the day slowly faded above the flaming city, it seemed to him that a new dawn was already breaking." (D, p. 514) Jean says farewell to his beloved Henriette, and goes out into the world as one of Zola's few bearers of hope, one of the few members of the Rougon-Macquart family who are entrusted with the responsibility of building a better future.

Zola's literary account of Paris burning is meaningful for Zola's cycle as a whole, and perhaps more generally for the phenomenon of the 'spectacle of catastrophe', because it exposes a constitutive tension: 'Catastrophe' and 'spectacle' cannot be grouped together without initiating a paradoxical dynamic. The one postulates distance, the other all-encompassing involvement and fatal affectedness; the one establishes a hierarchized constellation that the other brings to a collapse – and vice versa. As the success story of the cultural institution theater illustrates, spectacle can very effectively redirect and appropriate the energy of destruction by framing catastrophe and achieving a tragic or cathartic effect. When catastrophe, however, dominantly implies cosmic dimensions, as it does towards the end of the 19th century, spectacle's framing potential loses cogency. The question of whether Zola, the implied author of the *Rougon-Macquart*, watches and narrates the catastrophic shipwreck of the Second Empire as an "undisturbed and reflective observer", standing "unimperiled on the solid ground of the shore", or is himself drawn into the midst of things cannot be answered. The position apart that his representative in the fictional world, Doctor Pascal, had so long claimed for himself and that had made his project of scientifically describing his family (the Rougon-Macquarts!) possible turns out to have been an illusion: The cycle ends with Pascal dying of a hereditary illness. However, the tension between spectacle and catastrophe, between distance and exposition, to the violence of superior forces, between triumph and failure, fuels a literary project that, as a result, performs both: the spectacle of catastrophe and the catastrophe of spectacle.

1 *Cassell's History of the War between France and Germany 1870–1871*, vol. 1. London: Cassell 1873, p. 207.
2 Émile Zola: *La Débâcle*, transl. from the French by Elinor Dorday. Oxford: Oxford UP 2000 (hereafter: D). All page references in the main text are to this edition.
3 Hans Blumenberg: *Shipwreck with Spectator. Paradigm of a Metaphor for Existence*, transl. from the German by Steven Rendall. Cambridge: MIT Press 1997, p. 25.
4 Ibid.
5 Ibid., p. 17.
6 Ibid.
7 Immanuel Kant: *Critique of the Power of Judgment*, transl. from the German by Paul Guyer / Eric Matthews. Cambridge: Cambridge UP 2000, pp. 144–145.
8 Cf. "2 V. intr. (Le sujet désigne une rivière gelée). Dégeler brusquement, la couche de glace se fractionnant avant d'être emportée par le courant." (*Le Grand Robert de la langue française*, ed. by Alain Rey. Paris: Dictionnaires le Robert 2001, s. v. Débâcler.)
9 Émile Zola: *The Fortune of the Rougons*, transl. from the French by Brian Nelson. Oxford: Oxford UP 2012, p. 24.
10 Ibid., p. 28.
11 Ibid.
12 Blumenberg: *Shipwreck with Spectator*, p. 17.

Fig. 1: Bird's Eye View of Coney Island by Night (postcard by P. Sanders, 1906).

The Rise and Fall of Coney Island

Amusement, Catastrophe and the Dead Fire of Consumption

Giulia Palladini

> A fire broke out backstage in a theatre.
> The clown came out to warn the public;
> they thought it was a joke and applauded.
> He repeated it; the acclaim was even greater.
> I think that's just how the world will come to an end:
> to general applause from wits who believe it's a joke.[1]

A moon and a starry sky indicate the particular time of the day at which the image is set. In this landscape, however, numerous lights shine throughout the nocturnal darkness, as do their nuanced reflections on the water. Glimmering among the boats at the small pier, a symphony of red and yellow punctuates the image, constituting for the viewer an ephemeral architecture of light, which counterbalances the majestic shapes that otherwise dominate the picture. The cornerstone of the majestic buildings is the high beacon tower in the background, overlooking the bridge. On the left-hand side, the pier houses a great ballroom, its windows facing the ocean. On the right-hand side, passers-by stroll along the boardwalk between the lagoon and a sumptuous façade with a large archway at its center, from which the courtyard behind can be accessed.

The climax of the image, however, is not the high-rise tower, but rather the cornerstone of the ephemeral architecture of light: It is the intense cloud of flames and smoke emerging from within the building blocks. Everything in the image seems to be have been carefully orchestrated to stage this element as the main attraction for the viewer: In this bird's eye view of Coney Island overlooking the water, the fire has pride of place.

This detail is significant for the story this article is going to tell, which this image more or less accidentally condenses. Fire also has pride of place in this narrative, both as an attraction and as an omen of sorts for the fate of Coney Island, the legendary empire of pleasure conceived to "amuse the millions"[2] at the beginning of New York's urban modernity: a place imagined and produced as a delimited territory of unlimited consumption. Located at the far end of Brooklyn on a narrow peninsula extending into the ocean, Coney Island was established as a leisure area at the turn of the century, and continued to perform this function, with varying success, until the 1960s, surviving to this day more as a locus of nostalgia than as a productive enterprise. Comprising a beach resort and a wide variety of entertainment offers, Coney Island's golden age was between 1900 and 1912, when its three iconic amusement parks – Steeplechase, Luna Park and Dreamland – were in full operation, attracting more than 100,000 visitors a day during the summer season.[3] From very early on, Coney Island came to be referred to as 'The City of Fire', an expression used, for example, by Maxim Gorky, who visited the place in 1907 and famously described it, both disappointed and strangely fascinated, in an article entitled "Boredom" published in the newspaper *The Independent*.[4] This nickname conjured up an image of Coney Island as it appeared from Manhattan: that of a town of sparkling lights emerging as a flame from the ocean itself.

Fire, therefore, was always already a staple in the terminology and imagination associated with Coney Island. This reference is also alluded to in this illustration from 1906. But the picture potentially conjures up more than just this. I will regard it as an image that unwittingly conveys a set of historical references that exceed the time and purpose of this particular representation: as the imaginary archival remains of a stratified history which, at the time the picture was produced, had not yet fully taken place.

As a matter of fact, the image of the fire in the square lends itself to different interpretations, depending on the particular standpoint of the observer. Someone encountering this picture without any knowledge of either the subject being represented or of the purpose for which it was produced might assume that the blaze is an accident occurring in an otherwise harmonious landscape: a fire captured at the moment it is just about to conflagrate over the peaceful pier, and whose danger the surrounding environment is still unaware of. A careful observation of the image, however, also reveals that attempts to tame the fire are already at work: against the mist of fire and smoke rising toward the sky, the image also portrays jets of water streaming toward the blaze, graphically countering the flames with steady gushes coming from below. Among the flames, it is also possible to recognize the point where the fire originated: a building.

However, for an observer looking at this picture in 1906, at the time it was produced, this image had a radically different meaning. For that observer, the fire was a clear reference to the attraction that, in the 1904 and 1905 summer seasons, had been the most popular at Coney Island: Fighting the Flames, which regularly took place at Dreamland. Employing a cast of 4,000 people playing firemen and actors and performed for a crowd of around 1,500 spectators, Fighting the Flames was the re-enactment of a fire disaster taking place in a building block, staged in a meticulously reconstructed, plausible urban scene. For 20 minutes, a five-story hotel was set ablaze and rescued during an immersive performance, where spectators played (although from a safe distance) the part of witnesses. Further evidence of the popularity of this attraction is the short film *Fighting the Flames – Dreamland,* produced in August 1904 by the American Mutoscope & Biograph Company, which reproduced a fragment of the show. The promotional materials for the film described the salient features of the attraction in great detail, presented as the ultimate example of 'sensational realism':

The entertainment has all the excitement of a genuine fire. The conflagration is preceded by familiar scenes of every-day life in a busy city. Across the city square pass trolley cars, delivery wagons, coupes and pushcart vendors, while busy people complete the scene of life and activity in a metropolitan city. A well-equipped fire department is ready for emergency, and when the alarm is sounded that a five-story hotel is on fire, the engines, hose wagons, water tower, hook and ladder truck and battalion chief's wagon crowd one another as they rush to the scene of the conflagration. What the audience sees is a raging fire, with excitable people clinging to the windows, others forced to the fire-escapes, where escape is cut off by the flames below. The firemen play the part of heroes. By the use of scaling ladders, while the extension ladder is being raised, the firemen mount the building floor by floor, calm the inmates, bringing some to the ground by means of the scaling ladders and fire escape ropes. While this part of the scene is enacted the life-net has been placed in position. Frenzied people jump from the fire-escapes into the net from every floor. As one man jumps for the net from the roof, an explosion is heard and the roof falls in. All this time the engines have been pumping water into the building and upon the flames. The conflagration is gotten under control and all lives have been saved.[5]

Numerous illustrated postcards were produced to advertise *Fighting the Flames*: Some present a frontal image of the building on fire, with the crowd witnessing the rescue and the firemen heroically at work. Others, in turn, present the attraction in the broader environment of Dreamland, doubling in representation the tension between reality and fiction, which was intrinsic to the attraction. The 1906 *Bird's Eye View of Coney Island by Night* that opened this essay is an illustrated postcard of this kind: one of the postcards that park visitors could purchase as a souvenir of their leisure experience or send to their friends and relatives at home. Significantly, the golden age of Coney Island coincided with the establishment of a large tourist industry. Within this context, images of Coney Island were produced and put to work in the marketing and consumption of cultural memory in the forms of touristic postcards and memorabilia. As Richard Snow reports, "200,000 [post]cards were mailed from Coney in a single day of September 1906".[6]

However, for someone looking at this picture today, more than a century later, and with the long history of Coney Island in mind, besides being a souvenir of this legendary fire attraction, this picture is also a powerful detonator of historical recollections of the many fires that, for its part, Coney Island attracted to itself throughout its history. The most famous in 1911, which has gone down as the biggest fire in New York history to date, fatally destroyed Dreamland, the park portrayed in this postcard, at the peak of its splendor, performing the hubris of taming the blaze that was regularly ignited for public amusement. In a sense, then, interpreting the picture as the scenario of an imminent conflagration, which would later turn the empire of pleasure into a wasteland, was not too far from reality – especially since 'reality' in the history and legend of Coney Island has intrinsically blurred and overlapped with fiction.

The story of the complex relationship between the fire disasters staged at Coney Island and the catastrophic fires that repeatedly burned down its precarious architectures of amusement comprises many episodes, all of which could be considered distinctive examples of such blurring. Displaying and experimenting with what Rem Koolhaas has called the "Technology of the Fantastic",[7] Coney Island embodied an alternative world, where imagination was given form and marketed as experience. At Steeplechase Park (founded in 1897), visitors could give themselves over to the pleasure of sliding down gigantic chutes, experiencing the vertigo of height and speed, and bumping into each other on rides like the Human Roulette Wheel. At Luna Park (founded in 1903), dubbed Electric Eden because it was illuminated by

250,000 electric lights, visitors wandered into a surreal, exotic architectural space while undertaking simulated adventures such as The Trip to the Moon or Twenty Thousand Leagues Under the Sea. At Dreamland (founded in 1904), a majestic cosmogony featuring explicit biblical references (significantly framing the leisure experience between the poles of *creation* and *destruction*) welcomed the visitors, offering them the chance to travel through time, space, and human knowledge, encompassing attractions as diverse as a gigantic model of Venice, a Japanese tea room, the 'Midget City' of Lilliputia (housing a community of 100 midgets) and the Incubator Building (where premature children were on display in newly invented incubators).

At Luna Park and Dreamland, a great number of historical disasters from different historical periods were recreated and offered up for public amusement. Besides the fire attraction Fire and Flames (which functioned similarly to Fighting the Flames, but on a smaller scale), Luna Park featured, for example, a show about the floods and hurricane that had devastated Galveston, Texas, in 1900, a town reconstructed in miniature and routinely destroyed in performances using real and fake water, large sheets of painted fabric, and lighting and mechanical effects, while a lecturer explained the sequence of events. At Dreamland, visitors could witness The Fall of Pompeii, comfortably sitting in a reconstructed Greek temple, while the legendary eruption of Vesuvius was recreated using mechanical equipment with a spectacular fireworks finale. In the space of one day at Coney Island a visitor could potentially undertake time travel from one catastrophe to another, from the San Francisco earthquake to the burnings of Rome and Moscow, from the devastating 1902 eruption of Mount Pelée in Martinique to US naval battles and episodes from the Boer War.

Considering the greater spectacular effects displayed in these other attractions, it might seem surprising that audiences considered Fighting the Flames and Fire and Flames to be the most appealing – all the more so since the majority of visitors to Coney Island were working-class citizens who faced hard housing conditions in everyday life, "living in constant fear of fire in ramshackle, deathtrap tenements",[8] quite similar to the ones routinely set ablaze in the attractions. As Kevin Baker suggests, to a certain extent, these citizens "were there to see the pageant of their lives and their times played out before them".[9] More than a catastrophic phantasmagoria, the attraction was a ritual, where visitors came to terms with the hardship and congestion of the metropolitan experience, which at the time was new to many, constructing its own mythology, in which firemen played the part of heroes from the beginning. Before a paid fire department was established in New York in 1865, volunteer firefighters had performed a crucial role in society as well as in the growing American ideology of community and human mastery over adverse conditions.

Spectacular fires also characterized the history of Coney Island. A brief tour through such history should touch upon at least a few of the events that routinely destroyed its ambitious fantasies of amusement. Even before the foundation of Steeplechase, a series of fires destroyed various newly founded hotels in the beach area at Coney Island and, in 1903, a devastating blaze erased 14 square blocks on the Bowery, the site of a number of entertainment venues. In July 1907, Steeplechase burned down in 18 hours due to a lit cigarette accidentally thrown into a waste basket. In 1911, the legendary fire that devastated Dreamland was sparked by the explosion of a light bulb, fatally located on a ride named Hell's Gate. The firemen were also unable to tame the fire due to a flaw in the recently installed hydrant system. Half of Luna Park burned down in 1944, and it was finally torn down in 1949. Even more relevant than this partial chronology is the fact that some of these catastrophic events themselves became instances of spectacle, either perceived, marketed or consumed as such.

For example, the day after Steeplechase burned down, its founder George C. Tilyou posted the following sign at the site where his park had once been:

> To enquiring friends: I have troubles today that I had not yesterday. I had troubles yesterday which I have not today. On this site will be built a bigger, better, Steeplechase Park. Admission to the burning ruins – Ten cents.[10]

Indeed, before Tilyou later rebuilt the park on a much greater scale, he made the most of the disaster, starting by charging admission to the debris of Steeplechase, turning 'catastrophic reality' into 'spectacle', just as Coney Island's many other staged catastrophes did during the same period. The 1911 Dreamland fire, in turn, was perceived as a spectacle from the very moment it happened: Suspecting that it was just one more catastrophic attraction, news reporters from Manhattan printed the news with a 24-hour delay. "Dreamland", Koolhaas remarks,

> had succeeded so well in cutting itself loose from the world that Manhattan's newspapers refused to believe in the authenticity of the final disaster even as their editors see its flames and smoke from their office windows.[11]

However, once the news was announced, this charred site was also immediately turned into an attraction. As the article "Ruins Help Draw 350,000 to Coney" reported, published two days after the fire, the impresario Samuel W. Gumpertz organized "all that [was] left of Dreamland" to be exhibited for a paying audience:

> [T]he great waste, five blocks square, was considered an attraction, and it was reckoned that the desire to see the piles of blackened timbers and bent steel helped bringing 350,000 people to the island.[12]

Visitors paid their dimes to see the living remains of the entertainment that once was, namely the few animals from Joseph's Ferrari Trained Wild Animal Arena that had survived the catastrophe, along with numbers performed on the ruins by some of the 'freaks' from The Dreamland Circus Sideshow. Furthermore, half-burned pictures of Little Hip, the famous performing elephant that had died in the flames were sold

> as bona fide relics of the fire. They appear to have been genuine enough pictures of the elephant, but someone wandering through the wreckage came across a small boy crouched behind a pile of timber with a candle in one hand and a photograph in the another. He was singing [*sic*] the edges of the photograph and preparing it for the market.[13]

So, not only were real catastrophes exhibited as attractions, but to complicate matters even further, blurring the lines between fiction and reality, memorabilia of the catastrophe was manufactured from scratch as evidence of one more lesson from the history of Coney Island: that illusion, in spectacle, pays far more than authenticity, in good and bad fate alike.

Keeping in mind this manufactured memorabilia, I want to go back to the bird's eye view from 1906 where this essay started. That postcard, in fact, had also been manufactured with the intent of making entertainment endure after the moment of its *consumption*: It was meant to double and re-stage a leisure experience that, once the weekend was over and the masses of visitors had left Coney, was eaten up, disappeared as experience, alongside the dimes paid for it. After the blaze in Fighting the Flames had been heroically tamed in performance and all lives saved, working-class citizens could go back to the 'reality' of the "ramshackle, deathtrap tenements" to which the new, iconic metropolis of American industrial capitalism relegated their work time, while organizing the market where their leisure time could be spent, in the phantasmagoria of the consumption of 'the City of Fire'. Although the connection is not made explicit, the powerful etymological relation between *consumption* and the play of fire exhibited at Coney Island appears nowhere clearer that in the beautiful critique written by Gorky after his first visit to the place. After describing the wonderful deception of the City of Fire seen from the distance, at a first glance, once at the parks, Gorky encounters the dreadful allegory of human life's subjection to the power of capital: "[T]he fiery scintillation of Coney Island", he writes, "burns but does not consume".[14] That is, the spectacle of consumption in which the masses of workers participated was meant to be endless, as a "dead fire", which by its own nature had little to do with "the desire of a beautiful, a sublime fire, which should free the people from the slavery of a varied boredom".[15] Within this logic, endless consumption was to be replicated by manufactured goods that, like the 1906 postcard, would artificially reproduce an experience, prolonging the limitedness of its costly pleasure. The counter-image of fire imagined by Gorky was one that would not have to be paid for: It was "a merry dancing and shouting and singing" where the soul "would see a passionate play of motley tongues of fire; it would have joyousness and life",[16] in place of a compulsive urge to consume. The fire would be a force of conflagration coming from within, not sold to the masses and exceeding the limited time of a weekend: a fire igniting ideas about different life possibilities outside the phantasmagoria of American capitalism that first created the conditions for, and then displayed, its own disasters.

1 Søren Kierkegaard: *Either/Or. A Fragment of Life*, transl. from the Danish by Alastair Hannay. London: Penguin 2004, p. 49.
2 "Amusing the millions" was the title of an article written by Frederic Thompson, co-founder of Luna Park, describing the philosophy of his amusement business. Frederic Thompson: Amusing the Millions. In: *Everybody's Magazine* 19 (September 1907), pp. 378–386.
3 Louis J. Parascandola / John Parascandola: Introduction. In L. J. P. / J. P. (eds): *A Coney Island Reader: Through the Dizzy Gates of Illusion*. New York: Columbia UP 2015, pp. 1–50, here p. 1.
4 Maxim Gorky: Boredom. In: *The Independent*, August 8, 1907, pp. 309–317.
5 Synopsis of *Fighting the Flames – Dreamland* (1904), from Biograph promotional materials, qtd. in Lynn Kathleen Sally: *Fighting the Flames: The Spectacular Performance of Fire at Coney Island*. New York / London: Routledge, pp. 85–86.
6 Richard Snow: *Coney Island: A Postcard Journey to the City of Fire*. New York: Brightwaters 1984, p. 20.
7 Rem Koolhaas: *Delirious New York: A Retroactive Manifesto for Manhattan*. Oxford: Oxford UP 1978, p. 29.
8 Kevin Baker: Foreword. In: Parascandola / Parascandola (eds): *Coney Island Reader*, pp. XIII–XVIII, here p. XVI.
9 Ibid.
10 Quoted in Edo McCullough: *Good Old Coney Island: A Sentimental Journey into the Past*. New York: Fordham UP 2000, p. 202
11 Koolhaas: *Delirious New York*, p. 76.
12 Ruins Help Draw 350,000 to Coney. In: *New York Times*, May 29, 1911. Reprinted in: *A Coney Island Reader*, p. 164.
13 Ibid., p. 166.
14 Gorky: Boredom, p. 309.
15 Ibid., p. 311.
16 Ibid.

Fig. 1: B-29 airplane "Necessary Evil".

When Necessary Evil Is Evil All the Same

Jean-Pierre Dupuy

On the morning of August 6, 1945, three B-29s took off from the tiny island of Tinian in the Marianna islands. Their destination was the harbor of Hiroshima in southern Japan. One of them was named Enola Gay, and it was carrying the Little Boy atomic bomb. One of the other two carried the team of scientists in charge of observing and measuring the effects of the bomb's explosion. It had no name, but after its return to Guam, it was named Necessary Evil, as shown in the image above. Hence, the contribution made by science to the massacre was placed under the honorable label of ethics. The cocktail of science, death and sex that one sees in the image is insipid compared with this hijacking of moral philosophy.

Indeed, in the minds of many people – including, it would appear even today, a very large majority of Americans – Hiroshima is the classic example of a necessary evil. Having invested itself with the power to determine, if not the best of all possible worlds, then at least the least bad among them, America placed the bombing of civilians and their murder in the hundreds of thousands on one side of the scales of justice, and, on the other, an invasion of the Japanese archipelago that, it was said, would have cost the lives of a half a million American soldiers. Moral necessity, it was argued, required that America choose to put an end to the war as quickly as possible, even if this meant shattering everything that until then had constituted the most elementary rules of just war once and for all. Moral philosophers call this a consequentialist argument: When the issue is one of surpassingly great importance, deontological norms – so called because they express a duty to respect absolute imperatives, no matter what the cost or effects of doing this may be – must yield to the calculus of consequences.

In the decades since, however, persons of great integrity and intellect have insisted on the intrinsic immorality of atomic weapons in general, and the ignominy of bombing Hiroshima and Nagasaki in particular. In 1956, the Oxford philosopher and Catholic thinker Elizabeth Anscombe made an enlightening comparison that threw into stark relief the horrors to which consequentialist reasoning leads when it is taken to its logical conclusion. Let us suppose, she said, that the Allies had thought at the beginning of 1945 that, in order to break the Germans' will to resist and to compel them to surrender rapidly and unconditionally, thus sparing the lives of a great many Allied soldiers, it was necessary to carry out the massacre of hundreds of thousands of civilians, women and children included, in two cities in the Ruhr. Two questions arise: Firstly, what difference would there have been, morally speaking, between this and what the Nazis did in Czechoslovakia and Poland? Secondly, what difference would there have been, morally speaking, between this and the atomic bombing of Hiroshima and Nagasaki?[1]

In the face of horror, moral philosophy is forced to resort to analogies of this sort, for it has nothing other than logical consistency on which to base the validity of its arguments. In the event, this minimal requirement of consistency did not suffice to rule out the nuclear option nor to condemn it afterwards. Why? One answer is that, because the Americans won the war against Japan, their victory seemed in retrospect to justify the course of action that they followed. This argument must not be mistaken for cynicism. It involves what philosophers call the problem of moral luck. The moral judgment that is passed on a decision made under conditions of radical uncertainty depends on what occurs *after* the relevant action has been taken – something that may have been completely unforeseeable, even as a probabilistic matter.

Robert McNamara memorably described this predicament in the extraordinary set of interviews conducted by the documentarian Errol Morris and released as a film under a most Clausewitzian title, *The Fog of War* (2003). Before serving as Secretary of Defense under Presidents Kennedy and Johnson, McNamara had been an advisor to General Curtis LeMay during the war in the Pacific, who was responsible for the firebombing of 67 cities in Imperial Japan, a campaign that culminated in the dropping of the two atomic bombs. On the night of March 9–10, 1945, alone, 100,000 civilians perished in Tokyo, burned to death. McNamara approvingly reported LeMay's stunningly lucid verdict: "If we'd lost the war, we'd all have been prosecuted as war criminals."

Another possible answer is that consequentialist morality served in this instance only as a convenient pretext. A 'revisionist' school of American historians led by Gar Alperovitz has pleaded this case with great conviction, arguing that, in July 1945, Japan was at the point of capitulation.[2] Two conditions would have had to be satisfied in order to obtain immediate surrender: Firstly, President Truman would have had to agree to an immediate declaration of war on Japan by the Soviet Union; secondly, Japanese surrender would have had to have been accompanied by an American promise that the Emperor would be allowed to continue to sit on his throne. Truman refused both conditions at the conference in Potsdam, a few days after July 16, 1945. On that day, the President had received 'good news'. The bomb was ready – as the successful test at Alamogordo had brilliantly demonstrated.

Alperovitz concludes that Truman sought to steal a march on the Soviets before they were prepared to intervene militarily in the Japanese archipelago. The Americans played the nuclear card, in other words, not to force Japan to surrender, but to impress the Russians. In this case, the Cold War had been launched on the strength of an ethical abomination and the Japanese reduced to the level of guinea pigs, for the bomb was not in fact necessary to obtain surrender. Other historians argue that, whether or not necessary, it was not a sufficient condition for obtaining surrender.

The historian Barton J. Bernstein has proposed a "new synthesis" that departs from both official and the revisionist accounts.[3] The day after Nagasaki, War Minister General Korechika Anami and the Vice Chief of the Naval General Staff, Admiral Takijiro Ōnishi, urged the Emperor to authorize a "special attack [*kamikaze*] effort", even though this would mean putting as many as 20 million Japanese lives at risk, by their own estimate, in the name of ultimate victory. In that event, two bombs would not suffice. So convinced were the Americans of the need to detonate a third device, Bernstein says, that the announcement of surrender on August 14 – apparently the result of chance and reversals of allegiance at the highest level of the Japanese government that are still poorly understood by historians – came as an utter surprise. But Bernstein takes the argument one step further: Of the six options available to the Americans to force the Japanese to surrender without invading the archipelago, five had been rather cursorily analyzed, individually and in combination, and then rejected by Truman and his advisors: continuing with the conventional bombing campaign, supplemented by a naval blockade; carrying out unofficial negotiations with the enemy; modifying the terms of surrender, including a guarantee that the emperor system would be preserved; awaiting Russian entry into the war; performing a non-combat demonstration of the atomic bomb. As for the sixth option, the military use of the bomb – it was never discussed, not even for a moment: it was simply taken for granted. The bombing of Hiroshima and Nagasaki derived from the bomb's very existence. From an ethical point of view, Bernstein's findings are more terrible yet than those of Alperovitz: Dropping the atomic bomb, perhaps the gravest decision ever made in modern history, was not something that had actually been decided upon.

These revisionist interpretations do not exhaust the questions that need to be asked. There are at least two more. Firstly, how are we to make sense of the bombing of Hiroshima – and, more troubling still, of Nagasaki – which is to say the monstrously absurd determination to persist in infamy? Secondly, how could the consequentialist veneer of the official justification for these acts – that they were extremely regrettable, but a moral necessity just the same – have been accepted as a lawful pretext, when it should have been seen instead as the most execrable and appalling excuse imaginable?

It behooves here to introduce the figure of the German philosopher Günther Anders, one of Heidegger's former students and the first husband of his favorite student, political philosopher Hannah Arendt. Anders, a German Jew who had emigrated to France and then to America, and then came back to Europe in 1950 – everywhere an exile, the wandering Jew – recognized that on August 6, 1945, human history had entered into a new phase: its last. Or rather, that the sixth day of August was only a *rehearsal* for the ninth – what he called the 'Nagasaki syndrome'. Once it had occurred, thereby introducing the impossible into reality, the dropping of the first atomic bomb over a civilian population opened the door to more atrocities, in the same way that an earthquake is followed by a series of aftershocks. History became obsolete that day, as Anders put it. Now that humanity was capable of destroying itself, nothing would ever cause it to lose this "negative all-powerfulness", not even general disarmament, not even the total denuclearization of the world's arsenals. Now that apocalypse had been inscribed in our future as fate, the best we could do was to indefinitely postpone the final moment. We were living under a suspended sentence, as it were: a stay of execution. In August 1945, Anders said, humanity entered into the era of the reprieve (*die Frist*) and the second death of all that had existed. Since the meaning of the past depended on future actions, the obsolescence of the future, its programmed end, signified for Anders not that the past no longer had any meaning, but that it had never had any to begin with.[4]

Ascertaining the rationality and the morality of the destruction of Hiroshima and Nagasaki amounts to treating nuclear weapons as a means in the service of an end. A means loses itself in its end as a river loses itself in the sea and ends up being completely absorbed by it. But the bomb exceeds all ends that can be given to it or found for it. The question whether the end justifies the means suddenly became obsolete, like everything else. Why was the bomb used? Because it *existed.* The simple fact of its existence was a threat, or rather a promise that it would be used. Why has the moral horror of its use not been perceived? What accounts for this "blindness in the face of apocalypse"?[5] Because beyond certain thresholds, our power of doing (*herstellen*) infinitely exceeds our capacity for feeling and imagining (*vorstellen*). It is this irreducible gap that Anders called the "Promethean discrepancy".[6] The which is 'too great' leaves us cold, he adds, as does the fact that no human being was capable of imagining something of such horrifying magnitude: the elimination of millions of people.

Hannah Arendt diagnosed the evil in Eichmann as thoughtlessness or lack of imagination.[7] Anders showed that this was not the weakness of one person in particular; it was the weakness of all people, when their capacity for invention and destruction was disproportionately enlarged in relation to the human condition.[8]

In 1958, Günther Anders went to Hiroshima and Nagasaki to take part in the Fourth World Conference against Atomic and Hydrogen bombs. After many exchanges with survivors of the catastrophe, he noted in his diary:

> Their steadfast resolve not to speak of those who were to blame, not to say that the event had been caused by human beings; *not to harbor the least resentment, even though they were the victims of the greatest of crimes* – this really is too much for me, it passes all understanding.

He then adds: "They constantly speak of the catastrophe as if it were an earthquake or a tidal wave. They use the Japanese word, *tsunami.*"[9]

The evil that inhabits 'nuclear peace' is not the product of any malign intention. It is the inspiration for passages of terrifying insight in Anders's book, *Hiroshima ist überall* (*Hiroshima is everywhere*), words that send a chill down our spine:

> The fantastic character of the situation quite simply takes one's breath away. At the very moment when the world becomes apocalyptic, and this owing to our own fault, it presents the image [...] of a paradise inhabited by murderers without malice and victims without hatred. Nowhere is there any trace of malice, there is only rubble.[10]

And Anders prophesies:

> No war in history will have been more devoid of hatred than the war by tele-murder that is to come [...]. [T]his absence of hatred will be the most inhuman absence of hatred that has ever existed; absence of hatred and absence of scruples will henceforth be one and the same.[11]

Violence without hatred is so inhuman that it amounts to a transcendence of sorts – perhaps the only transcendence still left to us.

1 G.E.M. Anscombe: Mr. Truman's Degree. In: *Collected Philosophical Papers,* vol. 3: Ethics, Religion, and Politics. Minneapolis: University of Minnesota Press 1981, pp. 62–71. The title of this essay refers to Oxford's awarding of an honorary degree to President Truman in June 1956.

2 Gar Alperovitz: *The Decision to Use the Atomic Bomb and the Architecture of an American Myth*. New York: Knopf 1995.

3 Barton J. Bernstein: Understanding the Atomic Bomb and the Japanese Surrender: Missed Opportunities, Little-Known Near Disasters, and Modern Memory. In: *Diplomatic History* 19:2 (spring 1995), pp. 227–273, here p. 254.

4 Cf. Günther Anders: *Hiroshima ist überall.* Munich: Beck 1995.

5 Günther Anders: *Die Antiquiertheit des Menschen 1. Über die Seele im Zeitalter der zweiten industriellen Revolution*. Munich: Beck 1956, p. 263, passim.

6 Ibid., p. 267, passim.

7 Cf. Hannah Arendt: *Eichmann in Jerusalem. A Report on the Banality of Evil.* London: Penguin 1978.

8 Cf. Anders: *Die Antiquiertheit des Menschen 1*, p. 267.

9 Anders: *Hiroshima ist überall*, p. 84 (transl. by J-P.D.; emphasis added).

10 Ibid., p. 87.

11 Ibid., p. 114.

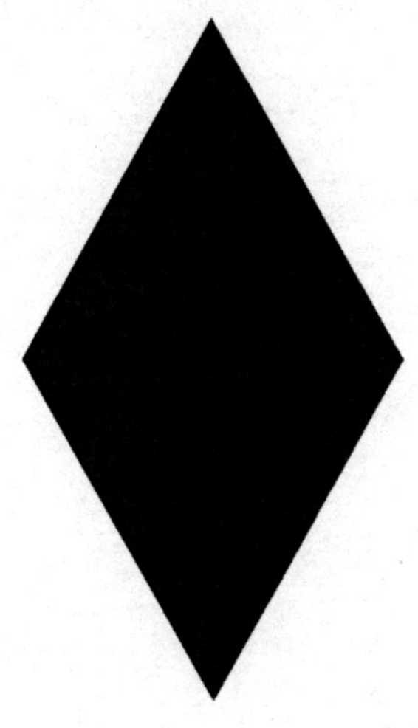

Fig. 1: Black Rhombus.

Endless Catastrophe

Maurice Blanchot and the Fragments of Disaster

Martina Bengert

What do we see? A black surface, an even black square shape made up of four sides of the same length. In geometry, a shape like this standing up on the tip of a longer diagonal is called a rhombus, diamond or lozenge. In this shape, it also appears in numerous heraldic contexts. Another context of application for the diamond shape is typography, where it is often presented as an alternative bullet point to a dash, solid circle or square. In Maurice Blanchot's 1980 book *The Writing of the Disaster* (*L'écriture du désastre*), a total of 403 diamond-shaped symbols are used to precede 403 fragments, creating a series or list. By having one of these diamonds precede my text, I would like to emphasize one of the phenomena of both the content and structure of *The Writing of the Disaster*: This one diamond represents all the other diamonds in the book that, as typographical symbols, are subject to uniformity. This one diamond (and the text it draws attention to) is all of the diamonds and can thus not be reduced to any of them. Presented individually, it makes the impression of an image or a symbol, which calls for interpretation. But when used as a bullet point within the text body without any context, it fades to black and is swallowed up in meaninglessness as a typographical symbol. Thus, within and by means of the diamond shape, an unstoppable oscillation can be seen between the promise of an abundance of meaning and the performance of meaninglessness, between participation in the symbolic order and its dissolution. Insofar as the diamond is positioned as a generic diamond at the beginning, we begin with what is marked as an in-between space (e.g. between two fragments). The beginning thus starts with the diamond shape as an interval, that is, with the simultaneity of interruption and continuity, beginning and end. This in-between space is neither singular nor spectacular, but rather the actualization of a repetition that Blanchot describes as the writing of the disaster.

The aim of what will follow is to demonstrate that Blanchot's disaster is not a spectacular catastrophe, but rather that its force unfolds as something neither temporally datable nor geographically locatable in the realm of the unspectacular and ahistorical. With continual reference to the diamond and its oscillation, I will outline this by focusing on the paradigmatic techniques of the text – fragmentation, repetition, recombination and displacement – and thus show that *The Writing of the Disaster* is a text whose a-centric center is the disaster that traverses, proliferates and further fragments the fragments in the form of an anarchic web of dis-placement and non-sense.

Fragmentation, destruction and disaster

Writing in splinters and fragments – the *Writing of the Disaster* – is, as I propose, writing that displays its own destruction, hovering between being unholy and unwhole: It is an expression of what is no longer whole, what has never been whole or intact, or of what will never be whole again. One of the possible translations of disaster is the French *désastre*. In the epilogue to his translation of *The Writing of the Disaster*, Gerhard Poppenberg highlights the ambivalence of Blanchot's *désastre* as *Unheil* (in the sense of the catastrophic) and as something that is not whole and unscathed, something *Unheiles* (in the sense of being both fragmented and wounded). *The Writing of the Disaster* is therefore something of a "practice in calamity [...] a way of conceiving of inner conflict and existential insecurity".[1] As something calamitous and unwhole, the disaster refers to the fragment and its interim status between remnant (rest, ruin) and something unfinished (project, draft) – to use the terms from Friedrich Schlegel's *Athenaeum* Fragment 22. By signifying calamity ('calamity' is also a translation for the Hebrew word *shoah*), however, it does not refer to a totality in a positive sense as in, for example, Early German Romanticism,[2] but rather to a negative totality that is devoid of self-sufficiency and has no internal closure. The disaster as unwhole/unholy is what remains when everything else is destroyed, namely the naked truth that things will somehow go on. Thus, the fragments cannot be semantically contained in the form of visible ruinous remains of a past time, but rather break through such restraint on the discursive level using a fragmenting structure that no longer presumes the existence of the ruin, but continues to ruin, that is, to fragment itself in an interplay of fragments. In other words, the ruin as noun and as effect of the disaster is replaced by an incessant discursive process that ruins meaning, unity and order. The fragment is transferred to a mode of fragmentary writing that self-referentially practices fragmentation at the level of its own discursive constitution.[3]

The 403 fragments alone institute a never-ending repetition of beginning and ending. In the eternal return of creation and destruction, the fragments present themselves as untenable modes of positing that lead nowhere. This ceaseless iteration is framed or confined by the term *désastre* which stands at the beginning and at the very end of this fragment collection, or better yet, this dispersion of fragments. However, the fact that the disaster constitutes the confinement of the fragments does not lead to any unity of what is said, but rather creates a destructive-apocalyptic framework toward which everything gravitates and from which everything emanates. It is both the condition and the objective and, as both calamitous and unwhole, cannot be understood as the one or the other.

"The disaster ruins everything, all the while leaving everything intact."[4] This is how the fragment, which is often quoted in Blanchot research, begins. Whereas the first fragment starts with "Le désastre [...]", thus placing a definite article in front of the disaster, indicating that it is possible to label 'the disaster', the last fragment ends in the French original with pure disaster, which does not allow for the use of any article: "*Solitude qui rayonne, vide du ciel, mort différée: désastre.*"[5] The other nouns do not possess any article either, nor can they bear one. 'Shining solitude', 'void of the sky', 'deferred death' are found on the left side of the colon whereby, at the end of *The Writing of the Disaster*, a final definition and a final doubling is created, which appears to summarize the remaining text but which, upon closer inspection, radically dissolves it by transgressing any ending. By way of the disaster, something shines through language and exceeds it, insofar as the disaster places itself at the end and thus lets the end itself emerge as a mode of positing. There are differences between the beginning and the end of *The Writing of the Disaster*. However, they cannot be located at the semantic level, but rather are recognizable as a linguistic displacement.

Whereas the first fragment is a grammatically complete sentence, the last fragment depicts the fragmentary in its inner structure as an incomplete and broken sentence and thus becomes a twice-fragmented ending by means of auto-affection. The only verb in the sentence does not become the predicate, but only exists in a relative sentence and, as previously mentioned, the articles (in the original French version) are missing within this elliptical equation. A further difference to the first sentence is the fact that the entire last fragment is set in italics. In Blanchot's oeuvre, something written in italics usually signals a quotation or a different epistemological level. Even though it does not constitute a referenceable quote, setting certain passages in italics can be understood as marking another manner of speaking. Due to the italics, the last fragment is evocative of a quote or rather highlights its status as that of improper discourse, a writing that questions itself and always remains in reserve.

Repetition I: Quotes without origin

> If quotations, in their fragmenting force, destroy in advance the texts from which they are not only severed but which they exalt till these texts become nothing but severance, then the fragment without a text, or any context, is radically unquotable. (WD, p. 37; ED, p. 64)

According to this definition of the quote, the destructive force residing within each quote, insofar as it has been taken out of its context and implanted within another one, means that fragments are absolutely unquotable. After all, fragments are specifically characterized by their independence as well as their interchangeability and, in this manner, are not bound to their context. Inasmuch as the writing of the disaster is fed by numerous quotes, which themselves were ripped from other texts for this purpose, the fragmenting dynamic of the disaster that destroys everything also manifests itself in the same manner.

The Writing of the Disaster contains various modes of quoting, or rather, of adding voices to the text. There are quotes marked by quotation marks that have, however, been altered by Blanchot, even though these alterations are not always properly indicated. Some quotes are set in italics, and some are not. According to the French citation method, italicizing is normally used to express the fact that the part of the text in question is a quote from someone else. Within *The Writing of the Disaster*, however, italicizing marks a fundamental non-originality, which encompasses more than the level of signifier and signified. This unreliability is programmatic, insofar as it thwarts the notion of the systematic as well as the illusion of originality and origin. Page numbers and exact bibliographical references are never used. If the quotes are marked but do not contain any concrete reference, for example to a name or at least to some initials, then they become stray fragments within the fragment. It marks that their origin is somewhere else, although it is not mentioned. The following quote is an example: "The pain of our times: 'An emaciated man, with head dropped and shoulders curved, on whose face and whose eyes not a trace of a thought to be seen.' 'Our looks were turned to the ground.'" (WD, p. 90; ED, p. 129).

This French, slightly modified quote originates from the story *Survival in Auschwitz* by Primo Levi, a Holocaust survivor who wrote down the experiences he had at Auschwitz between 1945 and 1947 directly after World War II but who is not mentioned by name. Both the author and the man remain hidden behind these two sentences, thus marking the anonymity of victims and witnesses. Furthermore, Blanchot shifts the quoted words dating from 1947 into ahistoricity by explaining that the following passage expresses the pain of "notre temps" ("our times"). Even though it was published 30 years later, in Blanchot's fragment, Primo Levi's words retain their significance, but are uprooted and expropriated in order to refer from their singularity to the preceding or underlying disaster. That is the power of the writing of disaster. By using Levi's quote in *The Writing of the Disaster* to introduce a series of fragments that all revolve around the Holocaust and the concentration camps, Blanchot opens up a context that allows us to place the quote within the context of Holocaust literature, even without knowing the author's name. This contradicts any contingency or arbitrariness in the fragments of disaster and thus relentlessly insists upon the fundamental instability of any attribution, classification or reference.

Holocaust

Blanchot describes the Holocaust as the "absolute event of history".

> *The unknown name, alien to naming: The holocaust, the absolute event of history – which is a date in history – that utter-burn where all history took fire, where the movement of Meaning was swallowed up, where the gift, which knows nothing of forgiving or of consent, shattered without giving place to anything that can be affirmed, that can be denied – gift of very passivity, gift of what cannot be given.* (WD, p. 47; ED, p. 80)

An absolute event is characterized, among other things, by the fact that it cannot be defined. The definition itself would reduce the extent and absoluteness of such an event. The term Holocaust (Hebrew: *olah*, Latin: *holocaustum*) comes from Greek *holókauston* (noun: *holokautoma*, *holos* = whole; *kausis* = fire, burning), which can be translated as 'completely burned'. The "toute-brûlure" (utter-burn) as 'total incineration' refers back to the word's etymology and emphasizes the completeness of the obliteration of history as a zero point that defies the historic datability of the Holocaust. Before its meaning as a label for the incomprehensible murder of Jews during World War II, the term was used in the context of sacrificial rituals during which the slaughtered animals would not be eaten but, as part of a purifying ritual, completely burned upon an altar for a sacrificial offering. Since the end of the 19th century, it has been used to describe the mass murder of ethnic groups. Since the 12th century, it has described pogroms against Jews.[6] Even when everything has been burned, something remains, albeit just ashes. Blanchot's term for this appears to be the disaster. What has been killed or destroyed remains, but in a different form. The fragments of the disaster carry their own death with them along with the traces of the genocide carried out by the National Socialists. However, they rarely do this through direct reference, because doing so would create fixability, which would turn the 'absolute event' into a relative or singular event. Even if *the* Holocaust is historically datable, and Blanchot apparently makes reference to the genocide of the Jews, there are still numerous other historically datable 'total incinerations' that resonate throughout Blanchot's use of *the* Holocaust.[7] Furthermore, the term 'Holocaust' as a word can only insufficiently describe the atrocities behind its historical locatability.

I read *The Writing of the Disaster* as an achronological history that consists not of catastrophes or other singular events, but of fragments beyond any logical outcome of a sequence of events. These fragments cannot and are not supposed to be memorized and thus be brought into a stable context – for they create a mode of rejecting any completion. For Blanchot, this is the only possible form of writing after World War II. The most notable incisions into historical writing (natural catastrophes, wars, even the Holocaust) are not the disaster. They are insufficient attempts to name an uncontainable atrocity.[8] This is why the fragments are not numbered either: The uniform diamond confronts us with the iteration of the disaster again and again. This confrontation must begin anew at all times and everywhere.[9]

Repetition II: One word hides another

On the first pages of *The Writing of the Disaster*, the word "le désastre" repeats itself in an almost neurotic, traumatized form. With nearly each fragment, a new description of how the disaster is or is not, of what it does or can do, commences: "The disaster is related to forgetfulness" (WD, p. 8; ED, p. 10), "The disaster has passed already beyond danger, even when we are under the threat of --" (WD, p. 9; ED, p. 12), "The disaster is the gift, it gives disaster" (WD, p. 9; ED, p. 13), "The disaster is not somber" (WD, p. 10; ED, p. 14).

None of these attempts to approach the disaster achieves a stable attribution of value. Due to the way various definitions are strung together, these attempts are instead presented in their ephemerality and are diluted and scattered in their truth as singular definitions. Insofar as statements are made about the disaster, their lifespan extends only until the next diamond, which means until the beginning of the subsequent fragment. Each attempt to explain is re-evaluated and re-contextualized by the next one so that none of them can reach any type of conclusion; instead, they all reflect, complement and fragment each other in an echo-like pattern. The disaster thus becomes a process, as formulated by Leslie Hill taking up Emmanuel Levinas' comments on Blanchot's *désastre*: The noun *désastre* receives a verb-like meaning.[10] Accordingly, the inexorable movement of the disaster affects the character of the word itself and releases itself from being a fixed grammatical category, transforming into a becoming (in the Deleuzian sense) and the destruction of linguistic reference. In its realization, the fragmentary writing of the disaster thus simultaneously dissolves itself and, in this manner, links writing with death. Polyphony (numerous voices revolving around the disaster) and polysemy (numerous meanings attributed to the disaster) are disseminated, that is, scattered and fragmented within themselves. As the serial fragments of disaster that transcribe each other within the *The Writing of the Disaster* show, the disaster resists definition. Instead, the impossibility of being distinctly defined demonstrates one crucial effect of the disaster: Every writing *of* the disaster and every writing *about* the disaster must fail, as it constantly fragments itself. Furthermore, this state of exception regarding disjunction and the ever-deferred reference becomes normality.

Repetition III: Contemplating the reduplication of one's own words

Repetition is an omnipresent procedure in Blanchot's writing, taking place at practically every level imaginable. A rather obvious example is the constant editing of his texts, where the new version is not supposed to replace the first version, rather, they coexist. Thus, *Thomas the Obscure* (*Thomas l'Obscur*) was published in two different versions, first as a novel and later as what Blanchot terms '*récit*'.[11]

Each fragment in *The Writing of the Disaster* does indeed posit particular propositions and occasionally even assumes an aphoristic character. Yet, through the repetition of similar aspects in the subsequent fragment, a dynamic of interruption and continuation is generated, as I have already shown, with regard to the coexisting descriptions and definitions of the *désastre*. I read this form of repetition as a distancing *from* and a criticism *of* numerous figures of thought and concepts of Western philosophy and intellectual history (among them the concepts by Plato, Hegel, Marx, Schelling, Schlegel, but also Nietzsche who Blanchot, as is well-known, very much respected) and, even more fundamentally, of a specific logic of the taproot – to mention the opposing model to Gilles Deleuze and Félix Guattari's rhizome.

Diverse ways to conceive of the world and make sense of it are quoted in the form of fragments of equal value: Interspersed between passages from the great thinkers mentioned above are also quotations from Blanchot's own texts. Such is the case in a fragment in which Blanchot inserts a quote from *The Space of Literature* (*L'espace littéraire*, 1955) and one from *Friendship (L'Amitié*, 1971), both of which had already been published in other places.[12] In the following, I am *not* quoting Blanchot's auto-quotation, i.e. the reduplication of his own discourse, but rather his meta-reflection on the reason for repeating something that has already been thought or stated:

> Why this recollection? Why [...] these words seem to need to be taken up again, repeated, in order to escape the meaning which animates them, and to be turned away from themselves, away from the discourse which employs them? (WD, p. 59; ED, p. 97)

Repetition and recurrence are ways for words to escape meaning and the power of discourse, i.e. their origins, objectives and purpose, since they prevent their definite localization and instead defer every localization to another, coexisting locatability. Blanchot, however, emphasizes the danger of claims to intellectual power and self-legitimization that the repeated use of words implies, when he continues:

> But taken up anew they reintroduce an assurance to which one thought one had ceased to subscribe. They have an air of truth – they aspire to coherence, they say: you thought all this long ago; you are thus authorized to think it again. They restore this reasonable continuity which forms systems [...] Thus they prevent the invisible ruin which the perpetual wake, outside consciousness-unconsciousness, gives back to the neuter. (WD, p. 59; ED, p. 97)

The danger of repetition is that it could be seen as an affirmation of words that have already been uttered. At different moments in time, these might be seen to constitute identity and coherence and thus become the foundation of particular (closed) systems (of meaning). In this case, the secretly unfolding process of ruin would become blocked and the unwhole/unholy of history and of language would be concealed. In order to avoid this and avoid becoming the basis of a new ideology itself, the repetition must expose, distort and disable itself by revealing itself to be a non-identical doubling of what has already been written, not least by way of meta-textual or self-referential comments.

Diamond and star – what we do not (immediately) see

The fragmentary writing, the self-referentiality of language, the de-hierarchization of discourse based on the fragmentary structure, the neurotic-ruminant repetition and variation of different topoi and concepts, and the foregrounding of improper discourse by way of quotes – all of these processes belong to the writing of the disaster. However, the processes listed are not the disaster, but express that they are effects of the disaster (lat. *desastrum*) or of the 'disastering'. The word 'disastering' again points towards the verb-like function noted by Levinas with regard to Blanchot's term. It also offers the possibility of letting the star appear while simultaneously hiding it. This not only takes place according to the etymological analysis that divides 'dis' and 'aster', but also in the process of reading the word 'disaster' where *astrum* can be seen to appear and disappear. According to this reading, the disaster refers to a de-starring or to being de-starred, to the removal of the star or to that which no longer has any star.

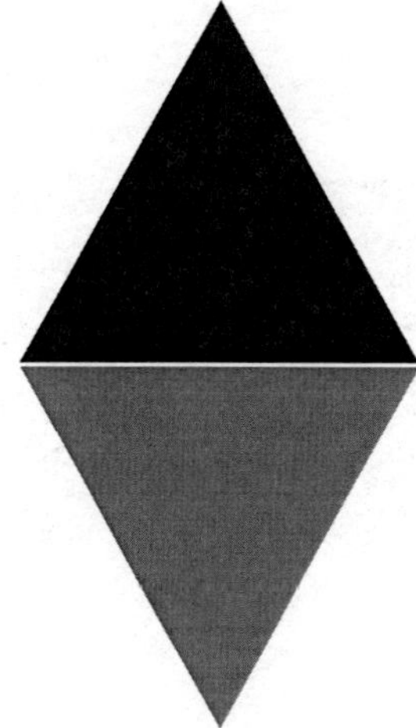

Fig. 2: Diamond.

At this point, I would like to return once more to the diamond that preceded my text as a typographical symbol and/or geometric shape, which is repeatedly referred to throughout the fragments. The blackening of its surface makes it impossible to geometrically analyze its shape, as it hides the two triangles that share one of their sides in the middle of the figure, creating a symmetrical axis (Fig. 2).

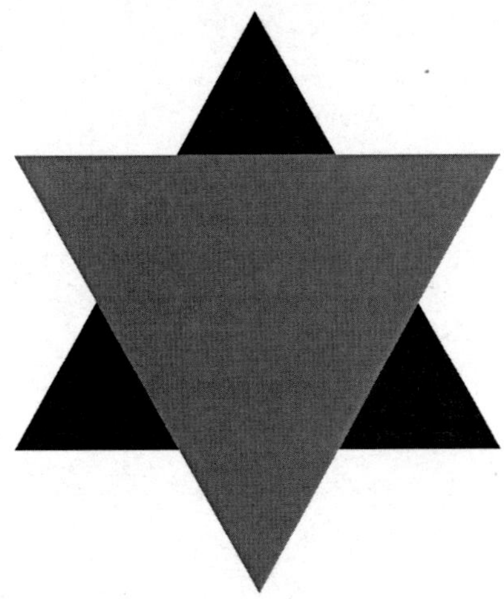

Fig. 3: Hexagram.

The black diamond of *The Writing of the Disaster* not only contains these two mirrored triangles, but also a hexagram that emerges when the two triangles shift and overlap (Fig. 3).
The resulting geometric shape links together the following two stars, both bearing a historical signature (Fig. 4 & 5).
As the Jewish scholar Gershom Scholem showed in his detailed historical analysis in *Das Davidschild. Geschichte eines Symbols* (*The Shield of David. History of a Symbol*),[13] the Shield of David (as a hexagram) has a long tradition in Jewish magic, where it was used in particular as a protective shield against enemies, but also against fires. Another line of development is its career as a print character.[14] What is remarkable in this context is that Scholem provides proof that the stable association between the hexagram and Jewish self-identification only began to establish itself in the heraldry of the 17th century. The 19th century then saw the Shield of David spread considerably, turning it into the Jewish equivalent of the Christian cross.[15] The crucial point in Scholem's argument is that the hexagram did not originally stand for Judaism (as the cross did for Christianity), but was retrospectively transformed into a sign of Jewish identity due to its popularity as a magical and typographical symbol. The National Socialists, of course, played a not inconsiderable part in the 'success' of the hexagram during the 20th century, when they introduced the Yellow Star (see illustration) on September 9, 1941, as a compulsory symbol to marginalize and stigmatize Jews in Germany. To this day, the Star of David, positioned between two blue stripes across a white background, forms the center of the Israeli flag. Thus, on the one hand, it can be interpreted as an overwriting of the Yellow Star that counters systematic annihilation with the prospect of a future for

Fig. 4: Yellow Star ("Judenstern").

Fig. 5: Shield of David.

Israel. On the other hand, the flag of Israel, with the Star of David and its overlapping triangles, which dates back to 1948, is linked to this symbol's long tradition, which is now clearly a symbol of Judaist self-identification.[16]

As I would like to argue in conclusion, Blanchot's black diamonds in the *Writing of the Disaster* contain, at least potentially, the hexagram. In this way, they also enfold a possible transition from a mere typographical sign to the hexagrammatic symbol of the Star of David, which paradigmatically performs the transition of the typographical into the symbolic. There is a structure hidden within the diamond that allows for historical concretization, but which Blanchot refrains from making explicit.[17] Being a meaningless typographical sign while offering itself to a reading as a symbol that splits, shifts and blackens the Star of David, the diamond performs the undecidability of the inexorable *différance* of the *Writing of the Disaster*. What we see is a black diamond, a displaced and blackened star that is not visible as such, but can be reconstructed and actualized. Just as Blanchot's disaster in the *Writing of the Disaster* makes numerous connections with the Holocaust and the Shoah without ever being a synonym for these historical events, so too is the Star of David evoked in every diamond of the 403 fragments without ever actually being present. The disaster is an untellable catastrophe, unspectacular and timeless, and accordingly, all the more severe.

Translation from the German by Michael C. Noto

1 Gerhard Poppenberg, postscript to the translation of: Maurice Blanchot: *Die Schrift des Desasters*, transl. from French to German by Gerhard Poppenberg / Hinrich Weidemann. Munich: Fink 2005, p. 185.

2 "A project is the subjective embryo of a developing object. A perfect project should be at once completely subjective and completely objective, should be an indivisible and living individual. In its origin: completely subjective and original, only possible in precisely this sense; in its character: completely objective, physically and morally necessary. The feeling for projects – which one might call fragments of the future – is distinguishable from the feeling for fragments of the past only by its direction: progressive in the former, regressive in the latter. What is essential is to be able to idealize and realize objects immediately and simultaneously: to complete them and in part carry them out within oneself. Since transcendental is precisely whatever relates to the joining or separating of the ideal and the real, one might very well say that the feeling for fragments and projects is the transcendental element of the historical spirit." (Friedrich Schlegel: *Philosophical Fragments*, transl. from the German by Peter Firchow. Minneapolis / London: University of Minnesota Press 1991, pp. 19–20 (Athenaeum Fragment 22); *Charakteristiken und Kritiken I. 1796–1801*. In: F. S.: *Kritische Friedrich-Schlegel-Ausgabe*, vol. 2, ed. by Ernst Behler. Paderborn: Schöningh 1967, pp. 168–169.)

3 For the term "écriture fragmentaire", see Maurice Blanchot: Nietzsche and Fragmentary Writing. In: M. B.: *The Infinite Conversation*, transl. from the French by Susan Hanson. Minneapolis / London: The University of Minnesota Press 1993, pp. 151–170; *L'entretien infini*. Paris: Gallimard 1969, pp. 227–255.

4 Maurice Blanchot: *The Writing of the Disaster*, transl. from the French by Ann Smock. Lincoln: University of Nebraska Press 1986, p. 7; *L'écriture du désastre*. Paris: Gallimard 1980, p. 7. These works will be abbreviated in following references as WD and ED.

5 The English translation does not do justice to this complete waiving of any article: "Shining solitude, the void of the sky, a deferred death; disaster" (WD, p. 146; ED, p. 219).

6 Cf. David M. Crowe: *The Holocaust: Roots, History and Aftermath*. Colorado: Westview 2008, p. 1.

7 We are reminded, for example, of the genocide in Armenia in 1915.

8 This explains the disaster's proximity to other figures of the notion of the incomprehensible by Blanchot, among them the outside (*dehors*), the other night (*autre* nuit) or the neutrum/neutral (*neutre*).

9 Incidentally, preceding the text with bullet points is another characteristic in Blanchot's writings, for example in *Awaiting Oblivion* (*L'attente l'oubli*, 1962) where numerous bullet points (e. g. ±±) precede fragments like a coat of arms. Even in *The Step Not Beyond* (*Le pas au-delà*, 1973), fragments are arranged using (more simplified) bullet points, in which this text along with *The Writing of the Disaster* melt into one another and prove to be a more comprehensive iteration structure within the works of Maurice Blanchot.

10 Cf. Leslie Hill: *Maurice Blanchot and Fragmentary Writing. A Change of Epoch*. London: Continuum 2012, p. 300.

11 Maurice Blanchot: *Thomas l'Obscur. Roman* [1941]. Paris: Gallimard 2005; and Maurice Blanchot: *Thomas l'Obscur*. Paris: Gallimard 1950 (English translation: *Thomas the Obscure*, transl. from the French by Robert Lamberton. New York: Lewis 1973). Regarding the two versions of *Thomas the Obscure* see also: Martina Bengert: *Nachtdenken. Maurice Blanchots "Thomas l'Obscur"*. Tübingen: Narr 2017.

12 Cf. Hill: *Blanchot and Fragmentary Writing*, p. 305.

13 Gershom Scholem: *Das Davidschild. Geschichte eines Symbols*, transl. from the Hebrew by Gerold Necker. Berlin: Jüdischer Verlag 2010. This text version is a translation of the expanded second Hebrew edition from 2008, which integrates the changes Scholem made to his 1963 self-translated version. The very first version of the book about the Shield of David was published in 1948. (English translation: *The Star of David: History of a Symbol* In: G. S.: *The Messianic Idea in Judaism and Other Essays*. New York: Schocken 1971, pp. 257–281.)

14 Cf. ibid., pp. 40–42.

15 Ibid., p. 47.

16 Cf. in addition the following exhibit catalogue: Wolf Stegemann / Johanna Eichmann (eds): *Der Davidstern: Zeichen der Schmach – Symbol der Hoffnung*. Dorsten: Dokumentationszentrum für jüdische Geschichte und Religion 1991.

17 Leslie Hill presents a wide range of potential meanings for the hash in *The Writing of the Disaster*, among them the heraldry of the hash in the navy as well as possible references to Paul Valérys fragment collection *Rhumbs* (cf. Hill: *Blanchot and Fragmentary Writing*, pp. 287–289).

Fig. 1: Francisco de Goya y Lucientes: *Los Desastres de la Guerra* (1810–1815), plate 69 (wash, etching, aquatint, burnisher, drypoint, 15.5 x 20.1 cm). Museo del Prado, Madrid.

Spectacular Catastrophes and Unspectacular Disasters

Francisco de Goya y Lucientes and Maurice Blanchot

Vittoria Borsò

Plate 69 of Goya's *Los Desastres de la Guerra* (*The Disasters of War*) appears to be unique in the series of etchings that, according to its thematic focus, is structured into three groups: Plates 1–47 represent violent scenes of the Independence War (1808–1814) against Napoleon's troops who had invaded Spain in 1808; plates 58–64 focus on the famine that hit Madrid in 1811–12; and numbers 65–82 demonstrate the deception suffered by Goya and his group of Spanish liberals after the restoration of Bourbon absolute monarchy by Ferdinand VII, who had promised to rule with a written constitution.[1] Produced between 1810 and 1815 but published posthumously in 1863, the plates appear to be the equivalent of the work of a modern war correspondent and photographer, covering stories firsthand from a war zone and providing witness testimony to the atrocities of the war. Plate 69 shows a skeletal figure that has just written the word *nada* (nothing) on a white page. The plate's title is *Nada. Ello dirá* (*Nothing: The Event Will Tell*). The degradation of humans and the earth's devastation shown in the preceding plates seem to culminate in plate 69 and its nihilistic reference. As part of the last thematic group, which Goya calls "caprichos enfáticos", this reference has been interpreted in relation to the outcome of the war, not only with respect to the suffering during the war and its aftermath, but also with regard to the political and social situation in 1815. Like *Capricho 43*, plate 69 also plays a pivotal role within the series. It is a response to the cruelties of the past as shown in the first 68 plates and an opening toward a present and a future that are overwhelmed by the catastrophes of the past. The catastrophes are still present in the spectral masks looming over the surrounding space, materializing the presence of a traumatic memory that seems to construct a haunting image of

Fig. 2: Francisco de Goya y Lucientes: *Los Desastres de la Guerra*, plate 1 (etching, drypoint, burin, and burnisher, 17.6 x 22.0 cm.). Museo del Prado, Madrid.

the future. In this respect, plate 69 corresponds to the imaginary of a catastrophic spectacle that reinforces the modern sense of catastrophe as integral to the progress of civilization[2] as well as to the vanishing of the past in line with the new sense of temporality emerging in the 18th century. This interpretation becomes even more evident when one compares plate 69 with plate 1, titled *Tristes presentimientos de lo que ha de acontecer* (*Sad presentiments of what must come to pass*) which, although produced during the last period, was chosen by Goya as the opener of the series. Plate 1 shows a man kneeling with his eyes gazing up to the heavens and his hands spread out. Both the reference to Goya's painting *Christ in the Garden of Gethsemane* (*Cristo en el huerto de los olivos*, 1819) as well as the plate's difference to this commissioned artwork, an altarpiece at the Escuelas Pías de San Antón, are incontestable. In the painting, Christ is praying and looking toward the light falling from heaven and to an angel who brings him a chalice as a sign of the will of the Father and his future sacrifice, which appears to be inevitable. In plate 1, by contrast, the figure is in the midst of a stony desert and a gloomy environment where not even the spectral figures of plate 69 or other etchings emerge from the dark clouds. The expression in the man's eyes is uncertain; it oscillates between objection and resignation. Nevertheless, there is still a future to expect despite the pessimistic mood.

Plates 1 and 69, which present the cruel disintegration of human life before and after the catastrophe of the war respectively, should also be considered not only in comparison with the gouache that was made in preparation of plate 69, but also as a study for the complete series *Los Desastres de la Guerra*. The gouache appears to represent the place where the disaster has just occurred. In fact, the space is dark, shadowy and obscure; all we see is the head of a screaming person lying on the ground, on the surface of the earth. It is the last remnant of complete destruction, a survivor who is not yet dead. The difference between plates 1 and 69 and the gouache is remarkable and shows a progressive loss of transcendence. If the heaven of the *Christ in the Garden of Gethsemane* materializes a transcendent God who is as opaque as the expression of the figure in plate 1, who represents the beginning of the war, and its aftermath in plate 69, the wasteland reveals destitution, the ruin of transcendence and a decline into a nihilistic situation. Thus, mankind is now reduced to its skeletal state, lying on the ground. No eye looks toward the sky. No future is possible, except that of a haunting future signalized by dreaded specters that emerge from the clouds as the memory of the unforgettable. It is the memory of the catastrophe that Walter Benjamin would envision in 1938, in his ninth thesis on the philosophy of history. According to the 'angel of history', the political history of Western culture is a continuous path toward the annihilation of life. Nevertheless, the concept of catastrophe gives rise to messianic hope and to a new temporal foundation.[3] Such progress must be found in the idea of catastrophe. In fact, to recognize the status quo as catastrophic is to conceive of a set of conditions of possible experiences that could also be "chips of Messianic time"[4]. With the specters of the past, plate 69 thus implies

Fig. 3: Francisco de Goya y Lucientes: *Los Desastres de la Guerra*, gouache in preparation of plate 69 (grey-brown wash, gouache, touches of white chalk on blue laid paper, 20.0 x 25.7 cm). Museo del Prado, Madrid.

the possible reversibility of history, the turning away from or the reversal of a calamitous past, i. e. the catastrophe of the catastrophe that corresponds with the modern concept of time, offering a "revolutionary chance", i. e. the potentiality of a new beginning and a radical change. Thus, the present is grounded in the act of remembering a tragic past, and the consciousness of an ongoing catastrophe can interrupt the time of progress. The potentiality of the future is characterized by what the present is not.

However, in contrast to plate 69, the gouache negates any messianic sliver of hope. In this image, the world is reduced to a wasteland where only a remnant is witness to the disaster. Nevertheless, in the gouache, the darkness includes an empty white space that appears to the left of the image as part of the environment. This other space is therefore not transcendent. In this dark, ravaged place, another space reveals itself which is yet to be written. It appears as the dense materiality of white brushstrokes, and this intense materiality alone provokes the experience of an immanent "smooth space".[5] Due to the materiality of its manifestation, it could be a white stone waiting to be written.

It would be a blatant mistake to understand this description as in anticipation of Deleuze and Guattari's "smooth space". Rather, what remains at stake in the study is the quality of the space as a scene of disaster. It is a space without an outside or transcendence, not even the transcendence of the past specters that emerge from the dark clouds in plate 69 and in many other etchings. The gouache as a previous study for the series *Los Desastres de la Guerra* goes beyond any contextual reference and is instead a general imagination of disaster that is close to the ontological condition that Maurice Blanchot will formulate in relation to the devastation of World War II. The following quotes taken from *The Writing of the Disaster*[6] seem to be, in some respects, an *ekphrasis* of Goya's gouache study:

> Blackness and void, responding to the suddenness of the opening and giving themselves unalloyed, announce the revelation of the outside by absence, loss and the lack of any beyond. (WD, p. 115)
>
> Shining solitude, the void of the sky, a deferred death: disaster. (WD, p. 146)

Blanchot emphasizes the uncovering of an absolutely empty sky, provoking "the vertiginous knowledge that nothing is what there is, and first of all nothing beyond" (WD, p. 72). In fact, in the etymology of disaster, the prefix 'dis' means a lack of stars and planets. If its astrological meaning relates to a calamity blamed on an unfavorable planetary position, and if its theological meaning addresses providence, Blanchot transforms its theological foundation into an ontological and immanent meaning. In contrast to the catastrophe that implies not only destruction, but also a chance to change paths, the disaster is the irreversible loss of belief in any power or in any salvation of value (cf. WD, p. 13). At the beginning, Blanchot establishes that disaster stands for an infinite threat; it removes us from the asylum of (Heideggerian) thinking about death, dissuading us from any catastrophic or tragic interpretation (cf. WD, p. 14). Disaster is, thus, an absolute and nihilistic desolation. Nevertheless, precisely this forsaking of any objective order, which also corresponds to the scene in Goya's gouache, provides the basis for another quality of space to take shape. Like the unwritten, material, white space in the gouache, Blanchot thus appears to emphasize that precisely this radical negation implied in the disaster opens up to the potentiality of life:

> Extinguished eyes flash suddenly with a wild glimmer for a crust of bread, 'even if the sense that one is going to die moments later still subsists' and there is no longer any question of nourishment. This glimmer [*lueur*] or spark [*éclat*] illuminates nothing living. And yet, with this look that is a last look, bread is given to us as a bread: a gift, beyond all reason, all values exterminated, in nihilistic desolation, and all objective order renounced, maintains the fragile chance of life through the sanctification of 'eating' (nothing 'sacred', let us be clear), something that is given unreservedly [*sans partage*] by whoever dies as a consequence ('Of great importance is the mouthful of food' [*Grand est le manger*] says Levinas, after a Jewish saying). (WD, p. 14)

In the above quote and in several fragments, it is evident that this shift to another, perhaps post-human space, is not only conceivable on the basis of Judaism as a prototype of a displaced monotheism, but also as the result of a devastating historical calamity, that is, the Shoah, which was a kind of violence that let humans fall into a bare and dying life. It was a disaster that devoured humanity.[7] Blanchot stresses that the disaster gives rise to a form of consciousness and remembrance that is different to the catastrophe. Disaster confronts us with what Levinas called the retrocession of "il y a", of any value or order. It is an existence without a (social) world. Nevertheless, negativity becomes an opening for another space and another way of thinking: "Inasmuch as the disaster is thought, it is nondisastrous thought. It is the thought of the outside" (WD, p. 6). Thus, as a technique of the dispossession of subjectivity, of the dis-empowerment of power, and of the detachment of any detachment (cf. WD, p. 12), negativity becomes a technique for affirming life. During the disaster, the event that affirms life is possible, which is felt at once in all its fragility and its whole glimmer of hope. What differs from the catastrophe is precisely the potential that emanates from the disaster to recognize the fragile possibility of life by sanctifying the act of 'eating' as its most elementary need, a need that is common to all living beings in the broadest sense – including humans, animals and non-humans. This both narrow and broad sense of the living emerges from the disaster, precisely from the complete elimination of transcendental belief.

Thus, disaster is a never-finished process associated with the particular experience of the immanence of a "wasteland", in which "the relation of an I to power has the form of power's loss" (WD, p. 12). In Blanchot's *Writing of the Disaster* after World War II, the scene of disaster is the condition for linguistic operations to abandon self-affirmation. Creation is dispossession and dis-identification; the creative energy comes from exteriority, as we can see in the above quote by Blanchot, where linguistic intensity responds to the appeal of "something that is given unreservedly".

In fact, the scene of disaster transforms subjectivity in a radical way. Blanchot refers to Levinas' claims about the passivity of the subject, in that for Levinas death is "suffering", understood as the event that destroys the supremacy of the subject.[8] For Levinas, death includes the "impossibility of the nothing" insofar as it does not belong to "me" and is therefore an infinite process of dying.[9] Consequently, for Blanchot too, the disaster is a spectral experience of the eternal return of what was not a concrete event in the past (cf. WD, p. 17). Thus, the writing of the disaster is not only a response to what we cannot remember, but is also continuously revived as the impersonal souvenir, remembrance without the subject that takes the place of oblivion.[10] Oblivion thus designates the 'beyond of the possible', the unforgettable Other. It is the Blanchovian *quelqu'un*, issued from an inhuman, unimaginable, non-original site. The "I", the "me" and the "he" are never anything at all, are always signifiers of the Other, 'who' is always outside any concept of otherness. Such ontological exile opens upon another space where 'everything has disappeared'. In this space, the subject is always outside of itself, always compromised by the 'neuter' that it essentially is.

Following on from the imaginary of catastrophe and disaster that we have found in Goya's aesthetics at the end of the 18th century after the French revolution and in the aftermath of the Spanish Independence War, and in Blanchot's *Writing of the Disaster* after World War II, two different ways of dealing with nihilistic desolation will now be considered: catastrophe and disaster. The spatio-temporal configuration of the disaster differs from that of the catastrophe. Both open up to an indeterminate space that maintains the awakening of the subject as the consciousness of the potential imminent annihilation. But in the process of imagining disaster, the messianic moment is either impossible, or the messianic is unspectacular; it is related to the view of a pre-individual, elementary need that Blanchot calls the "neuter"[11]. The space of disaster opens up to the poverty of a condition in which not only fragility is imagined, but also the intensity of life as an ontological relationality to the Other. The nihilistic experience of disaster is the 'original' scene of an illumination that reduces life to the poverty of its being and produces the basis for a shift to immanence to occur. In addition, Blanchot underscores the consistent struggle for a relational ontology that is also a seminal moment in intellectual history after 1945, specifically in the work of Maurice Blanchot, Samuel Beckett, Jean-Luc Nancy and, with respect to contemporary 'Italian Thought', in the work of Roberto Esposito and his notion of the "Impersonal"[12] that has been conceived of along the lines of Blanchot's 'neuter'.

By contrast, the *stréphō* ('I turn') of catastrophe implies the potential to change the path of a future history and therefore the messianic redemption of history. Catastrophe involves remembrance and thus also includes a splinter of the messianic, which may mark the threshold to another configuration of social space and history. Here, remembering a spectral, traumatic past, which is also a cataphoric reference to a haunting future, is the way in which catastrophe itself performs the interruption of temporality as the event of a possible turning of paths. This pattern of thought is evident in Giorgio Agamben's work, which is based on the role of the catastrophe in Benjamin's philosophic theses. For Agamben, the messianic is the remnant that fractures temporality, giving rise to a *kairos*, an intensive *Jetztzeit* ('now-time'), where subjects may even become the agents of a spectacular or terroristic 'artwork' that can bring the political and technological catastrophe to collapse.

Catastrophe and disaster – two modalities of nihilism and two different patterns of thinking

Heidegger's essay on nihilism, "Nietzsche's Sentence: God is Dead" (1943), focuses on a disaster in which God is dead and the stars have fallen. The essay has two objectives: 1) to show that nihilism, as a destructive power, is the modality of Western history that will eventually lead to the catastrophic annihilation of Being; and thus 2) to separate historic nihilism from its ontological modality. Therefore, if, on the one hand, nihilism has been history's self-destructive dynamic, then, on the other, its purpose is to ensure that, in terms of ontology, "'Nothing is befalling Being'. The *nihil* of 'nihilism' means that Nothing is befalling Being [...] In the appearing of whatever is as such, Being itself remains wanting."[13]

This ontological reinterpretation transforms the catastrophic path of Western history into the potential for metaphysics itself to dis-appear and for ontology to emerge. Thus, only in the history of man can violence destroy lives; the nothing is nothing for the vitality of Being[14] – hence the Heideggerian differentiation between the murderous mode of historical nihilism and its ontological nothingness. In both Heidegger's language and his description of empty space, a desert that reminds us of both Blanchot's quote and Goya's study, the world presents itself as an open space and an energizing Being, which, in its linguistic intensity, continues to resist objectification by humans. This ontology will eventually require both another phenomenology and other techniques for both intensively and diffusely creating an awareness for the stream of material data that hits the subject.[15]

In the ontological interpretation of nihilism, we recognize the source of contemporary aesthetics, which fosters relationality, closeness and processuality on the material surface of writings and images – from Nancy[16] to Lyotard. Its relevance becomes more evident if we take into account the further transmutation of nihilism as an overturning principle of immanence itself, about which Deleuze concludes in his own reading of Nietzsche:

> Under the rule of nihilism, negation is the form and the content of the will to power [...] We had to get to the last man, then to the man who wants to die for negation *finally to turn against the reactive forces* and become an action that serves a higher affirmation.[17]

Nihilism must be conceived of as a transmutation, that is, as an "active becoming of forces, *a triumph of affirmation in the will to power*".[18] However, in catastrophe and disaster, we recognize two modalities of nihilism: the historical destruction and the ontological nothingness of the nothing, the latter implying a phenomenological shift toward ontological relationality. We can observe these modalities in two contemporary philosophers: Giorgio Agamben and Roberto Esposito.[19]

Taking only the first approach, Agamben applies Heidegger's axiom "Nothing can happen to the Being" exclusively to the openness of "Dasein" (as a life form that intertwines *bíos* and *zoë*), which can arise if a poietic subject or agent (*man without content*)[20] brings the annihilating politics to a collapse. This demonstrates the role of catastrophe in Agamben's thinking, which he draws from his reading of Benjamin. For Agamben, nihilism is the calamitous character of Western history, which, in his *Homo Sacer* project, is linked to the historically invariable matrix of the camp as the paradigm of modernity – dismissing both democracy and totalitarianism. By transforming Heidegger using Benjamin, he understands the nihilistic disaster as the catastrophe of historical temporality. In doing so, he fulfills the meaning of *katastrophein*, not as a coming to an end (*kata* = down), but as a turning or reversing of what is expected. It is the function of Bartleby's "I would prefer not to" and, more precisely, of the actions described in his book on profanations.[21] The subversive and even terroristic subject has the power to destroy or deconstruct the devastating matrix of politics in order to provide access to its openness. Agamben's elaboration on nihilism develops the deconstructive gesture of destitution carried out by catastrophe instead of shifting to the configuration of a post-humanistic or primordial topology where subjectivity is a process resulting from the existential relationality to the world.

Nothing can happen to 'Being' as an operation of transmutation (Deleuze).

In this second approach, the dynamics of life are neither intrinsic to the 'Being' nor to the subject; instead, they are part of "becoming" and to the multiplicity that arises from the outside of humans, from the environment. Understood as relationality, subjectivity paves the way for an operative ontology. It is, for instance, devastating for the subject to lose its own capacity to be transformed or altered by the environment, as new insights into biological and political immune system have shown.[22] This is the role of the outside of the inner ("le dehors dans le dedans") underlined by Blanchot.[23] The aforementioned "movement of infinite negation"[24] is a transmutation of nihilism, pointing to the impotence and powerlessness of subjects. Blanchot already underlines the "logical vertigo" that accompanies the movement of thought:

> It is nihilistic thought par excellence: it is how Nihilism surpasses itself absolutely by making itself definitively insurpassable. Eternal Return is not on the order of power [...] a reversal of all perspectives [...] The will that wills Nothingness.[25]

"To fail without fail is a sign of passivity", Blanchot claims in *Writing of the Disaster* (cf. WD, pp. 13–14). This kind of passivity opens itself up to a relational ontology and demands operations and mediations as developed by philosophers such as Gilbert Simondon, Gilles Deleuze, Jean-Luc Nancy, Roberto Esposito, and, of course, Bruno Latour. In a 2000 essay, Esposito considers the relationship between nihilism and community. Going back to the difference between nihilistic, destructive interpretation on the one hand and the constructive function of the 'nothing' as an ontological category on the other, Esposito claims the following: "The nihil does not mean the negation of the essence [of community, understood as absolute entity]. The essence of community itself is rather its nothing".[26] The nothing of the nothing is the metaphysical lack at the origin.[27] Or, to be precise, the 'nothing in common' as a foundation of community requires relations and operations in order to endure. Its potentiality lies in the transformation of onus and community, identity and immunity: The undoing of any principle including that of the "nothing" is the "transmutation" that allows Esposito to turn back to ("Zurücksetzen") the poverty of the essence of community as well subjectivity. Both move towards their own alterity. Both are submitted to an alteration originating in the liminal line that separates each one from what it cannot be. Esposito shows the impact of literature and arts on the configuration of a political practice that goes beyond the biopolitical captivity of life. This political practice requires intensity and radical changes in both the disposition and the position of humans towards the world, which provides space for the contingency of life. The indetermination of the "neuter" in the scene of disaster is not the effect of ruptures in spectacular catastrophes, but rather the unspectacular ontological condition that requires relationality to others, to mediators, and to operations and transformation chains in order to take shape. This interrupts the actual chain of terroristic action taken by subjects searching for redemption or for a messianic coup. This could also be the foundation of another kind of politics.

1 A liberal revolt in Spain was brutally suppressed by Ferdinand VII in the 1820s.

2 According to Derrida, for Rousseau (*Essai sur l'origine des langues*), progress equals catastrophe; catastrophe is, thus, an inherent part of what is referred to as progress (Jacques Derrida: *De la grammatologie*. Paris: Minuit 1967, p. 287).

3 Walter Benjamin: Theses on the Philosophy of History. In: W. B.: *Illuminations: Essays and Reflections,* ed. by Hannah Arendt, transl. from the German by Harry Zohn. New York: Schocken 1968, pp. 253–264, here pp. 257–258.

4 Ibid., p. 265.

5 A smooth space is "no longer a division of that which is distributed, but rather a division among those who distribute themselves in an open space—a space that is unlimited, or at least without precise limits" (Gilles Deleuze / Félix Guattari: *A Thousand Plateaus. Capitalism and Schizophrenia*, transl. from the French by Brian Massumi: Minneapolis: University of Minnesota Press 1987, p. 36).

6 Maurice Blanchot: The *Writing of the Disaster*, transl. from the French by Ann Smock. Lincoln: University of Nebraska Press 1995 (hereafter: WD); *L'écriture du désastre*. Paris: Gallimard 1980.

7 Reflections on disaster appear in Blanchot's complete works with respect to the space of writing (among others, Stéphane Mallarmé, Franz Kafka), as well as in reaction to political "disasters", for instance the civil war in Spain as narrated in André Malraux' *Espoir* (1934).

8 Emmanuel Levinas: *Le temps et l'autre*. Montpellier: Fata Morgana 1980, pp. 57, 62. In this respect, Levinas (and Blanchot) diverge from the Heideggerian experience of authenticity through the anxiety of death.

9 Ibid., p. 60.

10 "Souvenir impersonnel, le souvenir sans personne qui nous tient lieu d'oubli" (Maurice Blanchot: *L'attente, l'oubli* [1962]. Paris: Gallimard, 2000, p. 69).

11 The neuter is related to the *écriture* and means the indeterminate zone in which space, time, and language appear to have been snatched away from history and negativity, from *chronos* and *kairós*, and from human determination. Cf. Maurice Blanchot: *The Space of Literature*, transl. from the French by Ann Smock. Lincoln: University of Nebraska Press 1982.

12 Cf. Roberto Esposito: *Terza persona: Politica della vita e filosofia dell'impersonale*. Turin: Einaudi 2006.

13 Martin Heidegger: The Word of Nietzsche: "God Is Dead" [1943]. In: M. H.: *The Question Concerning Technology, and Other Essays*, transl. from the German by William Lovitt. New York: Harper & Row 1977, pp. 109–110.

14 "[...] [T]hinking in terms of values is radical killing [...]. The value-thinking of the metaphysics of the will to power is murderous in a most extreme sense, because it absolutely does not let Being itself take its rise, i. e., come into the vitality of its essence." (Ibid., p. 108.) Here is one of the very few moments when Heidegger uses the concept of "vitality" which he perhaps avoided due to the tendency toward vitalism in Germany; this underscores the extreme sense that presents the destruction as the destruction of life.

15 Jean-François Lyotard: *Peregrinations: Law, Form, Event*. New York: Columbia UP 1988.

16 Jean-Luc Nancy: *Listening* [2000], transl. from the French by Charlotte Mandell. New York: Fordham UP 2007.

17 Gilles Deleuze: *Pure Immanence. Essay on a Life*, intr. by John Rajchman, transl. from the French by Anne Boyman. New York: Zone 2001, pp. 82–83.

18 Ibid., p. 82. Deleuze demonstrates this with respect to the Overman [*Übermensch*]: "The Overman refers specifically to the gathering of all that can be affirmed, the superior form of what is, the figure that represents selective Being, its offspring and subjectivity. He is thus at the intersection of two genealogies. On the one hand, he is produced in man, through the intermediary of the last man and the man who wants to die, but beyond them, through a sort of wrenching apart and transformation of human essence." (Ibid., p. 91.)

19 Cf. Vittoria Borsò: Oltre la biopolitica. Per un lessico del vivente. In: Dario Gentili / Elettra Stimilli (eds): *Differenze Italiane. Politica e filosofia: mappe e sconfianementi*. Roma: Derive Approdi 2015, pp. 121–139; V. B.: Giorgio Agamben – tra disastro e catastrofe. Ontologia e estetica. In: Luca Viglialoro / Antonio Lucci (eds): *La vita delle forme. Saggi su Giorgio Agamben* [forthcoming].

20 Giorgio Agamben: *The Man without Content*, transl. from the Italian by Giorgia Albert. Stanford: Stanford UP 1999.

21 Giorgio Agamben: *Profanations* [2005], transl. from the Italian by Jeff Fort. New York: Zone 2007.

22 Roberto Esposito: *Immunitas: The Protection and Negation of Life*, transl. from the Italian by Zakiya Hanafi. Cambridge: Polity 2011, especially chapter V., "The Implant", pp. 145–177.

23 Michel Foucault: *Maurice Blanchot: The Thought from Outside*, transl. from the French by Brian Massumi. New York: Zone 1987, p. 13.

24 Cf. Maurice Blanchot: Reflections on Nihilism. In: M. B.: *The Infinite Conversation*, transl. from the French by Susan Hanson. Minneapolis / London: University of Minnesota Press 1993, p. 145.

25 Ibid., pp. 148–149. Passivity is not the opposite of activity, cf. WD, p. 13.

26 Roberto Esposito. Nichilismo e comunità. In: R. E.: *Nichilismo e politica*. Bari: Laterza 2000, pp. 24–25 (transl. by V. B.).

27 "The Being of community is the gap [...]: in common is only the lack, not the possession, the property, the appropriation" (ibid., p. 92, transl. by V. B.).

Fig. 1: Claudio Parmiggiani: *Untitled* (1970). Galleria d'Arte Moderna, Bologna 2003 (photo by Aurelio Amendola).

This Is the End

Notes on the Holes in Language and Other Catastrophes

Davide Caliaro

> Since the beginning of time
> words have had something to do
> with the end of the world.
> Without the end of the world
> there would be no words.[1]

I.

It could be an image of a labyrinth, made out of glass, with all its square corners and narrow passages. What is striking about this labyrinth is its borders. This might be due to the standpoint of the viewer, or it might be the result of the way it refracts the light, but the labyrinth seems to be on the edge of losing its own limits. They are trembling, and they make it impossible to say where the labyrinth actually starts and where it ends. And, inside, there is a figure. If the labyrinth seems to have been caught by the camera in the moment of its fading, then the anonymous figure looks like a dark enigmatic point within the labyrinth. Is that point a person? Is it an animal? The viewer is not allowed to know. And here we are, facing something like a catastrophe in action, with the borders fading, the certainty of identification showing its laughable side and leaving us with the deeper feeling that if we watch the image long enough, we will be caught in the fading of the labyrinth and, caught as we will be, the world itself, and us with it, will fade; it will in fact end.

II.

In 1967, the Italian anthropologist and cultural historian Ernesto de Martino published the essay "Apocalissi culturali e apocalissi psicopatologiche" ("Cultural and Psychopathological Apocalypses").[2] De Martino's main topic is the experience of the end of the world. He approaches this topic from two different and nevertheless intertwined perspectives. On the one hand, the end is understood as the expression of the ongoing cultural productivity of humankind. This productivity includes literature, philosophy, art etc. On the other hand, the end of the world is acknowledged as a specific feature of some kind of psychopathological disorder. De Martino's hypothesis is very clear: Cultural apocalypses function as a sort of exorcism. They are a cultural device through which humankind has been trying to work out and manage the risks implied in the experience that de Martino calls the experience of the loss of world. Cultural apocalypses are, in other words, a way to overcome the end-of-the-world crisis and, *ipso facto*, they reveal, at a cultural level, the assumption that "madness represents the permanent possibility that a sane mind is always and repeatedly called to fight against using its real cultural productivity".[3]

The experience of the end has nothing to do with the spectacular image of this experience that the contemporary imaginary has made us accustomed to. The end – according to de Martino – is not so much a cataclysmic event but rather a small, minor episode that might take place in everyday life. Something like an unapparent catastrophe.

In order to provide some examples of his understanding, de Martino makes reference to modern and contemporary literature. He refers to Hugo von Hofmannsthal, Jean-Paul Sartre and Alberto Moravia's works to point out some common features of experiences of the end of the world. This seems to be first and foremost the very unique moment when we feel we are losing our grasp on the world as such. For a never-ending instant, the world ceases to be *our* world. Such an event can start in the most unforeseen way: Our gaze might be fixed on an item, like a glass of beer, and, suddenly, that item seems to tremble and lose its limits. It dismisses every familiarity and imposes itself on us as something extraneous, unheard of. An uncanny element rises up in the heart of what is most familiar and domestic, to the point that the familiar item seems to "subtract itself from its obvious and domestic meaning, fading into nothingness".[4]

What I propose is to understand this kind of fading into nothingness and therefore the experience of the end of the world as a linguistic experience or, rather, as the experience of what we might call, as Samuel Beckett did, the holes in language. As a result of such a hypothesis, we might say that the trembling and fading of the limits of things, described by de Martino as essential moments in the experience of the end, are the very expression of mismatches and holes in language itself.

It is De Martino who directs us towards language as the key to interpreting the end of the world. On the one hand, this experience is characterized by the fact that "items become strange, [...] in the act of *dissociating from their names*".[5] On the other hand and at the same time, during this experience, "the *word* remains on my lips; it refuses to meet the thing".[6] The matter here is the catastrophic separation of word and world. It is a two-way separation: The thing departs from the name, thus pointing out an *impasse* in the act of naming itself and, at the same time but *vice versa*, the word does not encounter the thing, as if it were too weak or unwilling to say the thing itself. The literary genius Sartre – who de Martino quotes – seems to suggest that this separation is an inner matter of language. The word, Sartre writes, "remains on my lips".[7] All the attention here seems to be drawn toward the hesitation of the word that remains on the lips, as if such a hesitation is declaring the impossibility of the word's correspondence with its own supposed duty to say the reality, and, in doing so, declaring that something in the word itself cannot be reduced to the simplicity of expression and communication. Something remains in the word that remains on the lips, something without expression, something like a black hole that makes the word(l)d tremble.

In order to understand the overlap between the experience of the end and the holes in language, we need to address de Martino's understanding of the relationship between world and word. The assumption here is not in fact that of a naive realism, putting language on one side and reality on the other. Reality should not, in other words, be understood as the realm of bare facts, which are only caught in the net of language *ex post*. On the contrary, reality and language are always already intertwined. In his essay, de Martino calls this overlap the "fondo operativo domestico" (domestic operative base). He defines it as the "base of implicitly admitted relationships [...] which do not emerge at a conscious level".[8] Human beings, according to de Martino, live on the basis of a symbolic treasure that allows them to inhabit the world as *their* world. This treasure, dipped in the "obscurity of unconsciousness",[9] in which the memories that everyone accumulates are collected depending on the influences of social and cultural biography, can be understood as a symbolic text. Constituted by relations that remain mostly implicit, the operative base is the text into which human beings are inscribed from birth. It is right there, waiting for them, ready to ask them something in exchange for the possibility of entering the world as *their* world. Such a text is what introduces the world to man and at the same time man to the world. According to de Martino, "precisely this latent historicity of being [...] establishes and maintains that obviousness of the world [...] which makes us available for the here and now".[10] Only on the basis of such

an inscription into the text are human beings established as beings-in-the-world. That is the reason why he describes the text/base as operative – because without it man will be left with no *opus*, with no world. The nature of this text is essentially historico-linguistic: it finds its place within a genealogy constructed out of memories that are at the same time latent and impersonal: latent as they "do not emerge at a conscious level"[11] and impersonal as they recapitulate trans-generational social and cultural conditionings. It is, in other words, something like a sedimentary text or a *palimpsest*, as medieval copyists would have referred to it: a continuously written and rewritten text, in which the more recent piece of writing is written on top of the older one, signifiers over signifiers.
De Martino's implicit understanding of the end of the world as a linguistic experience is one consequence of such a hypothesis. If human beings gain access to the world through their own inscription into the text/operative base, and if such a text is of an essentially linguistic nature, then reality itself must somehow already be a product of language. The world and reality are, in other words, always and already *my* world and *my* reality, effects of the text. World and text thus seem to get closer and closer to one another, until they mutually overlap. Considering the end of the world as a matter of holes means, first and foremost, understanding it as a matter of holes in the text, that is to say of holes in the symbolic order we live in and thus in language itself.
Here, in these holes, something happens, something that cultural apocalypses describe as a trembling and fading of the world. However, a question arises here, and we could again use a Beckettian image to express it: What actually *trickles* in such holes?

III.

The semantic field de Martino uses to describe the experience of the end relates to the idea of falling. A certain insistence on plummeting and therefore on verticality seems to be more appropriate when it comes to speaking about the end. It might be a "shipwreck",[12] a "falling ending",[13] a "collapse"[14] or a "sinking",[15] but, in addition to this, the end is always simultaneously a swirling fall, as if such an experience could only be understood as the experience of a descending movement. Nevertheless, despite this tendency, some other traces are present in de Martino's text, traces of a different kind of movement, something like a counter-movement in which the fall is at the very same time the moment of a rising up.
This twofold movement is already at work in de Martino's essay when he refers to Hugo von Hofmannsthal and the letter von Hofmannsthal imagines to be written by Philip

Lord Chandos to Francis Bacon from Verulamio. This letter is another example of cultural apocalypse and it is a confirmation of the relationship between language and the experience of the end. Lord Chandos' experience of the end was characterized – according to de Martino – by the fact that "all contents of conversation were in the act of breaking apart, and breaking again and again, *in a vortex of disarticulations*, at the end of which there was only nothingness".[16] With an extremely vivid image, Lord Chandos himself tries to describe this experience: "Words were decomposing in my mouth like rotten mushrooms".[17] The experience of the end and the disarticulation of language, end and decomposition of the word, are here one and the same experience. Nevertheless, it is right here in the midst of such a vortex of disarticulations that something unexpected happens. In the moment that language faces its own mismatches and touches its own holes, something like an absolute instant seems to take place, in which the most minor, casual thing stands up and becomes

> the jug of an unheard-of revelation, from which something like a wave of superior life touching every phenomenon of everyday ambience was pouring out: a revelation too lively and intense for the word to fully express it.[18]

A certain kind of duplicity sets the rhythm of the experience of the end. If it has something to do with the collapse of language, with its failures and falls, at the same time such a failure is counterbalanced by the insurgence of something de Martino identifies as a wave of superior life, as if an unheard-of wave of life were pouring out or trickling from the holes in language.

Life is indeed the word de Martino uses when he wants to address what rises up in the midst of the fall – perhaps an impossible life: impossible to qualify, impossible to say, impossible to institute. It is impossible precisely because it is like a wave of superior life, pouring and overflowing from the mismatches of language, *too lively and intense for the word to fully express it*. A life dismissed of its own qualifications and titles, whose only attribute would be, perhaps, the exhausted attribution of nudity: During the experience of the end, things are indeed perceived "in the act of dissociating from their names [...] and *falling in the opaque thickness of a 'bare' existence*".[19] The necessity felt by de Martino to write the word *bare* between quotation marks underlines its status. Bare is that life that rises up during the fall of language, which is first and foremost exhausted, unfit for any attributions, extraneous to the possibility of being said entirely. Bare is then the most intimate description of a life that was already known by Greeks under the name of *zoe*. In ancient times, it was considered inferior and lacking. Slaves shared bare life with animals, and it was considered to be the biological substratum that only the power of *logos* could take to a higher level and save, instituting an actual human life, an actual *bios*, out of it: a non-instituted life, which simply lies at the bottom of the hierarchy and therefore does not really matter. It has been Giorgio Agamben's main contribution to 20th century political philosophy to highlight the ways that the paradigm of bare life has functioned in the Western tradition as well as its contemporary long-lasting modifications.[20] If we listen to de Martino and to the insurgence of bare existence in the collapse of language, we might nonetheless encounter a different understanding of such an existence than the one we inherited from Western tradition. And that is because bare life is not what is there first, the biological body on which only the cut of language exerts its power *ex post*. Rather, it is what reveals itself precisely within language and its mismatches – as if those holes were the best witnesses to the opening of a bare life in our lives; as if they were there revealing both our qualified life *and therefore* what de Martino calls "bare existence" *as well*,[21] as if the experience of the end of the world as a linguistic experience was the not-to-be-missed moment when we could touch another life, a bare one, into ours, a life too intense to be spoken and, at the same time, bare, stripped of every qualification, like a silent and unsignifiable urgency in each of our individual existences. De Martino's identification of the bond that ties together this impossible life – and the experience of the end – is thus crucial, as it seems to imply a different logic, maybe a different ontology compared to the one that has characterized our culture for such a long time. It has granted an infamous primogeniture to bare existence since time immemorial: The biological substratum is something we must get rid of, something that must be elevated in human beings by language, which turns *zoe* into *bios*. By contrast, de Martino tells us that bare existence is, with all its nudity, a superior life, something like a more intense life that is already there in the interstices and falls of our individual existences. This strong and simultaneously unsustainable thesis might be recapitulated as follows: Falls and mismatches are the places where a superior life occurs.

This bare and superior existence cannot be encountered if we attribute the familiar traits of individuality to it. It seems to be, on the contrary, much more complex and, at the same time, delicate than that. Indeed, it has no name, even if it is not fully without name. It has no individuality even if it is not fully alien to it. Very instructive is, in this sense, the way that Sartre – quoted by de Martino – describes a peculiar moment in Roquentin's experience of the end. This character in Sartre's *Nausée*, looking at himself in the mirror, says, "what I see is far below the monkey, at the limit of the plant world, at the level of octopus".[22] Here, Roquentin's life is invaded by an extraneous element. Again, the double movement of fall and rise is at work here: It moves down from human being to the monkey and down again to the plant, where something rises unexpectedly, something disgusting, an octopus, neither plant nor monkey. The human figure, the qualified life, the person of Roquentin himself is here in the act of collapsing but, nevertheless, it is Roquentin who speaks and *pronounces* the words: "what I see".[23] What we have here is, on the one hand, the insurgence of an impersonal and animal element, whose features remind us of an octopus. On the other hand, it is Roquentin himself who, in the first person, says, "I see".[24] This is where all the complexity of the bare existence de Martino speaks about resides: We experience it in the moment itself we experience a double negation. We cannot in fact say that life is our life since it falls outside the reign of individuality, but at the same time, we cannot say that life is not our life. We lose our supposed grasp on it, identification shows its inner laughable side, but nonetheless we feel that a life like this has something to do with our singularity, just like Roquentin feels that the image in the mirror has a secret and intimate bond with him, despite the fact that it could not be simply reduced to him. This is where something like a non-individual but nonetheless singular element seems to qualify the bare life we all share.

Finally, we might say that the catastrophe of the end of the world as de Martino describes it seems to be very different to what we might have expected. Not only is it a minor and unapparent episode that could actually occur (and does occur) everyday to everyone, it is also a revealing moment that speaks about language and life, and about the way they encounter one another. It tells us, despite all the newest and *à la page* contemporary theories about communication, that language is not just a plain tool, but rather that it is made up of holes, fractures, mismatches, which are linguistic but without expression, showing how language itself cannot be reduced to communication as it produces a blind spot, an enigmatic and unspeakable note within it. Moreover, the experience of the end also tells us something about the most intimate dimension of our existence as far as it resembles a bare life finding its place and rising up in the holes and mismatches of language.

It is a superior life, as de Martino addresses it, a more intense life and, at the same time, a life with no words and therefore no name. An existence that is a superior existence precisely because it touches me without being mine, impossible to be subsumed to any individual form of life.

It is here, where the world trembles in the encounter with its own minor and unapparent catastrophe and language meets its holes, that a superior life finally reveals itself, with the fearful but vital enigma that accompanies it.

1 Giorgio Manganelli: *Discorso dell'ombra e dello stemma o del lettore e dello scrittore considerati come dementi*. Milan: Rizzoli 1982.
2 Ernesto de Martino: Apocalissi culturali e apocalissi psicopatologiche. In: Lia de Martino (ed.): *Rituali della memoria. Poesie, riflessioni. Considerazioni in dialogo con Roberto Altamura*. Lecce: Argo 1997, pp. 125–158. All translations from the Italian are by D. C.
3 Ibid., p. 140.
4 Ibid., p. 133.
5 Ibid., p. 137 (emphasis added).
6 Ibid., p. 138 (emphasis added).
7 Ibid.
8 Ibid., p. 141.
9 Ibid.
10 Ibid.
11 Ibid.
12 Ibid., p. 133.
13 Ibid., p. 129.
14 Ibid., p. 133.
15 Ibid., p. 137.
16 Ibid., p. 136 (emphasis added).
17 Ibid.
18 Ibid., p.137.
19 De Martino: Apocalissi culturali, p. 137.
20 Cf. Giorgio Agamben: *Homo Sacer. Sovereign Power and Bare Life*. Stanford: Stanford UP 1998.
21 De Martino: Apocalissi culturali, p. 137.
22 Ibid.
23 Ibid.
24 Ibid.

Fig. 1a–c: Claude Lanzmann: *Shoah* (F 1985, opening scene). Screenshots from DVD.

Augenweide

Catastrophe, Spectacle and Linguistic Accidents in Claude Lanzmann's *Shoah*

Judith Kasper

I.

Catastrophe, spectacle, Shoah: How are these three terms related and what role do they play in Claude Lanzmann's film *Shoah*? What shape do 'spectacular turns' take in *Shoah* and how do the meanings of spectacle and catastrophe change in this ten-hour long film?[1]

With *Shoah,* Lanzmann purposely distanced his work from the spectacularization of the annihilation to be found in the American TV series *Holocaust* (1978) and in Spielberg's *Schindler's List* (1993), a movie released eight years after *Shoah*. Without getting into a lengthy discussion of fictionalization, the use of archival images or cinematographic approaches to deportation and concentration and extermination camps, let it be said that *Shoah* rejects fictionalization and does not make use of archival images.[2] For Lanzmann, the Shoah destroyed our ability to depict what happened. The film is 613 minutes long, which exceeds what we expect from a cinematic spectacle. Rather than depicting the spectacular narrative of a past catastrophe, the film is made up of testimonies recorded in the present. It brings out the difficulty of finding words to describe that catastrophe and therein also exposes the Shoah as a linguistic catastrophe.

The witnesses' stories unfold in their own time, in a rhythm the viewer is obliged to follow. Their words are wrested from but also broken by silence. Interrupted by their stuttering and tears, witnesses often speak in a non-native tongue. Sometimes the story is even told in a language that Lanzmann, the constantly present interviewer, does not understand. Interpretation is in itself a complex process of finding the right words, and this also takes time in the film. In the time spent searching for words and their translation, we are reminded of another catastrophe, that of Babel. Babel, in Primo Levi's words, was repeated in the National Socialists' camps and in the testimonies about the camps, leaving language disrupted and jagged.[3]

II.

The title of the film *Shoah* is itself a foreign word, which Shoshana Felman describes as follows:

> Shoah, the Hebrew word which, with the definitive article (here missing), designates "The Holocaust", but which, without the article, enigmatically and indefinitely means "catastrophe", here names the very foreignness of languages, the very namelessness of a catastrophe which cannot be possessed by any native tongue and which, within the language of translation, can only be named by the untranslatable: that which language, in its turn, cannot witness without splitting.[4]

Without its article, *Shoah* is a name, not a concept. While as a concept, *Shoah* can be translated as 'a' or 'the' catastrophe, as a name, *Shoah* denies translation and thus remains irreducibly foreign. As a name, *Shoah* cannot be integrated into a history of concepts, let alone that of catastrophe. Bringing together catastrophe and spectacle, *Shoah* is not an attempt to translate a Hebrew word into Greek or Latin, but to confront the asymmetry between two concepts and one name. In this asymmetrical relationship, something untranslatable remains. And even the apparently well-known concepts of 'catastrophe' and 'spectacle' are affected by what resists translation.

III.

Moreover, what remains untranslatable remains active, altering language from within. This is perhaps nowhere more apparent than in the word 'spectacle' itself. 'Spectacle' comes from the Latin *spectaculum,* which itself derives from *spectare* (to show). Its suffix, *culum*, means medium, instrument or the location of an action, a play or a performance. More narrowly, the word refers to the gladiator games in ancient Rome and, in a more general sense, means anything that draws attention to itself. The *Etymological Dictionary of the Latin Language* by the German philologist Alois Walde also mentions the term's etymological link to *pasco* (in German: *weiden*, in English: to graze). This connection between the pleasure of viewing a spectacle and the act of grazing persists in a striking way in the German word *Augenweide*. A composite consisting of *Augen* and *Weide*, 'eyes', and 'meadow' (*Weide* as a noun) or 'grazing' (*weiden* as a verb), *Augenweide* literally means a kind of 'visual grazing' but is more colloquially translated as 'a feast for the eyes'. While the term never appears as such in the film, it nevertheless brings together, particularly for a German viewer, connections that the film never makes explicit but are nevertheless part of its *mise en scène*. Speaking in an interview about the film's composition, Lanzmann described it less as a series of testimonies than as a kind of "musical piece where a theme appears at a lower level, disappears, comes back at a higher level or in full force, disappears, and so on. It was the only way to keep several parameters together."[5]

The musical metaphor draws attention to the resonance created among various levels and parameters, but also more specifically among different voices, visual landscapes, and camera angles and shots. The metaphor also shifts the focus from the content of any one particular testimony to the interactions among them. This makes it clear that the film's own testimony is not restricted to what is said by any one particular witness (least of all Lanzmann, who never speaks as a witness in the film) but consists in the resonance between testimonies and, moreover, in what is said 'between the lines'. Such testimony is not assumed or expressed by any one witness, lingering instead in the interstices of the film. A term like *Augenweide* belongs to this interstitial dimension. By focusing on this term, my contribution seeks to attune itself to what Felman describes as catastrophe, that which cannot be possessed by any native tongue or testified to by any one particular witness. Language is not only split, as Felman argues, but through Lanzmann's filmmaking is also *spliced* into an interlingual testimonial montage. The 'interlingual' is to be understood not only in its narrow verbal sense but, more capaciously, as the splicing together of words, images, colors and gestures – and of what falls between them.

In this context, the word *Augenweide* as it imposed itself upon me when I viewed the film, is to be understood less as a positive German term with a particular range of meanings and connotations than as the index of an unsettling foreignness, of that which cannot be possessed by any native tongue, of something that Lanzmann's film, engaging with the 'untranslatable', gives us to see and hear.

The word *Augenweide* is linked most obviously to the visual dimension of the film, more specifically to the appearance of landscapes, ranging from green meadows to rivers, dense wooded glades, and vast forests. The film begins with a scene set in an open field where cattle might graze. This is the forest glade of Chelmno. Simon Srebnik, one of only two remaining survivors of the extermination camp, returns there. He is shown singing a song, carried by a little boat toward the place the Nazi crimes took place. The sheer fact that an extermination camp where 400,000 people were killed now appears on the silver screen as a bucolic meadow is deeply unsettling. And so are many other long stills of an apparently virgin landscape – huge, intensely green meadows and endless woods in Poland. Only the camera's gaze, its raw insistence on something that cannot be seen anymore, brings to the spectator's mind the idea that here, in this place, hundreds of thousands of people, not so long ago, were killed in the most brutal way.

This opening scene of *Shoah* has been rightly called "the 'abysmal' scene of all of Shoah representations."[6] Historically, unlike other extermination camps, Chelmno was not a separate location surrounded by barbed wire and did not have any guard towers policing its parameters; it was literally incorporated into the landscape.[7] But there is another issue as well. As spectators, we witness the utter transformation of a catastrophic scene into a pastoral idyll: since antiquity, the meadow has been linked to the shepherd's song. There is no catastrophe *in* the image, but we, as spectators, witness the catastrophe *of* the image. The absence of any visual sign of annihilation makes the scene inevitably and strangely idyllic. Viewers almost immediately attribute a sort of allegoric meaning to this opening scene, assuming that Lanzmann wants to show us nature devoid of memory and the cruelty of erasing any trace of annihilation. But in doing so, we dismiss out of hand the idea that the opening scene is literally a meadow to graze on.

IV.

The opening images of the meadow – and of the many others that follow – are often associated with the depiction of a void. Georges Didi-Huberman thus writes the following about Lanzmann's *Shoah* and Alain Resnais' *Nuit et brouillard*:

> *Shoah* shocked us with that *empty clearing* at Chelmno, recognized only by Simon Srebnik, the survivor. *Nuit et brouillard* had shocked us with its *empty fields* traversed by extraordinary „*tracking shots with no subject*" [emphasis added, J. K.].[8]

By contrast, Ulrich Baer takes a semiotic approach when writing about the black-and-white images of Sobibor taken by the photographer Dirk Reinartz, which are very similar to the landscape scenes in *Shoah*:

> The nothingness depicted in this image [a meadow, J. K.] [...] becomes the referent to an event whose monstrosity also comes from the fact that every trace of its happening should have been completely erased. By drawing us into an image where no

> meaning can be revealed, we are put into relation with the emptying of referentiality.[9]

Those who say that these images depict a 'void' or 'nothingness' adopt a pathos-laden stance that in itself risks denying what the image literally depicts. It does not show a void, it shows a meadow.

In the translations and shifts that take place between the name *Shoah* and the catastrophe, the catastrophe and its images, the site of annihilation and the pasture, there is always something that 'stutters', something that hovers precariously between speech and silence. Such stuttering extends to the act of translation itself. We have already established that translation plays a central role in the film. What needs to be emphasized at this point is the way that translation distends time, opening up another – more unconscious – theatrical space, in which symptoms, echo effects and linguistic accidents surface.[10] This unconscious space, what Freud tellingly refers to as "the other scene", is associated with bizarrely theatrical experiences recounted by witnesses and equally surprising moments when Lanzmann himself frames situations in pointedly theatrical terms.

V.

Richard Glazar, a survivor of Treblinka, speaks in his eyewitness account of a "fantastic stage setting" ("phantastische Kulisse") when describing the burning of human beings. I cite his account both in the original German and in the published English transcript:

> und durch das Fenster, durch ein kleines Fenster,
> sahen wir immer die phantastische Feuersbrunst
> mit allen möglichen Farben:
> rot, gelb, grün, violett,
> und auf einmal stand auf,
> auf einer Pritsche,
> einer von dem wir wußten,
> er war Opernsänger in Warschau.
> Salve hat er geheißen, und hat …
> *Salve?*
> Und hat vor dieser … vor dieser phantastischen Kulisse
> Angefangen, ein Lied zu singen:
> Eli, Eli,
> warum hast du uns verlassen?
> Man hat uns ins Feuer gebracht,
> aber von deiner Heiligen Schrift wollte niemand ablassen.
> Er hat das Lied in Jiddisch gesungen

> Vor der Kulisse
> Des Feuers vom Scheiterhaufen,
> auf dem man
> eben damals im November 1942 angefangen hat,
> in Treblinka, Menschen zu verbrennen.[11]
>
> And from the window, we kept on watching the fantastic backdrop of flames of every imaginable color: red, yellow, green, purple. And suddenly one of us stood up. We knew … he'd been an opera singer in Warsaw. His name was Salve and facing that curtain of fire, he began chanting a song I didn't know: 'My God, my God, why hast Thou forsaken us? We have been thrust into the fire before, but we have never denied Thy Holy Law.' He sang in Yiddish, while behind him blazed the pyres on which they had begun then, in November 1942, to burn the bodies of Treblinka.[12]

What is striking with regard to the original is the omission of key terms in the translation. These include: the repetition of the term "phantastisch", used first with regard to the flames ("Feuersbrunst") and then with regard to the stage setting ("Kulisse"); the repetition of the word "Kulisse" itself; the repetition of the "window", which appears smaller in its second mention ("durch das Fenster, durch ein kleines Fenster"); and, last but not least, Lanzmann's pointedly ironic echoing of the name "Salve", meaning 'salvation'. The Warsaw singer Salve's performance of a Yiddish song heard and seen against the backdrop of burning bodies is in and of itself unbearable. Yet, what makes it even more unbearable is Glazar's description of the scene as a "colourful, strangely operatic spectacle". In contrast to the narrow focus of the window that, in Glazar's account, opens out onto the "fantastic backdrop of flames of every imaginable color", Lanzmann's camera pans into an extreme wide-angle shot of a winter landscape, a white field with black pines. All color drains from the image as Glazar speaks about the horrifically bright and colorful fire in Treblinka.

VI.

Whereas Lanzmann provides a powerful visual counterpoint to Glazar's unsettlingly theatrical language, the filmmaker himself has recourse to such language in a curiously skewed encounter with the Polish farmer Czeslaw Borowi, who claims to have seen everything. Unlike other encounters, this one with Borowi is mediated by an interpreter who does not so much translate as paraphrase the witness' words:

> Il est né ici, en 1923,
> et il y habite jusqu'à présent.
>
> *Il habitait exactement à cet endroit?*

Oui. Exactement ici.

Alors, donc, il était aux premières loges pour voir tout ca, là-bas?

Naturellement.

On pouvait s'approcher, on pouvait regarder à distance.[13]

He was born here in 1923, and has been here ever since. *He lived at this very spot?* Right here. *Then he had a front-row seat for what happened?* Naturally. You could go up close or watch from a distance.[14]

The way that Lanzmann has recourse to theatrical language, as evidenced by the phrase "aux premières loges" ("a front-row seat"), suggests that the experience being related is set more on the stage of his mind than in the world outside. Borowi did not just see "everything", he saw – or at least imagined – far more. Thus, he reports that the Jews "came in passenger cars, they were well dressed, in white shirts, there were flowers in the cars, and they played cards."[15]

There is also something excessive, even if it is involuntary, in Lanzmann's own language at this point. In his dialogue with the interpreter, conducted in the presence of the Polish farmers, a disturbing rhyme on the words "champ" and "camp" can be heard:

Paysans de Treblinka

Il avait un **champ** situé à cent mètres du **camp**.

Et il travaillait aussi pendant l'occupation.

*Il travaillait dans son **champ**?*

Oui.

Alors il a vu comment on asphyxiait les Juifs,

il a entendu comment ils criaient,

il a vu tout cela.

Il y avait une petite élévation de terrain

et de là, il pouvait voir pas mal de choses.

Qu'est-ce qu'il dit, lui?

On ne pouvait pas s'arrêter et regarder.

C'était interdit,

parce que les Ukainiens leur tiraient dessus.

*On leur permettait de travailler dans leur **champ***

*même si leur champ était à cent mètres du **camp**?*

On pouvait, oui, on pouvait,

de temps en temps il jetait un coup d'œil,

quand les Ukrainiens ne le regardaient pas.

Mais alors, il travaillait les yeux baissés?

Oui.[16]

He had a field under a hundred yards from the camp. He also worked during the German occupation. *He worked his field?* Yes. He saw how they were asphyxiated; he heard them scream; he saw

> that. There's a small hill; he could see quite a bit. *What did this one say?* They couldn't stop and watch. It was forbidden. The Ukrainians shot at them. *But they could work a field a hundred yards from the camp?* They could. So occasionally he could steal a glance if the Ukrainians weren't looking. *He worked with his eyes lowered?* Yes.[17]

What gets lost in the English translation and what Lanzmann takes particular care to emphasize is the unnerving way that "champ" and "camp" – field and camp – rhyme. A number of issues come together in this linguistic condensation. First and most obviously, the rhyme can be viewed as a symptom of the unimaginable proximity between the farmers' fields and the camp in which the Jews were asphyxiated. But the way that "champ" and "camp" rhyme also evokes the French word *chant* (song), which produces an association with Srebnik's singing in the pastoral setting in which the film opens.[18] The farmer's paraphrased speech combined with Lanzmann's questioning echo of it enter into the uncanny idyllic landscape of *Shoah*. Here, the rhymes are neither part of a beautiful chant nor that of an eyewitness account. They belong instead to what is staged in the 'other scene' of Lanzmann's film. Something seems to slip between "champ", "camp" and *chant*, something that cannot be grasped or imagined, but that the film gives us to witness.

Translation from the German by Marlene Klein

1 I am extremely grateful to Marlene Klein for her careful translation and to Michael G. Levine whose critical suggestions pushed me beyond my own limits and made this a much better essay than it otherwise might have been.
2 Cf. specifically *Le Genre humain* 36 (2001): L'Art et la mémoire des camps. Représenter, exterminer, ed. by Jean-Luc Nancy; Georges Didi-Huberman: *Images malgré tout*. Paris: Minuit 2003.
3 Cf. Primo Levi: *Se questo è un uomo*. Torino: Einaudi 1989, p. 33.
4 Shoshana Felman: In an Era of Testimony: Claude Lanzmann's *Shoah*. In: *Yale French Studies* 97 (2000), pp. 103–150, here p. 111.
5 Cf. ibid., p. 144.
6 Daniel Baranowski: *Simon Srebnik kehrt nach Chelmno zurück. Zur Lektüre der Shoah*. Würzburg: Könighausen & Neumann 2008, p. 19.
7 Cf. ibid., p. 20.
8 Georges Didi-Huberman: *Images in Spite of All: Four Photographs from Auschwitz*, transl. from the French by Shane B. Lillis. Chicago: University of Chicago Press 2008, p. 129.
9 Ulrich Baer: Zum Zeugen werden. Landschaftstradition und Shoah oder Die Grenzen der Geschichtsschreibung im Bild. In: U. B. (ed.): *'Niemand zeugt für den Zeugen'. Erinnerungskultur nach der Shoah*. Frankfurt am Main: Suhrkamp 2000, p. 251.
10 Cf. Ottmar Ette / Judith Kasper (eds): *Unfälle der Sprache. Literarische und philologische Erkundungen der Katastrophe*. Wien: Turia + Kant 2014.
11 Claude Lanzmann: *Shoah* (1985). 4 DVDs. Absolut Medien / arte, 2007–2010, here DVD 1, 0:30:13–0:32:53.
12 *Shoah. The Complete Text of the Acclaimed Holocaust Film by Claude Lanzmann*. English subtitles of the film by A. Whitelaw and W. Byron. New York: Da Capo 1995, pp. 9–10.
13 Lanzmann: *Shoah*, DVD 1, 0:53:04 – 0:53:24.
14 *Shoah. The Complete Text*, pp. 17–18.
15 Ibid., p. 29.
16 Lanzmann: *Shoah*, DVD 1, 0:54:47–0:55:35.
17 Ibid., 0:54:47–0:55:35. The English translation does not render what happens in this scene on a prosodic level (*Shoah. The Complete Text*, p. 19).
18 Cf. for the importance of singing in *Shoah* Shoshana Felman: *The Juridical Unconscious: Trials and Traumas in the Twentieth Century*. Boston: Harvard UP 2002, pp. 268–283.

Fig. 1: Pablo Picasso: *Guernica* (1937, oil on canvas, 349.3 x 776.6 cm).

“The Fact that Things Keep Going On Like This *Is* the Catastrophe”

The Spectacularization of 9/11 Compared with Pablo Picasso’s *Guernica*

Markus Ophälders

> Death, if that is what we want to call this non-actuality, is of all things the most dreadful, and to hold fast what is dead requires the greatest strength. Lacking strength, Beauty hates the Understanding for asking of her what she cannot do. But the life of Spirit is not the life that shrinks from death and keeps itself untouched by devastation, but rather the life that endures it and maintains itself in it. It wins its truth only when, in utter dismemberment, it finds itself. It is this power, not as something positive, which closes its eyes to the negative, as when we say of something that it is nothing or is false, and then, having done with it, turn away and pass on to something else; on the contrary, Spirit is this power only by looking the negative in the face, and tarrying with it. This tarrying with the negative is the magical power that converts it into being. This power is identical with what we earlier called the Subject, which by giving determinateness an existence in its own element supersedes abstract immediacy, i. e. the immediacy which barely is, and thus is authentic substance: that being or immediacy whose mediation is not outside of it but which is this mediation itself.[1]

9/11 was a spectacular catastrophe. In this sense, Stockhausen talked about it as “the greatest work of art imaginable for the whole cosmos”,[2] a sublime artwork that could have been created by Luzifer, a figure he conceived for his musical theater piece *Licht*. But, due to the pictures broadcasted onto televisions around the world, 9/11 was also one of the most spectacularized catastrophes. On the other hand, a very different way of coping with a similar catastrophe is represented in Picasso’s *Guernica*. The opposite to 9/11, though, is not the mere absence of any spectacle, i. e., that there is nothing to see. On the contrary, removed and spectacularized catastrophes converge in their mere, abstract immediacy. In both cases, the element of reality is missing, which always includes the possibility of avoiding what has happened as well. In fact, what may help salvation can only be found in the reality of the catastrophe itself.

Spectacularization does not actually expose reality; rather, it represents a special way of hiding it, because when reality is exposed in this way, it represents an ideological element. In fact, this form of representation seems to be realistic, because what can apparently be seen are just the immediate facts. However, what is suppressed along with the realistic element in this way is the fact that the seemingly direct reproduction of facts always produces the way they will be perceived as well. Thus, what seems to only be an exposition of catastrophic happenings is more likely over-exposed or even under-exposed abstract immediacy. In fact, a disaster is only a disaster if the element of reality is missing, because a realistic representation of facts always includes what could have been foreseen by mediation, reflection and by using other realistic means. But this is only half the truth and half the reality, because it lacks any reflection on the question of how the form of representation affects the content and how the things being represented will be perceived. In other words: As long as there are catastrophes and their more or less realistic representations, human history will still be subject to its natural necessities, because unforeseeable catastrophes are only possible in nature.

Furthermore, a spectacular disaster creates a total sensation comparable only with that of war and, consequently, death.[3] This is what Benjamin conceived of as the counterpart to the poverty of experience. The collective modern sensorium seeks sensory overload to keep feeling alive, at least in a certain way. However, Theodor W. Adorno believed that human feelings usually flee during the perception of catastrophe. Sensory perception and subjective feelings, or rather: imagination and fantasy, always look for the elements that might help them to avoid the disaster. Thus, together with intellectual reflection, they try to connect the catastrophic event with potential salvific elements, which can always be found within the catastrophe itself. This is what the realistic element consists of; it forces living subjects to intervene in order to change things, and this is precisely what art does. It represents the world as it is, but slightly shifted and displaced. It teaches us how to shift the emphasis within the constellation of catastrophic elements itself. Catastrophe and salvation are both part of a dialectical relationship. Or, as Hölderlin puts it: "But where danger is, grows / the saving power also."

("Wo aber Gefahr ist, wächst / Das Rettende auch.")[4] Hence Adorno's famous sentence, "There is no right life in the wrong one",[5] is not only a sort of categorical imperative, but also a sensory imperative: On the one hand, there is the false life and the pseudo-realistic, one-dimensional media for its representation and, on the other, the arts and their multitudinous polyphonic forms of expression. In fact, art also tries to reinsert the element of reality, or more precisely: It tries to redouble reality, which, at the same, is a kind of exit strategy. In this way, art tries to enable collective perception in order to cope with new and menacing phenomena, which are not comprehensible in the here and now. In other words: Art changes the constellation of the elements that form what we usually refer to as reality and, in doing so, realizes reality. It not only copies it, but symbolizes it as well.

This is also what Picasso was attempting to do by painting *Guernica*. He tried to reduce the gap between the new method of area bombing – launched in 1936 by the German Condor Legion during the Spanish Civil War – and its consequences, and the impossibility of the collective perceiving this phenomenon or thus understanding and explaining it in order to overcome it. However, the spectacular methods of television broadcasting are nothing more than compulsive repetition that leads nowhere, like neurotic symptoms. But using the means of mass neurosis provoked and continuously fed by mass communication systems, the powerful establishment is able to govern the masses. In terms of collective perception and communication, a curious fact about the contiguous relationship between *Guernica* and 9/11 is the following: In February 2003, former State Secretary Colin Powell failed to convince the United Nations Security Council that Saddam Hussein possessed weapons of mass destruction. Immediately afterwards, he held a press conference in the conference room, where a copy of *Guernica* could be seen. However, when Powell spoke to the journalists of the world, already more or less announcing the U.S. invasion of Iraq, this image had been covered up. There is reason to believe that the feeling was at work that this copy of *Guernica* might have ruined the military plans. It could have provided the realistic documentation to Powell's fictional speech; it could have been a sort of a "tell-tale heart", as Edgar Allan Poe might have said.

But mass communication and collectivity are by no means the same thing. Thus, in *Guernica*, the impossibility of communication between the nine figures – who, apart from the bull, are all crying – expresses a collective feeling but only in a negative way. While television images generate nothing but irrational fear, *Guernica* calls to the stage the attention of the viewer, who has to cope with the represented catastrophe or the catastrophic representation. In fact, this painting is catastrophic in itself: The relationship between form and content, color and design, figural and abstract representation, aesthetic / objective and spiritual / subjective factors is highly contradictory and incoherent. *Guernica* is also a representation of the conflict of representation. But it is not irrational nor does it create fear. Its inner conflicts create, as Max Imdahl points out, "a kind of coherency out of incoherencies, which stays above the contrasts and the oppositions".[6] Compared with television images, this is also a result of the different medium: *Guernica* not only requires contemplation, but also creates space and time for it in the first place, thus protecting the viewer by focusing his or her perceptive and reflexive faculties. On the other hand, the moving television pictures of 9/11 inhibit contemplation and therefore distract the viewer and prevent him or her from reflecting on or processing the catastrophe, and prohibit any other possible forms of reaction, either theoretical, artistic or practical. In this way, the viewer's relationship to the catastrophe remains abstract, because there is no way for it to be concretized, which is possible only by means of the conscious, sensory and thus subjective mediation of reality as a whole.

For this reason, the problem is not so much the difference between the concrete and realistic representation of a catastrophe on the one hand and its abstract and unrealistic representation on the other, but rather the relationship – which is to say: the difference between the two forms of distance the viewer obtains through representation in order to comprehend it, since distance is fundamental to every act of comprehension. Generally speaking, every form of representation creates distance, because re-presentation repeats an event that has already taken place and, by repeating it, also modifies it. Not only does it seem like the television images of 9/11 did not modify what they were representing – they only purported to reproduce it – it also seems as if they were not representing a past event, but rather that they were contemporaneous with what they were showing. Thus, in the case of the representation of 9/11, the distance was abstract and did not involve the element of reality as a whole. On the contrary, the represented form of reality does not comprise a conscious, critical search for salvation, but rather causes the viewer to flee into an abstract relationship, which precisely because it is abstract only seems to establish a distance and thus only apparently protects.

In the case of *Guernica*, there is a concrete, though problematic, shocking and even harmful relationship between viewer and image based on a distance, which might be bridged by comprehensible elements that are all problematic and full of suffering. However, all of these elements are part of reality as a whole and may even include salvation, although there is obviously no guarantee for it. This form of processing reality consists of creating and recreating connections or textures that obviously include imagination and fantasy. But it also involves imagination from another point of view: Because contemporary catastrophes – from World War I and the area bombing of Guernica up until the present – are in themselves abstract, they are no longer perceivable without imaginative processing and this can, obviously, only be performed by the arts. This can also include filmmaking, as the heart of this art form is montage. But in the case of 9/11, this was not that simple, as becomes apparent in the movie *World Trade Center* (2006), shot by Oliver Stone with Nicolas Cage included in the cast. Even in the project *11 minutes 9 seconds 1 image*, produced by Alain Brigand, only some of the 11 short cuts succeed in representing this catastrophe, which is symbolized in a way that creates distance, thus permitting the mediation of what really happens and the reaction of the viewer. Once more they only represent a sort of coactive repetition. But this is not only due to the inability of the directors or the cinematographic medium; it also serves the interests of power to keep the masses in a continuous state of fear.

As a matter of fact, a catastrophe is not only the perception of a nameless disaster, but rather always involves the possibility of avoidance as well (*kata' strophé*, *Not-wendigkeit*, not mere *Not*). In this sense, its structure might be compared to that of ancient myths: There is an irrational and destructive natural part (*Not*), but there is also a rational, human, realistic part, which allows us to escape destruction, like Ulysses' astuteness (*Wende*, *strophé*). This kind of structure not only characterizes ancient myth or contemporary human disasters, but is also precisely the structure of what might be defined as history of nature. Every catastrophe involves nature as well as history or politics simultaneously. Thus, as Adorno puts it: We have to consider history as nature precisely where it seems to be most historical. The history of mankind has not yet become truly human, despite the lucid consciousness of historical figures like Napoleon, for example. When asked by Goethe in Erfurt in 1808 what he thought about destiny, he answered: "What does one want now with fate, politics is fate!" ("Was will man jetzt mit dem Schicksal? Die Politik ist das Schicksal!").[7] This means that politics – in spite of fate – is a self-reflexive, lucid and conscious means to guide the way things are going. However, over a century later, facing total administration, alienation and the catastrophic consequences of technology developed in a totally rational way, Kafka substituted politics with destiny anew. This was possible because, instead of creating a favorable tension between rationality and nature, over the course of its cultural history, humankind has recreated blind natural constraints in the form of a second nature, which is even more menacing than the first one. Today, spectacular catastrophes, natural or political, are largely part of this second nature, which is no longer able to be self-reflexive or self-conscious. On the other hand, when Kafka rewrote myths like that of the sirens or penned stories like that of Sancho Pansa, he inserted, according to Benjamin, only a few simple, but salvific tricks into the originals. In doing so, he created fairytales for dialectics and demonstrated that even childish elements may help to turn around the catastrophe if they possess a realistic side, or better: if these elements affect the reality of the viewer or reader, leading to a distancing self-reflection and thus to dialectical action.[8]

The aestheticization and spectacularization of catastrophes do not always have to do with embellishment. They are present everywhere a catastrophe is represented, hiding the fact that it is a certain form of representation that is being used and, consequently, that this form decides the content. There is no such thing as bare facts beyond all interpretation. It is this kind of embellishment or pseudo-realism that modern art opposes and this opposition is based on an emphasis on form and technique. A lot of these sometimes quite unique and original techniques and formal aspects were put to work during the making of *Guernica* – to name just a few: the artistic genre of historical painting, which has always included the abstract representation of ideas; the parody of forms no longer possible like the triptych, the tympanum and the pietas; allegorical figuration; quotations from Picasso's own bullfights; the technique of collage; the exhibition of the fact that this painting was made by a subject and that therefore the feelings of the painter are perceptible (mostly in the lines of the design); the cubistic distortion of the space; the introduction of temporal and thus musical elements into a usually more static art form; and so on, up to a certain form of the sublime, in which all these techniques converge.[9]

However, none of this can be just the auto-representation of genius, otherwise *Guernica* would not have become *Guernica*. Instead, this painting tries – as Hugo von Hofmannsthal puts it – to make us read what has never been written. In order to achieve this, *Guernica* cannot be reduced to a mere representation and thus somebody's experience of a catastrophe. This painting also causes the viewer to experience catastrophe, an experience that becomes more and more perceivable during the process of trying to understand this picture. *Guernica* does not seem to be an abstract painting; everything in it is figural. We might even say that a body and a bodily presence force other bodies – in this case the body of the viewer – to position themselves by means of mainly tactile and optic perception. Everything in *Guernica* tells the viewer: "Look at me, I am a body", but the more we go on trying to watch and perceive something bodily, the less we are actually able to see. In the end, what we see is nothing. In this way, the viewer is exposed to continuous, alienating, distancing shocks, and his or her perception and thinking habits stop working the way they usually do. This is the particular form of the sublime in this painting, a kind of mental presence (*Geistesgegenwart*) that, according to Benjamin, is linked to the body. This mental presence is able to catch the little crack in the continuous catastrophe represented by human history and thus may yet achieve salvation, maybe the little flower and the broken sword, which is not a sword though, as it is made out of wood. Actually in the face of the continuity of catastrophe, the whole painting is characterized by discontinuity.

The sublime in *Guernica* manifests itself in the way that it involves our five senses and our bodies as a whole (we have to walk alongside the painting in order to contemplate it in its entirety), thus exposing our feelings and subjectivity to continuous shocks. If the single viewer reaches the central point in this catastrophe of experience – which is a point of no return – *Guernica* might even be able to recreate what Kant defined as a *sensus communis*, a common perception and even feeling among the viewers. The artistic use of language changes the language, as it is affected by what the artist is trying to give expression to and by that which has never been written. When we compare the initial stage of the painting with the last stage, we can see that Picasso turned the techniques of painting against themselves, and herein lies the beginning of the *kata' strophé* of *Guernica*. In the first stage, we can clearly see the painting's structuring, horizontal and vertical lines, levels and angles. It creates the impression of a precisely lateralized design, which has become totally distorted and discontinuous by the end. At the end of the process of perceiving the artwork, every viewer is alone with his or her experience and must realize that nothing can be seen in this picture. All that can be seen is nothingness. This *e contrario* forces every viewer to transcend nothingness, which is the impossibility of making the experience of *Guernica* comprehensible using only sensory perception. This corresponds with the impossibility of experiencing the course of history or even just individual historical facts today, because *Guernica* as a painting does not represent Guernica as a historical event, but rather history as a whole. Thus, we have to radically change the way we experience it, transcend it and turn it around in the sense of *kata' strophé*, and in doing so, simultaneously transcend *Guernica* as a painting, as we now realize that this artwork has to be destroyed in order to complete the catastrophe of what happened in Guernica and subsequently as a whole. This is the meaning of *Guernica* as a historical painting in which we can read what has never been written. This reading considers *Guernica* as a dialectical image by means of the mental presence created in the viewer in the way the painting redoubles reality and thus introduces symbolization. We have to turn history around, to "brush [it] against the grain",[10] as Benjamin would have said. In order to bring the catastrophe – that is, the entire course of history – to its completion, we do not have to keep travelling on the train whose direction is determined by the locomotive that Marx viewed as revolution and progress. Rather, we should desperately try to pull the emergency brake.

1 G. W. F. Hegel: *Phenomenology of Spirit*, transl. from the German by Arnold V. Miller. Oxford: Oxford UP 1977, p. 19 (translation modified); *Phänomenologie des Geistes*, ed. by Eva Moldenhauer / Karl Markus Michel. In: G. W. F. H.: *Werke*, vol. 3. Frankfurt am Main: Suhrkamp 1986, p. 36.

2 Qtd. in Julia Spinola: Höllensturz. In: *Frankfurter Allgemeine Zeitung*, September 19, 2001, p. 49 (English translations, unless indicated otherwise, by M. O.).

3 See Walter Benjamin: *The Arcade Project*, transl. from the German by H. Eiland / K. McLaughlin. Cambridge, MA / London: Harvard UP 2002, p. 801 [m 1 a, 5]; *Das Passagen-Werk. Gesammelte Schriften*, vol. 5. Frankfurt am Main: Suhrkamp 1991, p. 962. Stockhausen's statements about 9/11 can easily be read in this sense as well: "Minds achieving something in an act that we couldn't even dream of in music, people rehearsing like mad for ten years, preparing fanatically for a concert, and then dying; just imagine what happened there. You have people who are that focused on a performance and then 5,000 people are dispatched to the afterlife, in a single moment. I couldn't do that. By comparison, we composers are nothing." (qtd. in Spinola: Höllensturz, p. 49).

4 Friedrich Hölderlin: Patmos. In: F. H.: *Poems and Fragments*, transl. from the German by Michael Hamburger. Ann Arbor: The University of Michigan Press 1966, pp. 462-487, here pp. 462–463; Patmos. In: F. H.: *Sämtliche Werke. Große Stuttgarter Ausgabe*, ed. by Friedrich Beißner, vol. 2: Gedichte nach 1800. Stuttgart: Kohlhammer 1951, pp. 165–172, here p. 165.

5 Theodor W. Adorno: *Minima Moralia*, transl. from the German by Dennis Redmond, 2005. http://members.efn.org/~dredmond/MM1.html (accessed October 20, 2017); *Minima Moralia.*

Gesammelte Schriften, vol. 4, ed. by Rolf Tiedemann / Gretel Adorno / Susan Buck-Morss. Frankfurt am Main: Suhrkamp 1980, p. 43.

6 Max Imdahl: Zu Picassos Bild "Guernica". Inkohärenz und Kohärenz als Aspekte moderner Bildlichkeit. In: Rainer Warning / Winfried Wehle (eds): *Lyrik und Malerei der Avantgarde*. Munich: Fink 1982, p. 556.

7 Johann Wolfgang von Goethe: Unterredung mit Napoleon. In: Renate Grumach (ed.): *Goethe. Begegnungen und Gespräche*, vol. 6. Berlin / New York: De Gruyter 1999, p. 541.

8 Franz Kafka: The Truth about Sancho Panza. In: F. K.: *The Complete Stories*, ed. by Nahum N. Glatzer. New York: Schocken 1995, p. 430; Die Wahrheit über Sancho Pansa. In: F. K.: *Kritische Ausgabe. Nachgelassene Schriften und Fragmente II*, ed. by Jost Schillemit. Frankfurt am Main: Fischer 1992, p. 38.

9 For an extended analysis of *Guernica* see: Markus Ophälders: *Auswege sind Umwege*. Würzburg: Königshausen & Neumann 2012, pp. 119–140.

10 Walter Benjamin: On the Concept of History. In: W. B.: *Selected Writings*, ed. by Howard Eiland / Michael W. Jennings, transl. by Edmund Jephcott et al., vol. 4: 1938–1940. Cambridge, MA / London: Harvard UP 2006, pp. 389–411, here p. 392; Über den Begriff der Geschichte. In: W. B.: *Gesammelte Schriften*, vol. I.2, ed. by Rolf Tiedemann / Hermann Schweppenhäuser. Frankfurt am Main: Suhrkamp 1974, p. 697.

Fig. 1a–c: Maja Bajevic / Emanuel Licha: *Green, Green, Grass of Home* (2002). Video stills.

Where Did It Happen?

Gianluca Solla

> The tempest was so bloody that not even the grass grew.[1]

I.

There is nothing to see here. After all, what type of picture could give us an idea – albeit approximate – of a catastrophe? The picture can only show one thing: nothing but an expanse of something undetermined. In these pictures, it is an expanse of green grass. A patch of grass beyond the representative dimension of images and their spectacular use can only pass through this 'nothing but': There is nothing to see but the green grass ... You have to go through what is not there, the absence of a home, through the invisible traces of an absence. An absence that is not a lack (it lacks a home), as it appears from outside, but the experience that affects each of our images and every word we say.

It was a happy coincidence that drew my attention to a video from 2002, a piece by two artists: Maja Bajevic, a Bosnian artist from Sarajevo, and the French artist Emanuel Licha. The video is called: *Green, Green Grass of Home*. After the storm of the war, the grass no longer grows, yet here the grass grew back, covering everything. Maja Bajevic describes her apartment in Sarajevo before the war in former Yugoslavia. You cannot see the apartment, instead, her spoken description recounts her memories in great detail. Licha writes:

> SHE MOVES IN THE FIELD AS SHE WOULD WALK IN IT: SHE GOES FROM ONE ROOM TO THE OTHER, DESCRIBING IT AND TELLING ANECDOTES. FROM THIS DESCRIPTION I DREW A PLAN OF THIS APARTMENT THAT I HAD NEVER SEEN.[2]

We listen to the words of the artist describing a house that we can no longer see. Bajevic passes through the spaces by way of memory, blindly. Her story becomes a tracing; it becomes the image of what is not there: the absent image of what is no longer, of what is no more. She says: "Like there", making gestures in the air to show the placement of rooms, objects, doors and windows. What she does is in fact nothing other than walking through a meadow that is anonymous to us and without reference. The camera films her at a strange angle from above. Where did it happen? The story tells us that we are in Sarajevo, but – frankly – we could be anywhere: We see no horizon, no point of reference – only green, a green expanse. What she does is in fact nothing other than walking over a lawn that is anonymous to us and without reference. Here, as is usual in a park, there are some passers-by.

II.

Can images that show nothing adequately honor the memory of the anonymous in the sense intended by Walter Benjamin, for whom the memory of the "nameless" ("die Namenlosen") is more difficult to honor than memories of the famous? Can images like the green-on-green field in Sarajevo filmed by Bajevic and Licha be an example of what Benjamin, in his unpublished manuscript *On the Concept of History*, calls "historical construction" (dedicated to the memory of the anonymous)?[3]

In the European Union, migrants crossing the Mediterranean Sea are sometimes referred to as clandestine, illegal or irregular; in Algeria they are called *harragas* – those who burn – as many of them destroy their documents to avoid being repatriated. Many of these crossings are destined for failure and end on the seabed. (The bottom of the sea of my childhood, the sea that I was born facing and, in a certain sense, the sea at which I still live.) Like the green field of Sarajevo, the sea closes over the bodies of those who it swallows up in its depths.

Of course, we have images of these audacious crossings carried out by people who have nothing to lose. But how can an image describe the weight of the nothing of the night, when you put your life and the lives of your family members in danger to escape, to save something of your lives?

How can we approach the daily catastrophes that occur on the Mediterranean Sea every day? An overwhelming reality in front of which intervention by an intellectual, a university professor, can only be considered something like a comma, a dash, almost nothing, an almost imperceptible suspension of the voice between one shipwreck and the next, one rescue and another. It remains something like a trembling voice speaking a foreign language. But a comma reminds us of something persistent, something that does not come to end. It reminds us of an open question, something that does not end at all.

III.

Where did it happen? Where is it happening? When we are unable to localize an event – when an event is the impossibility of localization – but we are sure that something has happened and is still happening, namely when it has not finished happening and it is happening even now, we feel that there is a strange or remarkable overlapping ('strange' or 'remarkable' in the sense of the German *merkwürdig* or *denkwürdig*), an overlapping between certitude and incertitude, a division within the same experience.

The issue of what it means when we do not stop to listen to something that defies our usual understanding, when we are without a definite place in our knowledge, brings me to talk about a work of art that I saw recently. It was in October 2013 at Gabriele Soave's studio in Venice, and it came as a real surprise, like vertigo: 366 ash-grey rectangles painted on paper, each stamped with a number in a progressive sequence – a triptych of mourning and memory.

Soave's work reminded me of scenes from our TV screens in October 2013: 366 coffins lined up at a school gym on the island of Lampedusa, which were then loaded onto an Italian navy ship to be buried elsewhere. I can say without a doubt that I saw those coffins for the first time in Gabriele's studio, because there is something important that persists in his work, which deals with this issue not as a matter of fact, but as an exception. His work asks urgent questions, but with a slow insistence, a slowness all its own – unlike the news reports, anxious to move on to new stories. It is a question that touches us beyond the pathos we feel in the face of TV images.

One might say that, in this case, art 'acts' by underlining something, or rather that, thanks to the attention that the artwork creates, there is a fixation of the gaze on the event. However, this convergence does not have the character of synthesis, in that it is different or even incompatible. Movements and intensifications coexist, for example, the softness of the drawing with the hardness of the stamped number. When art exists beyond synthesis, it also disavows the possibility that the event can be 'finished', that it is ready to be

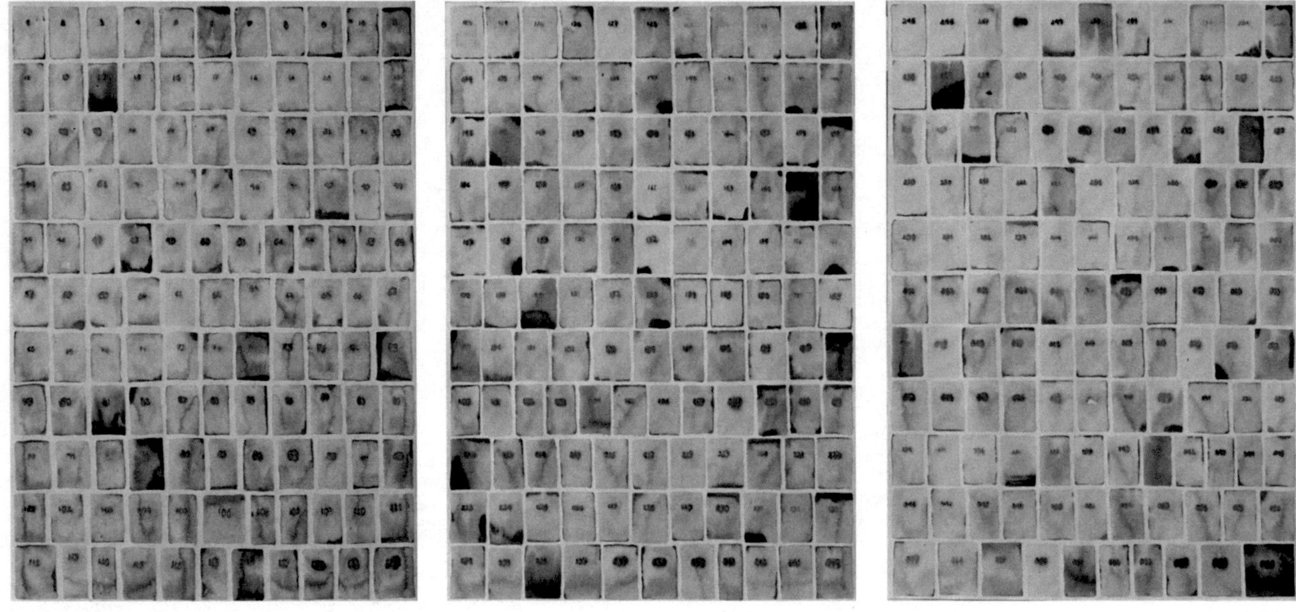

Fig. 2a–c: Gabriele Soave: *366* (triptych, 2013).

commemorated, i. e. forgotten. It helps us to understand the event as a never-ending question. It testifies to the materiality of what has happened, in contrast with the way we speedily scroll through images on a digital device.

What happens here is not about our perception of images – images that we forget just as easily as we watch. In terms of the order of representation, what happens in an artwork is much more about stretching out the images within us, in this case the presentation of a landscape made of water, ash and ink. In their silence, the 366 rectangles in the triptych register an enigma within us for which we have no ready answers. At first we are perplexed and astonished; it is then that questions may arise.

Art provokes questions that makes images possible that are seen quickly and then 'shelved' to continue to grow within us, extending the span of our attention to them. This is about the excess of images we should call 'vision'. To put it another way, it is less about seeing and more about the fact that something appears in what we have already been looking at the entire time without noticing. A better formula might be: seeing something we have already seen for the first time – beginning at the end, seeing something that was in front of our eyes the whole time.

IV.

Soave's artistic research, like all real research, takes place without giving consideration to academia or marketing. It is nothing less than a search for justice – one might say 'pictorial justice'. And in this context, justice is not separate from the need to pay homage: homage to numbers without a name or names without faces. It is about numbers that relate only to themselves and which take their only shape in a list, in an anonymous sequence. This is the only shape we can give to their catastrophe. 366 men, women and children. 366. In the hardness of this number we feel that something is irretrievably lost. We feel it in the decisiveness with which it is repeated in the news in the days following the disaster. We have the same feeling of loss in the insistence with which it is articulated in the work of Gabriele Soave, who only writes the number once, when it corresponds to the coffin of the same number. We feel that something is irretrievably lost, but also that, at the same time, something continues, something persists and insists on remaining there. Maybe it is a question, an unanswered one – a question about our time and about ourselves as inhabitants of this time.

While they were carrying out their extermination of the European Jews, what the Nazis wanted was to resolve the question once and for all, so that the material end of the Final Solution, the *Endlösung*, would coincide at least with the end of the question. After all, a final act or a final solution is defined precisely by its supposed ability to create an end, to act as if things really could be over. Perhaps nothing more than the fact that we do not know, and that we cannot know, speaks of the infinity of events, of the fact that things do not end. The survival of the catastrophe, this strange singular survival is precisely what has yet to be thought of, beyond sentimentalism, in the concept of catastrophe.

If we now come back to the crossing of the sea that the ancient Romans, with a mixture of pride and arrogance, called *mare nostrum*, we can see that catastrophe is not a concept from the judicial tradition notorious for being the domain of the distinction between norm and exception. Catastrophe opens up a third space. It is true that the sea was seen as an exception to this space, or as an element in which, precisely due to its features, the legal determinations that are used to regulate life on land do not have the same value.

It is easy for a jurist like Carl Schmitt to reduce this exceptional character of the sea to the regularity of the land, thinking of the war as the historical principle of continuity between land and sea. As he says in *Land and Sea*: "World history is the history of the wars waged by maritime powers against land or continental powers and by land powers against sea or maritime powers."[4] Every conflict appears to be solved on the horizon of military power; even the alleged and suspicious impropriety of the sea is recovered on the symbolic horizon of regularity, that is: on the horizon of the establishment of a new *nomos*, in Schmitt's words. This is another way of subverting the uncanny when faced with the unknown vastness of the water.

The newspaper articles about the sinking of the 366 are revealing. I cannot go into too much detail here, but these chronicles revive the more traditional image of the sea, "first, the sea as a naturally given boundary of the realm of human activities and, second, its demonization as the sphere of the unreckonable and lawless, in which it is difficult to find one's bearings", as Blumenberg describes it in *Shipwreck with Spectator: Paradigm of a Metaphor for Existence.* From this perspective, "[i]n this field of representation, shipwreck is something like the 'legitimate' result of seafaring [...]".[5]

It is this ancient suspicion about the sea and navigation, this alleged logical connection between navigation and shipwreck that underlies xenophobic statements in Europe: It is the others that are trying to cross the Mediterranean; why should we help them?

V.

The sea, formerly the cradle of European culture, has now become a rampart. We do not have a wall for a border like that between Mexico and the USA, we have a sea. Thus, one could say that the Schengen treaty has lowered borders within the EU and raised them as legal barriers that decide who is a simple migrant and who is entitled to refugee status. The EU's Operation Triton depends on that wall of water: Warships patrol the southernmost border of the EU. They are permitted up to 30 miles from the Italian coast (the previous mission allowed ships to rescue boats in distress, even close to the Libyan coast). And so, although it is presented as a rescue operation, it is in fact nothing but border control.

Nothing needs to happen here: The border has immunity, the ability to reject any danger that comes from outside. But the same controls lead our perception as far away from events as possible. They act as if nothing has happened. But in reality, what happens here is that our memory of what happens in our lives is transformed. Despite the glorification of the concept of the event, it is necessary here to say that the space of the event has now disappeared, perhaps only remaining for those who experience this history that Benjamin called the "the tradition of the oppressed" ("die Tradition der Unterdrückten").[6] There is in this sense a catastrophe of spectacle that coincides with the same cancellation of the spectacle after the spectacle itself has erased our vision.

However, there are traces, or more precisely some traces, that do indeed resist, and I would like to conclude by thinking about them. Given the sea's tendency to erase the signs of what has happened on its surface, it is as if nothing has happened:[7] flat, broken only by the waves, wiping out any memory of those routes and the human migrants that pass through them. It makes me think in particular about the attempt of the *Museo delle migrazioni* (Migration Museum) founded on the island of Lampedusa, a few miles away from the Libyan coast. It is estimated that, in the last 15 years, two hundred thousand migrants have arrived in Lampedusa. The museum describes the island as "[a] meeting point in the middle of the Mediterranean Sea which witnesses the passage of human beings, animals, cultures, and histories, incorporating transit as a reality of Lampedusa."[8] In fact, the aim of the museum project is to collect different traces of the passage of migrants, including those of boat wrecks that have come to this remote strip of Europe, so close to the African coast.

Here we put in place another archaeology that is less noble than that to which we are accustomed. This is one of the most decisive issues at stake in this collection. Here, there is a distinction between noble and less noble, or worthless tracks.

Here, the human becomes a product of its remains. Most artefacts are simple things (a box of baby milk, a damaged bible, lost photographs …) which might seem trivial or insignificant. Where anything can become an artefact, we cannot create a spectacular museum, but only a museum *sui generis*, a collection of human remains that calls into question the function of the museum as a place of entertainment. At the same time, this collection also testifies to a radical transformation that has taken place in the European landscape and that remains to be properly contemplated in all its implications. Of course, such a transformation of the landscape means a transformation of the space in which we live. In today's society, space appears to have been or to be an aseptic dimension in which history is only present in the secured and isolated spaces of a neutrally organized representation of the past.

This museum not only speaks to our need for knowledge but also raises questions about the way we perceive the time and space we traverse. It awakens us from an attitude of indifference to what happens thousands of kilometers away from shinier Europe. In this museum on Lampedusa, there is not much to see, but it gives us a lot to think about. By subtracting certain elements, it asks us to read an unequivocal story that cannot be defined and that is perhaps not even to be defined at all, but rather listened to instead as a constitutive part of our present. It is necessary to devise another means of reporting on what has happened and what we cannot see – to tell the story of what does not stop, of the memory of the nameless, whose uncanny traces remain beneath our present. There is no possible monument here; at most there can only be an involuntary monument. The Museum of Migration is an involuntary memorial to the sea where memory and oblivion coincide, where we are able to preserve the traces of men and women who the sea has returned to us and, at the same time, welcome those people who come from the sea. Perhaps it is only in such acts that take place at the extreme borders of Europe that we are able to assume the risk for the memory of the 'nameless', as it was pointed out by Walter Benjamin shortly before he fled from advancing Nazism as the only real task to think about in history.

1 *Lektionen in Finsternis* (*Lessons of Darkness*, UK / FR / DE 1992, D: Werner Herzog).

2 http://www.emanuel-licha.com/EN_greengreen02.html (accessed February 2, 2017).

3 Cf. Walter Benjamin: Paralipomena to "On the Concept of History", transl. from the German by Edmund Jephcott / Howard Eiland. In: W. B.: *Selected Writings*, vol. 4, ed. by Howard Eiland / Michael W. Jennings. Cambridge, MA: Harvard UP 2003, pp. 401–411, here p. 406; Über den Begriff der Geschichte [Anmerkungen]. In: W. B.: *Gesammelte Schriften*, vol. I.3, ed. by Rolf Tiedemann / Hermann Schweppenhäuser. Frankfurt am Main: Suhrkamp 1990, p. 1241.

4 Carl Schmitt: *Land and Sea*, transl. from the German by Simona Draghici. Washington D. C.: Plutarch 1997, p. 5; *Land und Meer. Eine weltgeschichtliche Betrachtung*. Köln: Hohenheim 1981, p. 16.

5 Hans Blumenberg: *Shipwreck with Spectator. Paradigm of a Metaphor for Existence*, transl. from the German by Steven Rendall. Cambridge, MA / London: The Press 1997, pp. 8, 10; *Schiffbruch mit Zuschauer. Paradigma einer Daseinsmetapher*. Frankfurt am Main: Suhrkamp 1979, pp. 10, 13.

6 Walter Benjamin: On the Concept of History, transl. from the German by Harry Zohn. In: W. B. *Selected Writings*, vol. 4, pp. 389–400, here p. 392; Über den Begriff der Geschichte. In: W. B.: *Gesammelte Schriften*, vol. I.2, ed. by Rolf Tiedemann / Hermann Schweppenhäuser. Frankfurt am Main: Suhrkamp 1990, pp. 693–704, here p. 697.

7 "Toward the end of the fifteenth book of *Dichtung und Wahrheit*, Goethe goes beyond the metaphorics of shipwreck, and even beyond that of the distance of life from the experience of failure. What happens on the sea, he says, is as if it did not happen. For this, he finds the metaphor of ships' courses across the sea that disappear without a trace." (Blumenberg: *Shipwreck with Spectator*, p. 58; *Schiffbruch mit Zuschauer*, pp. 56–57.)

8 The museum merged with the project *PortoM*: https://portommaremediterraneomigrazionimilitarizzazione.wordpress.com (accessed April 30, 2017).

Fig. 1: The “magic cave” in Lars von Trier’s *Melancholia* (DK 2011).

Cosmological Depression
On Lars von Trier's *Melancholia*

Jörn Etzold

Cinema and survival

Cinema has often dealt with spectacular catastrophes: falling skyscrapers, cities devastated by monsters, tsunamis rolling into downtown Manhattan ... Things fall apart. But there is always somebody who survives: It is the spectator, spellbound in darkness during the catastrophe, but slowly getting back to reality during the credit sequence and then stumbling out of the door, realizing that it is now night and that people are sitting around in bars. The spectators have made it out of it all, once again. Everything is in ruins, but they can head for a drink to calm down. Tomorrow is another day, and work is waiting.

In his reading of Walter Benjamin's *The Origin of German Tragic Drama*, the American literary scholar Samuel Weber points to a specific relationship between the modern figure of the spectator as a survivor and the rise of Protestantism. Benjamin, he notes, understood the disparate crowds assembled in baroque theaters as an assembly of sad spectators, watching an allegorical reanimation of a world that had been rendered empty and meaningless by Luther's verdict against good works. God was far away and no longer cared about what human beings did. Since then, all events had unfolded in a time that had fallen out of salvific history. "Something new arose", says Benjamin: "an empty world."[1] All the spectator could now hope for was to survive the catastrophes staged again and again before his very eyes.

A surprisingly similar description of the modern spectator was developed in the 1960s by the Situationist International, a France-based, anti-art avant-garde that, by then, had become a radical group of Marxist cultural critics. Guy Debord and Raoul Vaneigem, his co-conspirator at the time, characterized modern media and, above all, television and cinema as machines for the production of survival. Their focus was not on theology, but on economy – but we should keep in mind that, for the young Benjamin in his fragment "Capitalism as Religion", Protestantism was the name for Christianity's transformation into capitalism. For Debord and Vaneigem, cinema was one of the main tools of a "society of the spectacle", as Debord named it and, like all the other media, it was only an extension of the market economy and its underlying structure of reification. For Vaneigem, the fundamental operation of exchange of the "societies of alienation" was to give up "life" (*vie*) for "survival" (*survie*). Your time will be measured, you will be governed, but if you are lucky, you will at least stay alive: "Up till now surviving has prevented us from living."[2] So, the "society of the spectacle" urgently needed to produce an ongoing threat of death, as Vaneigem observed in allusion to Hegel's famous chapter on the master and slave in the *Phenomenology of Spirit.* In the Situationist era, this threat was produced by the Cold War as an internal split within the global society of the spectacle. Every catastrophe you survived in cinema, in front of your TV screen or in your own private atomic shelter in your garden (which served as illustrations in the journal volume that contains Vaneigem's article) proved to you that giving up "life" for "survival" had been a wise bet. In the empty world of the commodity, you could at least survive catastrophes on screen.

Cosmological depression

Lars von Trier's movie *Melancholia*[3] is about the most spectacular of all catastrophes: the end of the world, of life on earth and life as such – as Justine, one of the two sisters the film is centered around, senses: "[L]ife is only on earth, and not for long". It is a movie about a catastrophe that does not offer the slightest hope of survival of any kind, be it that of a jellyfish, a plant or a bacterium. As Peter Szendy underlines in *Apocalypse-Cinema*, in *Melancholia*, "*[t]he end of the movie is the end of the world*",[4] i. e. when the screen suddenly turns dark and even the music – Wagner's famous leitmotif from the overture of *Tristan and Isolde* – breaks off. In this movie, however, doomsday is not commanded by God's wrath or caused by human hubris. It is caused by Melancholia, a monstrous planet that approaches Earth in line with the simple and eternally foreseeable laws of the physics of idleness and gravity. "It's a planet that has been hiding behind the sun. And now it passes by us", explains Justine's little nephew Leo – who might well be the loneliest child in film history – to his aunt. The planet is blue, cold and completely unstoppable as it approaches Earth through the interstellar void.

But *Melancholia*, deeply protestant in its theme, style, music, images and allusions, is not a 'catastrophe movie' in the Hollywood style, like Roland Emmerich's spectacular works.

We do not see much destruction – no falling cities, no burning houses. When Melancholia hits the doomed Earth, it destroys everything very quickly and once and for all. Most of the movie is more reminiscent of von Trier's movies from the Dogma 95 period, often shot using a handheld camera that comes very close to the protagonists and their inner conflicts, their consciousness, their feelings – with the difference that the family structures, displayed in a psychological intensity typical of Dogma, relate to cosmological constellations, to the interstellar space that is empty, ice cold and hostile to all life. The film is centered around two sisters: Justine (played by Kirsten Dunst), whose catastrophic wedding is portrayed in the first part of the film, is a deeply depressed copywriter who works in the advertising industry; Claire, her sister (played by Charlotte Gainsbourg), is married to an extremely rich man named John, whose palace-like estate hosts the wedding as well the rest of the action. The couple has one young son, and Claire's main occupation seems to be to take care of both him and her sister. Neither she nor her husband seems to work. The film is divided into two parts: "Justine" shows the long wedding night degenerating into despair and separation and "Claire" the arrival of the planet Melancholia some weeks later. Justine, Claire, her husband, her son and the butler, "little father" (who will disappear at some point), are alone on the enormous estate, waiting for the announced "fly-by" of Melancholia that, according to scientists, will not affect earth. Most of the time, we can hear the horses neighing and stomping around in fear in the background. The two main parts are preceded by an eight-minute long overture to Wagner's music – a series of images that turns out to be from one of Justine's dreams. Birds fall from the sky; the geometrically arranged trees in the garden and the huge sundial in the middle cast two shadows in different directions; Justine raises her hands and sees little lambent flashes of electric light emerge from them, attracted by Melancholia. Unlike in Wagner, however, the music will not change over the course of the following two hours; the theme from the overture will be heard again and again, like a broken record. This is very consistent: *Melancholia* is a film about depression, and depression does not know any progress.

But while we see the catastrophic relationships in the sisters' family poisoning the marriage – the horrifying mother, evil and careworn, played by Charlotte Rampling, and the ridiculous, obscene and completely unhelpful father, played by John Hurt – and while, in the second part, depression gains a hold of Justine's body and soul and then falls off her, as she is about to be freed from all creaturely evil by the end of the world, the planet Melancholia approaches irrevocably from outer space. The icy, irreparable relations between the characters correspond with a cosmic happening of an all-encompassing magnitude that does not leave any hope for consolation of any kind either. Justine's depression, her failing efforts to finally embrace a bourgeois family life, the naïve and helpless endeavors of her groom to take her sadness from her (he buys a garden with apple trees and, in a quiet moment, offers her a photo that she forgets to take with her immediately afterwards), Claire's fear and her ridiculous attempts to keep family life going in the face of doomsday – all of these movements are interrelated by the cosmic catastrophe. It is the largest imaginable catastrophe for humankind and for life in general, but, on a larger scale, it is only one of the many cosmic catastrophes that have shaped our universe since the Big Bang that no eye ever saw.

This cosmic catastrophe 'doubles' the intimate, Dogma-style family drama, because Melancholia is mainly about what its title says: melancholia, the sentiment, to use Benjamin's formula once again, of "an empty world". In Justine, this sentiment has become a permanent condition. Since the end of the 19th century, the notion of "depression" has become increasingly common for its description and analysis. But, like melancholia, depression is not merely a psychological issue, but also a cosmological one. Far from being a trait of a psychologically convincing character or merely an illness that can be cured through proper therapy, depression speaks a final word about life *in general*: "Life on earth is evil." It is Justine who says this to her sister in the second part of the movie, when she is already completely sure that the planet will hit Earth and that nothing will survive. And of course, in doing so, Justine contradicts the Creator, if there ever was one, who looked at his creation every day once he had completed his work and "saw that it was good". Von Trier (who, like his main actress, knows what he is talking about) portrays depression as the final verdict on life as such – on life as the strange and somewhat unnecessary detour that leads to death anyway, which Freud evokes in *Beyond the Pleasure Principle*. And this verdict is issued from the perspective of the cosmos, its emptiness, its endless distances, its temperatures far below or above anything that any living organism could endure. From this cosmic perspective – the perspective of "natural history", to use a term Benjamin employs in an idiosyncratic way in the *Arcades Project* – life is just a very irrelevant exception, taking place during a very short period of time on what Schopenhauer called the "mouldy film"[5] of one tiny planet in some small solar system in the Milky Way. Hence, it is not "Justine" as a psychologically interesting character who issues this verdict on life: She is merely a medium for the articulation of the truth about an empty cosmos. Justine's eyes, icy blue as the approaching planet, long for a cosmic encounter with the an-organic and inanimate that will put an end to all the differences and difficulties that make up life, recognizing once and for all what Freud called "the most universal endeavour of all living substance – namely to return to the quiescence of the inorganic world."[6]

This is why Justine calms down near the end of the film, whereas her sister, the one who has cared for her all her life, gets lost in panic. At some point, not content with her husband's appeasements, Claire steals away from the family and tries to find out on the internet whether Melancholia will hit Earth or not. First, she types in "Melancholia" (which leads her to descriptions of a "mental disorder" and "symptoms, causes, diagnosis, and treatment information"), and then – during a search within "Melancholia" – she types in what she fears the most: "DEATH". This search not only leads her to Lav Diaz's *Death in the Land of Melancholia* (a hidden tribute to the Philippine filmmaker), but also to a page on Melancholia's "Dance of Death". It shows a diagram of the planet's slingshot orbit around Earth, into space and then back into a frontal collision, due to the effects of gravity (a path that is highly unlikely since its mass would be much greater than Earth's and therefore would attract Earth and not vice versa[7]).

This "dance of death" is exactly what the planet performs. First, it approaches Earth, but orbits around it. Then it gets smaller and smaller, as Claire can see through a device built by her son, a little wire sling that captures the actual size of the planet so that it can be compared a few minutes later if it has veered away or come closer. After its fly-by, the image of the planet inside the sling shrinks; everything gets better; the catastrophic mass of matter can now be framed – but then the planet *comes back* like a repressed trauma. When Claire looks through the sling twice the morning after the fly-by, by the second time, the planet has exceeded the frame that was supposed to contain it. Soon it will exceed all forms and all frames. For Claire, who is portrayed as the one who cares and keeps the family together, this excess is related to her greatest possible fear.

Justine, however, longs for this excess. At some point, when the planet is already close and is blurring the difference between night and day, shining a pale blue light, she bathes naked in its glow. Justine, who sent her worldly husband home at the end of the wedding night, now looks like a heavenly bride waiting for unification with her eternal groom, who will liberate her from all earthly suffering and pain, reminiscent of the Protestant Johann Sebastian Bach's *actus tragicus* (*Gottes Zeit ist die allerbeste Zeit,* BWV 106): *Ja komm, Herr Jesu, komm*. But she also resembles the Phrygian Niobe, who another protestant, Friedrich Hölderlin, evoked in his

"Remarks on 'Antigone'". Transformed into stone, Niobe assimilates into what Hölderlin calls the "eternally anti-human course of nature"[8] – which is here a cosmic meaninglessness, a mass of pure destructive matter that in and of itself cannot talk. Dunst's beautiful body turns into a lifeless sculpture as it waits for unification with the non-human, anti-human planet that will bring calm once and for all.

Melancholy and astrology

Melancholia came out in 2011, and not by accident. The idea of a hidden planet bound to hit and destroy Earth is taken from the modern myth of the "Nibiru cataclysm" that was spread by Nancy Lieder, a woman from Wisconsin, on her website *Zeta Talk*.[9] Claiming that she was able to receive messages from extraterrestrials from the Zeta Reticuli star system via an implant in her brain, Lieder announced in 1995 that the planet Nibiru, also called Planet X, would pass through our solar system in 2003 and cause a shift in the earth's poles, leading to the destruction of most of humanity. When the event did not take place, Lieder changed her prediction to 2012, thus linking her prophecy with the apocalyptic movements around the end of the 5,126 year-long cycle of the Mesoamerican Long Count calendar. On her homepage, she states that the planet has not been visible since 2003 as it is hidden behind the sun, but photos taken before that date show what is supposed to be Nibiru: a shadow near the sun, a gigantic, blurry object in the sky.

But the relationship between the condition of melancholia, or, depression, and stellar constellations in von Trier's movie is not only influenced by the Nibiru cataclysm – it has a long history. Walter Benjamin, in *The Origin of German Tragic Drama*, states that the "theory of melancholy has a very close connection with the doctrine of stellar influences."[10] Due to these uncontrollable influences, humans encounter "fate", which is why their creaturely, bare existence fell out of paradise and became ensnared in what Benjamin calls in a preceding text the "guilt context".[11] Astrology claims to understand the fateful influences that planets cast over men's lives. Since the renaissance, it has been "the ancient occidental residue of oriental paganism."[12]

But why are planets said to cast "fate" on men's lives? Tracing this long history, Raymond Klibansky, Erwin Panofsky and Fritz Saxl underline the fact that the planets were discovered by the Babylonians, whereas the Greeks only knew of two of them (which, in fact, were one: *Phosphoros* and *Hesperos*, the morning star and the evening star, both of which we now refer to as Venus). But for the Babylonians, the planets were also deities. Hence, they entered Greek knowledge in this form: as strange oriental deities, which the Greeks replaced with their own. As Klibansky, Panofsky and Saxl further note, the Greek deities that had been transformed into planets survived the decline of the polytheistic system more easily than those who had not and were only known to scholars.[13] It is due to this history that the planets are considered to be the bearers of ancient, cryptic, oriental powers that leap from early antiquity into the modern age. And while each planet is said to have a different influence on humans, the melancholic are possessed by Saturn, the Roman equivalent of the Greek titan Cronus, the father of Zeus – a highly ambivalent deity who is most famous for eating his children.

For Benjamin in *The Origin of German Tragic Drama*, the first and most powerful attempt in human history to escape the spell of fate and the "pagan" "guilt context" was Greek tragedy. In tragedy, man opposes the pagan gods, claims that he is better than them, and hence "[i]t was not in law but in tragedy that the head of genius lifted itself for the first time from the mist of guilt".[14] In a letter to Benjamin, his friend Florens Christian Rang, whom Benjamin consulted for his chapters on Greek tragedy, connected this guilt to the influence of the luminaries: "The tragedy is the disruption of astrology and therefore a breaking away out of astral destiny".[15] But in a way, it is precisely this condition of fate and destiny that tragedy sought to overcome that is 'updated' when Luther abandons the importance of good works and opens up the "empty world" of modernity. The ritual and institutional arrangements that had been believed to connect man to the transcendental, which, if observed, were thus able to free him from guilt and destiny, were now damaged. A new "guilt context" had now been installed, which is no longer guilt in the face of the gods but in the pure immanence of mankind, going under the name of capitalism. Benjamin speaks of "an element of German paganism and the grim belief in the subjection of man to fate"[16] that speaks from Luther's decision. Hence, from the viewpoint of dramaturgy, astrology would be a useful tool to develop intrigues of characters fallen into fate – something that the Catholic Calderón did with mastery and that Schiller, according to Benjamin, kept in mind. The writers of the German mourning play, however, as Benjamin notes, failed to do this.

Lars von Trier takes up the old dramaturgical motive of stellar influences, but in a very special way. Astrology has always tried to track the hidden influences that the planets cast on men's lives. It has never been about planets physically colliding with Earth or destroying life at all. Von Trier transgresses the borders of plots like Calderón and Schiller's, but he also goes further than Nestroy in *The Evil Spirit Lumpacivagabundus*, where a comet in the sky announces a looming doomsday and influences the destiny of the characters. More precisely, in radical protestant subjectivity, von Trier reverses the scheme of the influence of luminaries: It is not Justine who is attracted and steered by the planet, as a 'woman under the influence'. On the contrary, it is she, the lost soul and fallen creature, who attracts the planet with her creaturely loneliness and pure urge for the calm of the anorganic. As she and her groom are arriving late to their own wedding, she takes a long, longing look into the sky and sees Antares, which will soon be hidden by Melancholia – she will also be the first to remark upon it, during a ride the day after. The planet will come to her and celebrate another kind of wedding.

The magic cave

During the infamous press conference after the presentation of *Melancholia* at the 2011 festival in Cannes, von Trier was asked by a British journalist about his relationship to German romanticism, gothic and Nazi aesthetics. Von Trier began an alienating and absurdly comic monologue about discovering that his biological father was not the Jew Ulf Trier, but the German Fritz Michael Hartmann, "which also gave me some pleasure", and went on to confess his sympathy for Hitler and his attraction to Albert Speer. Beating his fist on the table, he concluded by stating: "OK, I am a Nazi". And when he was offered the grace of a last question to get out of it when another journalist asked him if he considered *Melancholia* to be his "answer to the Hollywood blockbuster" and if he could envision doing "something on a larger scale than this", he said: "Yes, that's what we Nazis ... We have a tendency to do things on a greater scale."[17] It is well known that von Trier was banned from Cannes – from the festival palace, that is – afterwards. But some critics have seen in the movie itself a strange annihilation fantasy, a dream of complete destruction strangely mixed with sexual energy – on a greater scale.

Is *Melancholia* a mere celebration of death and destruction, led by bottomless ennui and disgust for existence? Does it glorify, to use Hölderlin's words once again, "*the striving from this world to the other*" (whereas the "character" of Zeus, who overcame Cronus / Saturn, is to reverse it into a striving "*from another world to this one*")[18]? Does the movie celebrate a character whose depression is so deep that it can attract a planet to put an end to life in general once and for all? Does

Justine, the just one, stand for all the martyrs, lunatics and death-seekers of modernity?

At the end, the film seems to focus more and more on the little boy, Leo. Somewhat neutral, shy, and completely lost in space in his pajamas, this child – one of the last of his kind – senses that things are going horribly wrong. His mother is about to lose her mind while his father does not appear at all – he has already committed suicide in the stables, where Claire finds him and covers him with straw. He talks to Justine, "Auntie Steelbreaker", as he calls her: "Dad said there is nothing to do then, nowhere to hide." She answers: "If your Dad said that, then he's forgotten about something. He's forgotten about the magic cave." "Is that something everybody can make?" the child asks. "Aunt Steelbreaker can", answers Justine. During the world's last minutes, Justine and the child collect branches in the forest to construct this cave. At the end, when the planet is already filling the sky, the two sisters and the boy gather under the branches. Does the child believe, as Aunt Steelbreaker says, that this cave will protect him from the apocalypse? Has Justine made something up to ease his journey into annihilation? The scene is ambivalent. The hut does not protect anybody. When Melancholia crashes into Earth, flames sweep over it and, for a millisecond, we see the bodies in flames. But similar to Claire's rudimentary funeral for her husband, this hut is a last manifestation of something human in the face of the approaching apocalypse. Justine constructs something, builds something, a home or a shelter – a refuge at a point when there is literally nowhere to go. She makes her nephew believe that it will work. It may sound somewhat impassioned – and indeed it is – but in this final scene, von Trier opposes culture, make-believe, imagination and compassion to the dedifferentiation of the an-organic and the death drive.

What survives is the camera. And, for a few seconds longer, the soundtrack. After the screen has turned black and the music has suddenly stopped, we still hear sounds of destruction coming from nowhere, echoing for a few seconds in the blackness. And during these seconds, this blackness transforms from the interstellar void into the cozy, but public interior space of a cinema. "[N]ever have the credits of a film seemed so reassuring,"[19] writes Peter Szendy. The spectator has made it out of doomsday, once again. He can stumble out of the cinema and will find people hanging around in bars. Tomorrow is another day, and work awaits.

1 Walter Benjamin: *The Origin of German Tragic Drama*, transl. from the German by John Osborne. London / New York: Verso 2003, p. 139. "Etwas Neues entstand: eine leere Welt." (*Ursprung des deutschen Trauerspiels*. In: W. B.: *Gesammelte Schriften*, vol. 1, ed. by Rolf Tiedemann / Hermann Schweppenhäuser. Frankfurt am Main: Suhrkamp 1997, pp. 203–430, here p. 317.) See also Samuel Weber: Genealogy of Modernity: History, Myth and Allegory in Benjamin's Origin of the German Mourning Play. In: *Modern Language Notes* 106 (1991), pp. 465–500; S. W.: Storming the Work. Allegory and Theatricality in Benjamin's "Origin of the German Mourning Play". In: S. W.: *Theatricality as Medium*. New York: Fordham UP, pp. 160–180.

2 Raoul Vaneigem: Basic Banalities (Part 1), transl. from the French by Ken Knabb. In: Ken Knabb (ed.): *Situationist International Anthology*. Berkeley: Bureau of Public Secrets 2006, pp. 117–130, here p. 121; Banalités de base. In: *Internationale Situationniste* 7 (1962), pp. 272–281, here p. 275.

3 *Melancholia* (DK / SE / FR / DE 2011, D: Lars von Trier).

4 Peter Szendy: *Apocalypse-Cinema. 2012 and Other Ends of the World*, transl. from the French by Will Bishop. New York: Fordham UP 2015, p. 2 (italics in original); "*[L]a fin du film, c'est la fin du monde.*" *L'Apocalypse Cinéma. 2012 et autres fins du monde*. Nantes / Bordeaux: Capricci 2012, p. 9.

5 Arthur Schopenhauer: *The World as Will and Representation*, transl. from the German by E. F. J. Payne, vol. II. New York: Dover 1958, p. 3. "Kugeln, die inwendig heiß, mit erstarrter, kalter Rinde überzogen sind, auf der ein Schimmelüberzug lebende und erkennende Wesen erzeugt hat." (*Die Welt als Wille und Vorstellung*, vol. 2.1. Zurich: Diogenes 1977, p. 9.)

6 Sigmund Freud: Beyond the Pleasure Principle. In: S. F.: *The Standard Edition of the Complete Psychological Works*, ed. by James Strachey, vol. XVIII. London: The Hogarth Press and the Institute of Psychoanalysis 1955, pp. 1–64, here p. 62. "[D]as allgemeinste Streben alles Lebenden, zur Ruhe der anorganischen Welt zurückzukehren." (Jenseits des Lustprinzips. In: S. F.: *Gesammelte Werke*, vol. 13. Frankfurt am Main: Fischer 1987, pp. 1–69, here p. 68.)

7 See the discussion among experts under: http://physics.stackexchange.com/questions/15083/is-melancholias-orbit-impossible (accessed April 21, 2017).

8 Friedrich Hölderlin: Remarks on 'Antigone'. In: F. H.: *Essays and Letters on Theory*, transl. from the German and ed. by Thomas Pfau. Albany: State University of New York Press 1988, pp. 109–116, here p. 113. "[E]wig menschenfeindliche[r] Naturgang" (Anmerkungen zur Antigonä. In: F. H.: *Sämtliche Werke und Briefe*, vol. 3, ed. by Michael Knaupp. Munich: Hanser 1992, pp. 369–376, here p. 373).

9 http://www.zetatalk.com (accessed April 21, 2017). See also "Nibiru Cataclysm" on https://en.wikipedia.org/wiki/Nibiru_cataclysm (accessed April 21, 2017), where the following information is taken from.

10 Benjamin: *The Origin of German Tragic Drama*, p. 148. "Die Theorie der Melancholie steht in genauem Zusammenhang mit der Lehre von den Gestirneinflüssen." (*Ursprung des deutschen Trauerspiels*, p. 326.)

11 Walter Benjamin: Fate and Character. In: W. B.: *Reflections. Essays, Aphorisms, Autobiographical Writings*, ed. by Peter Demetz, transl. from the German by Edmund Jephcott. New York: Schocken 1986, pp. 304–311, here p. 308. "Schuldzusammenhang" (Schicksal und Charakter. In: W. B.: *Gesammelte Schriften*, vol. 2, ed. by Rolf Tiedemann / Hermann Schweppenhäuser. Frankfurt am Main: Suhrkamp 1991, pp. 171–179, here p. 175).

12 Benjamin: *The Origin of German Tragic Drama*, p.221. "[...] die Astrologie, de[r] alt[e] abendländisch[e] Rückstand des orientalischen Heidentums." (*Ursprung des deutschen Trauerspiels*, p.395.)

13 Cf. Raymond Klibansky / Erwin Panofsky / Fritz Saxl: *Saturn and Melancholy. Studies in the History of Natural Philosophy Religion and Art*. Nendeln: Kraus Reprint 1979, pp. 133–137.

14 Benjamin: Fate and Character, p.307. "Nicht das Recht, sondern die Tragödie war es, in der das Haupt des Genius aus dem Nebel der Schuld sich zum ersten Male erhob, denn in der Tragödie wird das dämonische Schicksal durchbrochen." (Schicksal und Charakter, pp. 174–175.) Benjamin will cite this phrase again in his book on German tragic drama.

15 "Die Tragödie ist der Bruch der Astrologie und also das Entlaufen aus dem Sternlauf-Geschick." (Florens Christian Rang: Agon und Theater, quoted in: Benjamin: *Gesammelte Schriften*, vol. 1, pp. 891–895, here p. 893.)

16 Benjamin: *The Origin of German Tragic Drama*, p.138. "Ein Stück germanischen Heidentums und finsteren Glaubens an die Schicksalsverfallenheit [...]" (Ursprung des deutschen Trauerspiels, p.317).

17 The video can be seen at: https://www.youtube.com/watch? v= QpUqpLh0iRw (accessed April 21, 2017).

18 Hölderlin: Remarks on Antigone, p.112. In German, he states he translates "Zeus" as "Vater der Erde, weil sein Charakter ist, der ewigen Tendenz entgegen, *das Streben aus dieser Welt in die andre* zu kehren *zu einem Streben aus einer andren Welt in diese*." (Anmerkungen zur Antigonä, p.372.)

19 Szendy: *Apocalypse-Cinema*, p.2. "[J]amais un générique du film ne m'a paru aussi rassurant." (*L'Apocalypse Cinéma*, p.10.)

List of Figures

Contributors

Martina Bengert is Assistant Professor of Spanish and French Literature at the Ludwig-Maximilians-Universität, Munich. Her research interests include German, French and Spanish mysticism, topology, French theory, psychoanalysis and theology. Selected publications: "Kryptische Gründung. Die Aushöhlung des Grundes und Blanchots literarische Krypta" (in: Maha El Hissy / Sascha Pöhlmann (eds): *Gründungsorte,* 2014); *Nachtdenken. Maurice Blanchots "Thomas l'Obscur"* (2017). She is currently working on a postdoctoral project entitled "Mystik und Neomystik. Seelentopologien bei Teresa de Ávila und Simone Weil".

Vittoria Borsò is Professor Emerita of Romance Literature at the Heinrich-Heine-Universität, Düsseldorf. Her research interests include modern French and Italian literature; biopolitics, ontology and the poetics of life in historical and contemporary texts; the theory of memory and media; visual cultures; topology and literary topographies; the theory of 'World Literature'; and Mexican culture and literature. Selected publications: *Die Kunst das Leben zu 'bewirtschaften'. Bíos zwischen Politik, Ökonomie und Ästhetik* (2013, coeditor with M. Cometa); *Bio-Poetics: Wissen und Leben – Wissen für das Leben: Herausforderungen einer affirmativen Biopolitik* (2014, editor); and *Lateinamerika anders denken. Literatur – Macht – Raum* (2015).

Davide Caliaro completed his PhD in Philosophy at the University of Verona, where he collaborates with the chair of the Philosophy of Religion. His fields of interest are the intersections between philosophy, psychoanalysis and political theology. Currently he is studying the relationship between prophecy and subjectivation. Selected publications: "L'Animale e il Messia. Appunti per una lettura teologico-politica del romanzo Teorema di Pier Paolo Pasolini" (in: G. Dalla Fior (ed.): *Comunicare Letteratura*, 2012); "Qualcosa si scrive, qualcosa si grida. Note su parola, burocrazia e bestiame umano" (introduction to Pierre Legendre: *Godere del Potere. Trattato sulla burocrazia patriota*, 2014); and "Incontrare il taglio. Note su interdetto, enigma e parola" (in: Gianluca Solla (ed.): *Cosa può un taglio? Filosofia, psicoanalisi e altre circoncisioni*, 2016).

Jörg Dünne is Professor of Romance Literature at the Humboldt-Universität, Berlin. His research interests include literature, space and cartography, cultural techniques, the history of geology in modern popular culture, early modern Spanish literature, French modernity and contemporary Argentine literature. Selected publications: *Die kartographische Imagination: Erinnern, Erzählen und Fingieren in der Frühen Neuzeit* (2011); *Handbuch Raum & Literatur* (2015, coeditor with Andreas Mahler); and *Die katastrophische Feerie. Geschichte, Geologie und Spektakel in der modernen französischen Literatur* (2016).

Jean-Pierre Dupuy is Professor Emeritus of Social and Political Philosophy at the École Polytechnique, Paris, and Professor of Political Science at Stanford University. He is a member of the French Academy of Technology and of the Conseil Général des Mines. He chairs the Ethics Committee of the French High Authority on Nuclear Safety and Security. Selected publications in English: *The Mechanization of the Mind* (2000); *On the Origins of Cognitive Science* (2009); *The Mark* *of the Sacred* (2013); *Economy and the Future. A Crisis of Faith* (2014); *A Short Treatise on the Metaphysics of Tsunamis* (2015); and *Enlightened Doomsaying* (to be published in 2018).

Jörn Etzold is Professor of Theater Studies at the Ruhr-Universität Bochum. His research interests include theater and political theory, layers of theater history, tragedy and the "mourning play", labor and artistic practice, and avant-gardes and neo-avant-gardes. Selected publications: *Die melancholische Revolution des Guy-Ernest Debord* (2009); *Nicht-Arbeit* (2011, coeditor with Martin Jörg Schäfer); and *rhythmos. Formen des Unbeständigen nach Hölderlin* (2016, coeditor with Moritz Hannemann).

Gesine Hindemith is Research Assistant for French and Italian literature at the University of Stuttgart. Her PhD thesis, *Sonographie – Akustische Texturen im französischen Autorenfilm*, was published in 2013. Her research interests include the relationship between affects and economy in literature; configurations of opera, tragedy and melodrama (17th to 20th century); historiography; and literature. She is currently working on a postdoctoral project entitled "(Dis)Grace and Sovereignty – Figurations of Tragedy by Jean Racine and Vittorio Alfieri".

Marie-Hélène Huet is a Affiliate Faculty member at the Massachusetts Institute of Technology and M. Taylor Pyne Professor Emerita of French at Princeton University. Selected publications: *Monstrous Imagination* (1993), winner of the Harry Levine prize in Comparative Literature; *Mourning Glory: The Will of the French Revolution* (1997); and *the Culture of Disaster* (2012). Her areas interests include the philosophy of the Enlightenment and European cultural history.

Walburga Hülk-Althoff is Professor of Romance Literatures at the University of Siegen. Several of her research projects in French and Italian literature and media have focused on modernity and avant-gardes. She has published studies on medieval literature and the literature of the 19th and 20th centuries, focussing on the dialog between literature, the sciences and the social history of literature. Selected publications: *Haussmann und die Folgen. Vom Boulevard zur Boulevardisierung* (coeditor with Gregor Schuhen, 2012); *Bewegung als Mythologie der Moderne: Vier Studien zu Baudelaire, Flaubert, Taine, Valéry* (2012); *Die Krise als Erzählung* (coeditor with Uta Fenske and Gregor Schuhen, 2013); *Bohème nach '68* (coeditor with Nicole Pöppel and Georg Stanitzek, 2015); and *Geteilte Städte/Villes divisées* (coeditor with Stephanie Schwerter, forthcoming). She also has a monography in progress, *Als Paris die Moderne erfand. Der Rausch der Jahre 1850 bis 1870* (forthcoming in 2019).

Judith Kasper teaches French, Italian and comparative literature at the Ludwig-Maximilians-Universität, Munich. Her research interests include Holocaust studies, trauma theory, psychoanalysis and philology, and lyric theory. Selected publications: *Sprachen des Vergessens. Proust, Perec und Barthes zwischen Verlust und Eingedenken* (2003); *Trauma e nostalgia. Per una lettura del concetto di Heimat* (2009); and *Der traumatisierte Raum. Insistenz, Inschrift, Montage bei Freud, Levi, Kertész, Sebald und Dante* (2016). She was also coeditor (with Ottmar Ette) of the volume *Unfälle der Sprache. Literarische und philologische Erkundungen der Katastrophe* (2014).

Françoise Lavocat is Professor of Comparative Literature at the Université Sorbonne Nouvelle – Paris 3. She was a fellow at the Wissenschaftskolleg zu Berlin (2014–2015), and is currently a member of the Institut Universitaire de France (2015–2020) and the Academia Europaea (since 2016). She specializes in theories of fiction (fact and fiction, possible worlds, characters), early modern literature and the narrative of catastrophes. Selected publications: *Arcadies malheureuses, aux origines du roman moderne* (1997); *La Syrinx au bûcher, Pan et les satyres à la renaissance et à l'âge baroque* (2005); *La théorie littéraire des mondes possibles* (editor, 2010); *Pestes Incendies, Naufrages, écritures du désastre au 17e siècle* (editor, 2010); and "Narratives of Catastrophe in the Early Modern Period: Awareness of Historicity and Emergence of Interpretative Viewpoints" (in: *Poetics Today* 33:3, 2013). Most recently, she published *Fait et fiction: pour une frontière* (2016).

Bettine Menke is Professor of Comparative Literature at the University of Erfurt. Her research interests include literature and theater, rhetoric and deconstruction, the mediality of theater, the scripturality of texts, concepts of media and cultural techniques, Walter Benjamin, and Franz Kafka. Selected publications: *Tragödie. Trauerspiel. Spektakel* (2007, coeditor with Christoph Menke); *Das Trauerspiel-Buch. Der Souverän – das Trauerspiel – Konstellationen – Ruinen* (2010); *Das Melodram: ein Medienbastard* (2013, coeditor with Armin Schäfer and Daniel Eschkötter); "Suspendierung des Auftritts; On/Off" (in: Juliane Vogel / Christopher Wild (eds): *Auftreten. Wege auf die Bühne*, 2014); "im auftreten/verschwinden – auf dem Schauplatz und anderswo" (in: *Zeitschrift für Medien- und Kulturforschung* 7:1, 2016); and *Flucht und Szene* (2018, coeditor with Juliane Vogel).

Markus Ophälders is Professor of the Aesthetics and Philosophy of Arts and Music at the University of Verona. His research interests include music, arts and literature, the philosophy of history and political philosophy as well as cultural studies. Selected publications: *Auswege sind Umwege* (2012); *Konstruktion von Erfahrung. Versuch über Walter Benjamin* (2015); *Dialettica dell'ironia romantica* (2016).

Giulia Palladini is Senior Lecturer in Drama, Theater and Performance at the University of Roehampton. Her research interests include theater history, critical theory, performance labor and free time, the archive, and materialist theories of artistic production. Selected publications: *The Scene of Foreplay: Theater, Labor and Leisure in 1960s New York* (2017); and *Lexicon for an Affective Archive* (2017, coeditor with Marco Pustianaz).

Kati Röttger is professor of Theater Studies at the University of Amsterdam. Her current research interests include international dramaturgy, theater and globalization, the history of technology and spectacle, and theater and philosophy. Selected publications: *Welt-Bild-Theater. Bildästhetik im Bühnenraum* (editor, 2014); "Occupying Scenes of Thinking: The Case of Antigone" (in: *Forum Modernes Theater* 47, 2016); *International Performance Research Pedagogies. Towards an Unconditional Discipline?* (2017, coeditor with Sruti Bala, Milija Gluhovic and Hanna Korsberg); and "Spectacle and Politics. Is there a Political Reality in the Spectacle of Society?" (in: Samir Gandesha / Johan F. Hartle (eds): *The Spell of Capital. Reification and Capital*, 2017).

Gianluca Solla teaches Philosophy at the University of Verona. His research currently focuses on the political implications of namelessness in history. His monographs include *L'ombra della libertà. Schelling e la teologia politica del nome proprio* (2003); German translation: *Schatten der Freiheit. Schelling und die Politische Theologie des Eigennamens*, 2006); *Nomi di nomi* (2006); *Marrani. Il debito segreto* (2008); and *Memoria dei senzanome* (2013).

Johannes Ungelenk is Research Assistant at the Ludwig-Maximilians-Universität, Munich. His research interests include literature and the weather, philology's relationship with love and touch, and critical theory. Selected publications: *Narcissus and Echo: A Political Reading of George Eliot's "Daniel Deronda"* (2012); *Sexes of Winds and Packs: Rethinking Feminism with Deleuze and Guattari* (2014); and *Literature and Weather: Shakespeare – Goethe – Zola* (forthcoming).

Funded by the Deutsche Forschungsgemeinschaft
(DFG, German Research Foundation) –
Projektnummer 191457833

German National Library Cataloguing in Publication Data
A catalogue record for this book is available from the German National Library:
http://dnb.d-nb.de

www.neofelis-verlag.de

Cover Design: Marija Skara, photo by Chantal Nederstigt
Editing & Typesetting: Neofelis Verlag (lw / ae)
Printed by PRESSEL Digitaler Produktionsdruck, Remshalden
Printed on FSC-certified paper.
ISBN (Print): 978-3-95808-122-2
ISBN (PDF): 978-3-95808-173-4